EXECUTIVE SUMMARY OF THE JANUARY 6TH COMMITTEE REPORT

Introductory Material to the Final Report of the Select Committee

EXECUTIVE SUMMARY OF THE JANUARY 6TH COMMITTEE REPORT

Introductory Material to the Final Report of the Select Committee

—

by the
Select Committee to Investigate the
January 6th Attack on the United States Capitol

United States House

QUID PRO BOOKS
New Orleans, Louisiana

The original work, absent the publisher's front matter, the new foreword, and the final publisher logo page, was produced in 2022 by the "Select Committee to Investigate the January 6th Attack on the United States Capitol, United States House." **No copyright is claimed in the original text of the report (as a government and public document), nor in any quoted statutes, regulation, or excerpts from transcripts.**

Foreword copyright © 2022 by Steven Alan Childress. All rights reserved.

Published in December 2022 by Quid Pro Books, an independent academic publisher of law, history, political science, and sociology.

ISBN 978-1-61027-469-2 (trade paperback)

QUID PRO BOOKS
QUID PRO, LLC
5860 Citrus Blvd., Suite D
New Orleans, Louisiana 70123
www.quidprobooks.com

The original work was released in one document on December 19, 2022, preliminary to the release of the Final Report on December 22, 2022. This printed reproduction is reduced in page size, and given the name of "Executive Summary" as commonly used by the press and the committee, but otherwise is an exact reproduction of the original report, entitled "Introductory Material to the Final Report." The original pagination is retained. See our "Publisher's Note."

As authors, the members of the Select Committee to Investigate the January 6th Attack on the United States Capitol are Bennie Thompson (Chair), Liz Cheney (Vice Chair), Zoe Lofgren, Adam Schiff, Adam Kinzinger, Pete Aguilar, Stephanie Murphy, Jamie Raskin, and Elaine Luria.

PUBLISHER'S NOTE

This book, other than the new foreword by Prof. Childress, is the introductory report of the House Select Committee. Its formal name, as issued December 19, 2022, is "Introductory Material to the Final Report," so that is our subtitle. But the popular media and Twitter refer to it consistently as an "Executive Summary" of the December 22 Final Report, so that is the main title we use for this publication.

The principal content of this book does not purport to be our own original "summary" or "analysis" of the Select Committee's introductory report. It *is* the introductory report (or the committee's "summary") itself, adding a foreword. We do not want the title of "Executive Summary," as popularly used in the media and by the committee itself (see below), to lead a reader into thinking the body of this book is an independent evaluation of the committee's work.

The body can be obtained directly and free from many online sources, including the House's website at *https://january6th.house.gov/report-executive-summary*. Note, too, that in that URL the committee refers to this document as an "executive summary." It can be read free as a letter-sized PDF. We offer it in book form, and in reduced page size to fit in the hand, for those who prefer to read it printed out and not as a "memo." It otherwise is an exact reproduction of the original, and its pagination is retained. We hope this book-style presentation, and new foreword, add value to the reader. At the least, presenting it as a book allows it to be kept on a bookshelf in a way that befits its status as an important historical record.

FOREWORD

This is a book form of the official introductory report (or "executive summary," as the press and other media consistently describe it) by the "Select Committee to Investigate the January 6th Attack on the United States Capitol, United States House," as issued on December 19, 2022. It was released preliminary to the committee's publication two days later of the complete and final report. It contains 154 pages of the committee's original text and endnotes. It is much longer and more detailed, more documented and supported, than most such "executive summaries" typically are.

We have presented it here in a properly-sized book form rather than as a letter-size memo, to enhance its manageable readability as an actual book. Still, this edition otherwise exactly reproduces the Select Committee's version and retains the citable pagination of the original work.

This executive summary introduces the report released December 22, 2022 — most likely the final one — by the House Select Committee to Investigate the January 6th Attack on the United States Capitol, informally known as the "J6 Committee." The committee is destined to be disbanded or replaced under a new Congress next month. Both this executive summary and the final report are in turn destined to be *this* Congress's — its 117th — last word on the subject.

The report, whether in this introductory form or the more complete final version, is history. It documents history, and it makes history. There's never been a Congressional Report memorializing mounds of documented evidence of an insurrection from within the United States government in a violent attempt to keep the current president in power against the lawful election of a political opponent. The breach of the U.S. Capitol and its carnage were awful, seen live by nearly everyone, but much was hidden and unknown about the day and the events leading up to it.

The committee's report is the first real effort at a comprehensive examination of all that, from a body having a certain amount of investigative prowess and subpoena power. Not every stone was turned, not every witness brought in to testify. A reader can certainly wish that more subpoenas were issued — and the ones that were, had been more boldly enforced. But the report's reach and depth, even in this summary form, is impressive; it should and will be taken seriously.

Reports of the kind serve as the foundation for the dialog and further investigations to follow. The Warren Report, an informal name for the product of the committee that examined the assassination of John F. Kennedy, Jr., did not satisfy everyone's curiosity about that shocking day in 1963, and it did not end the industry of skeptical publications about the assassination. If anything, it jump-started that industry. But the report still served as the essential basis for all the further examinations and reimaginings. At the very least, as a point of departure it could not be ignored.

This House Report will have a similar life. More information will come, mistakes will be found, and doubters of various fine-points will go public. But it will be the starting-point for those reflections and revisions. Even other official reports to come, such as one that may someday mark the end of the work by the Department of Justice's recently appointed Special Counsel, Jack Smith, will in some ways be a response to this report, not just a replacement of it. This documentation will outlast all efforts to make it irrelevant or discredited. It's just too detailed and supported by evidence to be treated as trivial or merely partisan.

This report certainly is political. How can it not be, since it deals with a deeply political event? But there's no real evidence that it's *partisan*. Or at least whatever partisanship may have influenced it origins and nudged its movements and focus (in the most cynical view of its mission) is dwarfed by the sheer proof of its product. The careful product seen here is ample evidence that the committee regarded it as serious and worthy of true engagement rather than gamesmanship.

A reader could wish that the committee had been "more" bipartisan, in the sense of having more Republican members present. But the committee was undoubtedly bipartisan as measured by the involvement and leadership by the members who were present. (For example, important statements along the way were jointly issued by Chairman Bennie Thompson (D-MS) and Vice Chair Liz Cheney (R-WY).) As to the GOP representatives, it is preposterous to think they were conducting themselves on this committee for the partisan goal of benefitting the Democratic Party. And it's quite clear that several un-serious members were kept off, ones that were openly and unabashedly committed to disruption. Some were clearly involved in a conflict of interest or were key witnesses behind-the-scenes (albeit refusing to tell what they knew, and herein referred to the House Ethics Committee because of that). So, any "more" bipartisanship would very likely have sabotaged the serious purpose of the investigation. It would have been form over substance. This proved too important an infamous historical moment to be treated as a political football.

More to the point, too much can be made of the mantra of bipartisanship. In such important matters or previous presidential scandals, that has never really been the norm — especially in recent years. Many examples exist of investigations by the "same party" or by the "opposing party," but you have to go back to Watergate to find appointments of high-level Special Prosecutors (Archibald Cox, then Leon Jaworski) who were also known to be Democrats (albeit Jaworski considered a conservative one). The DOJ under Trump, in appointing Robert Mueller to investigate the Trump campaign's Russian contacts and eventually Trump's own multiple actions of obstruction, made no effort to have Democratic representation. Same with special prosecutor-type work in investigations of Bill Clinton (both Robert Fiske and Kenneth Starr were Republicans) and George W. Bush (Patrick Fitzgerald, appointed by James Comey). Finally, at last, someone not a Republican has been appointed to be Special Counsel in matters related to Trump. But Jack Smith isn't even a Democrat; he's registered as an Independent.

It's time to stop acting as if the only objective, good-faith investigators belong to the Republican Party. Or as if the only true Republicans are those who joined the fervently Trump faction of the GOP. Even if this committee had not offered serious leadership and contributions by long-time and consistent Republicans Liz Cheney and Adam Kinzinger, its legitimacy will ultimately be measured by whether its conclusions are supported by the *evidence* it catalogs here and in the final report.

A point on "evidence," in this case evidence *law*: much was made by committee critics and all over Twitter (including the GOP House Judiciary Committee, who ought to know better) that various statements made by witnesses were "hearsay" and should not be taken as proof of the facts asserted. This was and is a complete misstatement of the hearsay rule, to the extent a congressional committee even needs to follow it.

It has never been the law that every second-hand or repeated statement is hearsay. Multiple ways exist for such repeated statements to be treated as non-hearsay. Most notably, statements made by a "party" (or their "co-conspirator") can be offered against the party without being defined as hearsay. Or a statement is not hearsay if it's not offered for the truth of what it asserts, but rather something else such as state of mind or awareness of a situation. Plus nearly thirty exceptions exist that permit statements that actually are hearsay to be admissible as evidence and regarded as proof of what the statement asserts. Any professor of evidence law, like me, can tell you that most (by *far*) of the quotes given by congressional witnesses as to what others said are not hearsay or would otherwise be admissible in court anyway under some recognized and long-time exception. Prisons are filled with people convicted on the basis of second-hand quotes from the witness chair, and no one has protested the fundamental unfairness for *them* of this common-law way of conducting evidentiary hearings and trials.

Much will also be made of the committee's referrals to the DOJ of criminal conduct: the four referrals made on December 19, for inciting an insurrection, conspiracy to defraud the United States, conspiracy to make a false statement, and obstruction of an official proceeding. These referrals are not valueless, and may be acted upon, but really they are more symbolic than substantive — since the DOJ has already begun to investigate these matters, has empaneled grand juries, and appointed Jack Smith for further work. They really don't need a referral. I am suggesting that, while the hot-flash news of the day may focus more on the referrals than the report, what will be an enduring account of history — and an *act* of history in itself — will be the report itself, whether in its complete form or in this lengthy introduction. It is presented here in book form to give it the seriousness it deserves.

STEVEN ALAN CHILDRESS
Conrad Meyer III Professor of Law
Tulane University Law School

New Orleans, Louisiana
December 22, 2022

Select Committee to Investigate the
JANUARY 6TH
Attack on the United States Capitol

Introductory Material

to the Final Report

of the Select Committee

On October 31, 2022, in a Federal courthouse in Washington, DC, Graydon Young testified against Stewart Rhodes and other members of the Oath Keepers militia group. The defendants had been charged with seditious conspiracy against the United States and other crimes related to the January 6, 2021, attack on Congress.[1]

In his testimony that day, Young explained to the jury how he and other Oath Keepers were provoked to travel to Washington by President Donald Trump's tweets and by Trump's false claims that the 2020 Presidential election was "stolen" from him.[2] And, in emotional testimony, Young acknowledged what he and others believed they were doing on January 6th: attacking Congress in the manner the French had attacked the Bastille at the outset of the French Revolution.[3] Reflecting on that day more than a year and half later, Young testified:

Prosecutor: And so how do you feel about the fact that you were pushing towards a line of police officers?

Young: Today I feel extremely ashamed and embarrassed....

Prosecutor: How did you feel at the time?

Young: I felt like, again, we were continuing in some kind of historical event to achieve a goal.

* * *

Prosecutor: Looking back now almost two years later, what would that make you as someone who was coming to D.C. to fight against the government?

Young: I guess I was [acting] like a traitor, somebody against my own government.[4]

Young's testimony was dramatic, but not unique. Many participants in the attack on the Capitol acknowledged that they had betrayed their own country:

- Reimler: "And I'm sorry to the people of this country for threatening the democracy that makes this country so great...My participation in the events that day were part of an attack on the rule of law."[5]

- Pert: "I know that the peaceful transition of power is to ensure the common good for our nation and that it is critical in protecting our country's security needs. I am truly sorry for my part and accept full responsibility for my actions."[6]

- Markofski: "My actions put me on the other side of the line from my brothers in the Army. The wrong side. Had I lived in the area, I would have been called up to defend the Capitol and restore order...My actions brought dishonor to my beloved U.S. Army National Guard."[7]

- Witcher: "Every member—every male member of my family has served in the military, in the Marine Corps, and most have saw combat. And I cast a shadow and cast embarrassment upon my family name and that legacy."[8]

- Edwards: "I am ashamed to be for the first time in my 68 years, standing before a judge, having pleaded guilty to committing a crime, ashamed to be associated with an attack on the United States Capitol, a symbol of American democracy and greatness that means a great deal to me."[9]

Hundreds of other participants in the January 6th attack have pleaded guilty, been convicted, or await trial for crimes related to their actions that day. And, like Young, hundreds of others have acknowledged exactly what provoked them to travel to Washington, and to engage in violence. For example:

- Ronald Sandlin, who threatened police officers in the Capitol saying, "[y]ou're going to die," posted on December 23, 2020: "I'm going to be there to show support for our president and to do my part to stop the steal and stand behind Trump when he decides to cross the rubicon. If you are a patriot I believe it's your duty to be there. I see it as my civic responsibility."[10]

- Garret Miller, who brought a gun to the Capitol on January 6th, explained: "I was in Washington, D.C. on January 6, 2021, because I believed I was following the instructions of former President Trump and he was my president and the commander-in-chief. His statements also had me believing the election was stolen from him."[11]

- John Douglas Wright explained that he brought busloads of people to Washington, DC, on January 6th "because [Trump] called me there, and he laid out what is happening in our government."[12]

- Lewis Cantwell testified: If "the President of the United States ... [is] out on TV telling the world that it was stolen, what else would I believe, as a patriotic American who voted for him and wants to continue to see the country thrive as I thought it was?"[13]

- Likewise, Stephen Ayres testified that "with everything the President was putting out" ahead of January 6th that "the election was rigged ... the votes were wrong and stuff... it just got into my head." "The President [was] calling on us to come" to Washington, DC.[14] Ayres "was hanging on every word he [President Trump] was saying"[15] Ayres posted that "Civil War will ensue" if President Trump did not stay in power after January 6th.[16]

The Committee has compiled hundreds of similar statements from participants in the January 6th attack.[17]

House Resolution 503 instructed the Select Committee to "investigate and report upon the facts, circumstances, and causes relating to the January 6, 2021, domestic terrorist attack upon the United States Capitol Complex" and to "issue a final report" containing "findings, conclusions, and recommendations for corrective measures." The Select Committee has conducted nine public hearings, presenting testimony from more than 70 witnesses. In structuring our investigation and hearings, we began with President Trump's contentions that the election was stolen and took testimony from nearly all of the President's principal advisors on this topic. We focused on the rulings of more than 60 Federal and State courts rejecting President Trump's and his supporters' efforts to reverse the electoral outcome.

Despite the rulings of these courts, we understood that millions of Americans still lack the information necessary to understand and evaluate what President Trump has told them about the election. For that reason, our hearings featured a number of members of President Trump's inner circle refuting his fraud claims and testifying that the election was *not* in fact stolen. In all, the Committee displayed the testimony of more than four dozen Republicans— by far the majority of witnesses in our hearings—including two of President Trump's former Attorneys General, his former White House Counsel, numerous members of his White House staff, and the highest-ranking members of his 2020 election campaign, including his campaign manager and his campaign general counsel. Even key individuals who worked closely with President Trump to try to overturn the 2020 election on January 6th ultimately *admitted* that they lacked actual evidence sufficient to change the election result, and they *admitted* that what they were attempting was unlawful.[18]

This Report supplies an immense volume of information and testimony assembled through the Select Committee's investigation, including information obtained following litigation in Federal district and appellate courts, as well as in the U.S. Supreme Court. Based upon this assembled evidence, the Committee has reached a series of specific findings,[19] including the following:

1. Beginning election night and continuing through January 6th and thereafter, Donald Trump purposely disseminated false allegations of fraud related to the 2020 Presidential election in order to aid his effort to overturn the election and for purposes of soliciting contributions. These false claims provoked his supporters to violence on January 6th.

2. Knowing that he and his supporters had lost dozens of election lawsuits, and despite his own senior advisors refuting his election fraud claims and urging him to concede his election loss, Donald Trump refused to accept the lawful result of the 2020 election. Rather than honor his constitutional obligation to "take Care that the Laws be faithfully executed," President Trump instead plotted to overturn the election outcome.

3. Despite knowing that such an action would be illegal, and that no State had or would submit an altered electoral slate, Donald Trump corruptly pressured Vice President Mike Pence to refuse to count electoral votes during Congress's joint session on January 6th.

4. Donald Trump sought to corrupt the U.S. Department of Justice by attempting to enlist Department officials to make purposely false statements and thereby aid his effort to overturn the Presidential election. After that effort failed, Donald Trump offered the position of Acting Attorney General to Jeff Clark knowing that Clark intended to disseminate false information aimed at overturning the election.

5. Without any evidentiary basis and contrary to State and Federal law, Donald Trump unlawfully pressured State officials and legislators to change the results of the election in their States.

6. Donald Trump oversaw an effort to obtain and transmit false electoral certificates to Congress and the National Archives.

7. Donald Trump pressured Members of Congress to object to valid slates of electors from several States.

8. Donald Trump purposely verified false information filed in Federal court.

9. Based on false allegations that the election was stolen, Donald Trump summoned tens of thousands of supporters to Washington for January 6th. Although these supporters were angry and some were armed, Donald Trump instructed them to march to the Capitol on January 6th to "take back" their country.

10. Knowing that a violent attack on the Capitol was underway and knowing that his words would incite further violence, Donald Trump purposely sent a social media message publicly condemning Vice President Pence at 2:24 p.m. on January 6th.

11. Knowing that violence was underway at the Capitol, and despite his duty to ensure that the laws are faithfully executed, Donald Trump refused repeated requests over a multiple hour period that he instruct his violent supporters to disperse and leave the Capitol, and instead watched the violent attack unfold on television. This failure to act perpetuated the violence at the Capitol and obstructed Congress's proceeding to count electoral votes.

12. Each of these actions by Donald Trump was taken in support of a multi-part conspiracy to overturn the lawful results of the 2020 Presidential election.

13. The intelligence community and law enforcement agencies did successfully detect the planning for potential violence on January 6th, including planning specifically by the Proud Boys and Oath Keeper militia groups who ultimately led the attack on the Capitol. As January 6th approached, the intelligence specifically identified the potential for violence at the U.S. Capitol. This intelligence was shared within the executive branch, including with the Secret Service and the President's National Security Council.

14. Intelligence gathered in advance of January 6th did not support a conclusion that Antifa or other left-wing groups would likely engage in a violent counter-demonstration, or attack Trump supporters on January 6th. Indeed, intelligence from January 5th indicated that some left-wing groups were instructing their members to "stay at home" and not attend on January 6th.[20] Ultimately, none of these groups was involved to any material extent with the attack on the Capitol on January 6th.

15. Neither the intelligence community nor law enforcement obtained intelligence in advance of January 6th on the full extent of the ongoing planning by President Trump, John Eastman, Rudolph Giuliani and their associates to overturn the certified election results. Such agencies apparently did not (and potentially could not) anticipate the provocation President Trump would offer the crowd in his Ellipse speech, that President Trump would "spontaneously" instruct the crowd to march to the Capitol, that President Trump would exacerbate the violent riot by sending his 2:24 p.m. tweet condemning Vice President Pence, or the full scale of the violence and lawlessness that would ensue. Nor did law enforcement anticipate that President Trump would refuse to direct his supporters to leave the Capitol once violence began. No intelligence community advance analysis predicted exactly how President Trump would behave; no such analysis recognized the full scale and extent of the threat to the Capitol on January 6th.

16. Hundreds of Capitol and DC Metropolitan police officers performed their duties bravely on January 6th, and America owes those individual immense gratitude for their courage in the defense of Congress and our Constitution. Without their bravery, January 6th would have been far worse. Although certain members of the Capitol Police leadership regarded their approach to January 6th as "all hands on deck," the Capitol Police leadership did not have sufficient assets in place to address the violent and lawless crowd.[21] Capitol Police leadership did not anticipate the scale of the violence that would ensue after President Trump instructed tens of thousands of his supporters in the Ellipse crowd to march to the Capitol, and then tweeted at 2:24 p.m. Although Chief Steven Sund raised the idea of National Guard support, the Capitol Police Board did not request Guard assistance prior to January 6th. The Metropolitan Police took an even more proactive approach to January 6th, and deployed roughly 800 officers, including responding to the emergency calls for help at the Capitol. Rioters still managed to break their line in certain locations, when the crowd surged forward in the immediate aftermath of Donald Trump's 2:24 p.m. tweet. The Department of Justice readied a group of Federal agents at Quantico and in the District of Columbia, anticipating that January 6th could become violent, and then deployed those agents once it became clear that police at the Capitol were overwhelmed. Agents from the Department of Homeland Security were also deployed to assist.

17. President Trump had authority and responsibility to direct deployment of the National Guard in the District of Columbia, but never gave any order to deploy the National Guard on January 6th or on any other day. Nor did he instruct any Federal law enforcement agency to assist. Because the authority to deploy the National Guard had been delegated to the Department of Defense, the Secretary of Defense could, and ultimately did deploy the Guard. Although evidence identifies a likely miscommunication between members of the civilian leadership in the Department of Defense impacting the timing of deployment, the Committee has found no evidence that the Department of Defense intentionally delayed deployment of the National Guard. The Select Committee recognizes that some at the Department had genuine concerns, counseling caution, that President Trump might give an illegal order to use the military in support of his efforts to overturn the election.

* * *

This Report begins with a factual overview framing each of these conclusions and summarizing what our investigation found. That overview is in turn supported by eight chapters identifying the very specific evidence of each of the principal elements of President Trump's multi-part plan to overturn the election, along with evidence regarding intelligence gathered before January 6th and security shortfalls that day.

Although the Committee's hearings were viewed live by tens of millions of Americans and widely publicized in nearly every major news source,[22] the Committee also recognizes that other news outlets and commentators have actively discouraged viewers from watching, and that millions of other Americans have not yet seen the actual evidence addressed by this Report. Accordingly, the Committee is also releasing video summaries of relevant evidence on each major topic investigated.

This Report also examines the legal implications of Donald Trump and his co-conspirators' conduct and includes criminal referrals to the Department of Justice regarding President Trump and certain other individuals. The criminal referrals build upon three relevant rulings issued by a Federal district court and explain in detail how the facts found support further evaluation by the Department of Justice of specific criminal charges. To assist the public in understanding the nature and importance of this material, this Report also contains sections identifying how the Committee has evaluated the credibility of its witnesses and suggests that the Department of Justice further examine possible efforts to obstruct our investigation. We also note that more than 30 witnesses invoked their Fifth Amendment privilege against self-incrimination, others invoked Executive Privilege or categorically refused to appear (including Steve Bannon, who has since been convicted of contempt of Congress).

Finally, this report identifies a series of legislative recommendations, including the Presidential Election Reform Act, which has already passed the House of Representatives.

EXECUTIVE SUMMARY: OVERVIEW OF THE EVIDENCE DEVELOPED

In the Committee's hearings, we presented evidence of what ultimately became a multi-part plan to overturn the 2020 Presidential election. That evidence has led to an overriding and straight-forward conclusion: the central cause of January 6th was one man, former President Donald Trump, who many others followed. None of the events of January 6th would have happened without him.

THE BIG LIE

In the weeks before election day 2020, Donald Trump's campaign experts, including his campaign manager Bill Stepien, advised him that the election results would not be fully known on election night.[23] This was because certain States would not begin to count absentee and other mail-in votes until election day or after election-day polls had closed.[24] Because Republican voters tend to vote in greater numbers on election day and Democratic voters tend to vote in greater numbers in advance of election day, it was widely anticipated that Donald Trump could initially appear to have a lead, but that the continued counting of mail-in, absentee and other votes beginning election night would erode and could overcome that perceived lead.[25] Thus, as President Trump's campaign manager cautioned, understanding the results of the 2020 election would be a lengthy "process," and an initial appearance of a Trump lead could be a "red mirage."[26] This was not unique to the 2020 election; similar scenarios had played out in prior elections as well.[27]

Prior to the 2020 election, Donald Trump's campaign manager Bill Stepien, along with House Republican Leader Kevin McCarthy, urged President Trump to embrace mail-in voting as potentially beneficial to the Trump campaign.[28] Presidential advisor and son-in-law Jared Kushner recounted others giving Donald Trump the same advice: "[M]ail in ballots could be a good thing for us if we looked at it correctly."[29] Multiple States, including Florida, had successfully utilized mail-in voting in prior elections, and in 2020.[30] Trump White House Counselor Hope Hicks testified: "I think he [President Trump] understood that a lot of people vote via absentee ballot in places like Florida and have for a long time and that it's worked fine."[31] Donald Trump won in numerous States that allowed no-excuse absentee voting in 2020, including Alaska, Florida, Idaho, Iowa, Kansas, Montana, North Carolina, North Dakota, Ohio, Oklahoma, South Dakota, and Wyoming.[32]

On election night 2020, the election returns were reported in almost exactly the way that Stepien and other Trump Campaign experts predicted, with the counting of mail-in and absentee ballots gradually diminishing President Trump's perceived lead. As the evening progressed, President Trump called in his campaign team to discuss the results. Stepien and other campaign experts advised him that the results of the election would not be known for some time, and that he could not truthfully declare victory.[33] "It was far too early to be making any calls like that. Ballots—ballots were still being counted. Ballots were still going to be counted for days."[34]

Campaign Senior Advisor Jason Miller told the Select Committee that he argued against declaring victory at that time as well, because "it was too early to say one way [or] the other" still who had won.[35] Stepien advised Trump to say that "votes were still being counted. It's too early to tell, too early to call the race but, you know, we are proud of the race we run - we ran and we, you know, think we're—think we're in a good position" and would say more in the coming days.[36]

President Trump refused, and instead said this in his public remarks that evening: "This is a fraud on the American public. This is an embarrassment to our country. We were getting ready to win this election. Frankly, we did win this election. We did win this election.... We want all voting to stop."[37] And on the morning of November 5th, he tweeted "STOP THE COUNT!"[38] Halting the counting of votes at that point would have violated both State and Federal laws.[39]

According to testimony received by the Select Committee, the only advisor present who supported President Trump's inclination to declare victory was Rudolph Giuliani, who appeared to be inebriated.[40] President Trump's Attorney General, Bill Barr, who had earlier left the election night gathering, perceived the President's statement this way:

> [R]ight out of the box on election night, the President claimed that there was major fraud underway. I mean, this happened, as far as I could tell, before there was actually any potential of looking at evidence. He claimed there was major fraud. And it seemed to be based on the dynamic that, at the end of the evening, a lot of Democratic votes came in which changed the vote counts in certain States, and that seemed to be the basis for this broad claim that there was major fraud. And I didn't think much of that, because people had been talking for weeks and everyone understood for weeks that that was going to be what happened on election night....[41]

President Trump's decision to declare victory falsely on election night and, unlawfully, to call for the vote counting to stop, was not a spontaneous decision. It was premeditated. The Committee has assembled a range of evidence of Trump's preplanning for a false declaration of victory. This includes multiple written communications on October 31 and November 3, 2020, to the White House by Judicial Watch President Tom Fitton.[42] This evidence demonstrates that Fitton was in direct contact with Trump and understood that Trump would falsely declare victory on election night and call for vote counting to stop. The evidence also includes an audio recording of President Trump's advisor Steve Bannon, who said this on October 31, 2020, to a group of his associates from China:

> And what Trump's gonna do is just declare victory, right? He's gonna declare victory. But that doesn't mean he's a winner. He's just gonna say he's a winner... The Democrats - more of our people vote early that count. Theirs

vote in mail. And so they're gonna have a natural disadvantage, and Trump's going to take advantage of it – that's our strategy. He's gonna declare himself a winner. So when you wake up Wednesday morning, it's going to be a firestorm.... Also, if Trump, if Trump is losing, by 10 or 11 o'clock at night, it's going to be even crazier. No, because he's gonna sit right there and say 'They stole it. I'm directing the Attorney General to shut down all ballot places in all 50 states. It's going to be, no, he's not going out easy. If Trump – if Biden's winning, Trump is going to do some crazy shit.[43]

Also in advance of the election, Roger Stone, another outside advisor to President Trump, made this statement:

I really do suspect it will still be up in the air. When that happens, the key thing to do is to claim victory. Possession is nine-tenths of the law. No, we won. Fuck you, Sorry. Over. We won. You're wrong. Fuck you.[44]

On election day, Vice President Pence's staff, including his Chief of Staff and Counsel, became concerned that President Trump might falsely claim victory that evening. The Vice President's Counsel, Greg Jacob, testified about their concern that the Vice President might be asked improperly to echo such a false statement.[45] Jacob drafted a memorandum with this specific recommendation: "[I]t is essential that the Vice President not be perceived by the public as having decided questions concerning disputed electoral votes prior to the full development of all relevant facts."[46]

Millions of Americans believed that Trump was telling the truth on election night – that Trump actually had proof the election was stolen and that the ongoing counting of votes was an act of fraud.

As votes were being counted in the days after the election, President Trump's senior campaign advisors informed him that his chances of success were almost zero.

Former Trump Campaign Manager Bill Stepien testified that he had come to this conclusion by November 7th, and told President Trump:

Committee Staff: What was your view on the state of the election at that point?

Stepien: You know, very, very, very bleak. You know, I – we told him – the group that went over there outlined, you know, my belief and chances for success at this point. And then we pegged that at, you know, 5, maybe 10 percent based on recounts that were – that, you know, either were automatically initiated or could be – could be initiated based on, you know, realistic legal challenges, not all the legal challenges that eventually were pursued. But, you know, it was – you know, my belief is that it was a very, very – 5 to 10 percent is not a very good optimistic outlook.[47]

Trump Campaign Senior Advisor Jason Miller testified to the Committee about this exchange:

Miller: I was in the Oval Office. And at some point in the conversation Matt Oczkowski, who was the lead data person, was brought on, and I remember he delivered to the President in pretty blunt terms that he was going to lose.

Committee Staff: And that was based, Mr. Miller, on Matt and the data team's assessment of this sort of county-by-county, State-by-State results as reported?

Miller: Correct.[48]

In one of the Select Committee's hearings, former Fox News political editor Chris Stirewalt was asked what the chance President Trump had of winning the election after November 7th, when the votes were tallied and every news organization had called the race for now-President Biden. His response: "None."[49]

As the Committee's hearings demonstrated, President Trump made a series of statements to White House staff and others during this time period indicating his understanding that he had lost.[50] President Trump also took consequential actions reflecting his understanding that he would be leaving office on January 20th. For example, President Trump personally signed a Memorandum and Order instructing his Department of Defense to withdraw all military forces from Somalia by December 31, 2020, and from Afghanistan by January 15, 2021.[51] General Keith Kellogg (ret.), who had been appointed by President Trump as Chief of Staff for the National Security Council and was Vice President Pence's National Security Advisor on January 6th, told the Select Committee that "[a]n immediate departure that that memo said would have been catastrophic. It's the same thing what President Biden went through. It would have been a debacle."[52]

In the weeks that followed the election, President Trump's campaign experts and his senior Justice Department officials were informing him and others in the White House that there was no genuine evidence of fraud sufficient to change the results of the election. For example, former Attorney General Bill Barr testified:

And I repeatedly told the President in no uncertain terms that I did not see evidence of fraud, you know, that would have affected the outcome of the election. And, frankly, a year and a half later, I haven't seen anything to change my mind on that.[53]

Former Trump Campaign lawyer Alex Cannon, who was asked to oversee incoming information about voter fraud and set up a voter fraud tip line, told the Select Committee about a pertinent call with White House Chief of Staff Mark Meadows in November 2020:

Cannon: So I remember a call with Mr. Meadows where Mr. Meadows was asking me what I was finding and if I was finding anything. And I remember sharing with him that we weren't finding anything that would be sufficient to change the results in any of the key States.

Committee Staff: When was that conversation?

Cannon: Probably in November. Mid- to late November....

Committee Staff: And what was Mr. Meadows's reaction to that information?

Cannon: I believe the words he used were: "So there is no there there?"[54]

President Trump's Campaign Manager Bill Stepien recalled that President Trump was being told "wild allegations" and that it was the campaign's job to "track [the allegations] down":

Committee Staff: You said that you were very confident that you were telling the President the truth in your dealings with [him]. And had your team been able to verify any of these allegations of fraud, would you have reported those to the President?

Stepien: Sure.

Committee Staff: Did you ever have to report that –

Stepien: One of my frustrations would be that, you know, people would throw out, you know, these reports, these allegations, these things that they heard or saw in a State, and they'd tell President Trump. And, you know, it would be the campaign's job to track down the information, the facts. And, you know, President Trump, you know – if someone's saying, hey, you know, all these votes aren't counted or were miscounted, you know, if you're down in a State like Arizona, you liked hearing that. It would be our job to track it down and come up dry because the allegation didn't prove to be true. And we'd have to, you know, relay the news that, yeah, that tip that someone told you about those votes or that fraud or, you know, nothing came of it.

That would be our job as, you know, the truth telling squad and, you know, not – not a fun job to be, you know, much – it's an easier job to be telling the President about, you know, wild allegations. It's a harder job to be telling him on the back end that, yeah, that wasn't true.

Committee Staff: How did he react to those types of conversations where you [told] him that an allegation or another wasn't true?

Stepien: He was—he had—usually he had pretty clear eyes. Like, he understood, you know – you know, we told him where we thought the race was, and I think he was pretty realistic with our viewpoint, in agreement with our viewpoint of kind of the forecast and the uphill climb we thought he had.[55]

Trump Campaign Senior Advisor Jason Miller told the Committee that he informed President Trump "several" times that "specific to election day fraud and irregularities, there were not enough to overturn the election."[56]

Vice President Pence has also said publicly that he told President Trump there was no basis to allege that the election was stolen. When a reporter recently asked "Did you ever point blank say to the President [that] we lost this election?," Pence responded that "I did... Many times."[57] Pence has also explained:

There was never evidence of widespread fraud. I don't believe fraud changed the outcome of the election. But the President and the campaign had every right to have those examined in court. But I told the President that, once those legal challenges played out, he should simply accept the outcome of the election and move on.[58]

The General Counsel of President Trump's campaign, Matthew Morgan, informed members of the White House staff, and likely many others, of the campaign's conclusion that none of the allegation of fraud and irregularities could be sufficient to change the outcome of the election:

What was generally discussed on that topic was whether the fraud, maladministration, abuse, or irregularities, if aggregated and read most favorably to the campaign, would that be outcome determinative. And I think everyone's assessment in the room, at least amongst the staff, Marc Short, myself, and Greg Jacob, was that it was not sufficient to be outcome determinative.[59]

In a meeting on November 23rd, Barr told President Trump that the Justice Department was doing its duty by investigating every fraud allegation "if it's specific, credible, and could've affected the outcome," but that "they're just not meritorious. They're not panning out"[60]

Barr then told the Associated Press on December 1st that the Department had "not seen fraud on a scale that could have effected a different outcome in the election."[61] Next, he reiterated this point in private meetings with the President both that afternoon and on December 14th, as well as in his final press conference as Attorney General later that month.[62] The Department of Homeland Security had reached a similar determination 2 weeks earlier: **"There is no evidence that any voting system deleted or lost votes, changed votes, or was in any way compromised."**[63]

In addition, multiple other high ranking Justice Department personnel appointed by President Trump also informed him repeatedly that the allegations were false. As January 6th drew closer, Acting Attorney General Rosen and Acting Deputy Attorney General Donoghue had calls with President Trump on almost a daily basis explaining in detail what the Department's investigations showed.[64] Acting Deputy Attorney General Richard Donoghue told the Select Committee that he and Acting Attorney General Rosen tried "to put it in very clear terms to the President. And I said something to the effect of 'Sir, we've done dozens of investigations, hundreds of interviews. The major allegations are not supported by the evidence developed. We've looked in Georgia, Pennsylvania, Michigan, Nevada. We're doing our job.'"[65] On December 31st, Donoghue recalls telling the President that "people keep telling you these things and they turn out not to be true."[66] And then on January 3rd, Donoghue reiterated this point with the President:

[A]s in previous conservations, we would say to him, you know, "We checked that out, and there's nothing to it."[67]

Acting Attorney General Rosen testified before the Select Committee that "the common element" of all of his communications with President Trump was President Trump urging the Department to find widespread fraud that did not actually exist. None of the Department's investigations identified any genuine fraud sufficient to impact the election outcome:

During my tenure as the Acting Attorney General, which began on December 24 of [2020], the Department of Justice maintained the position, publicly announced by former Attorney General William Barr, that the Department had been presented with no evidence of widespread voter fraud in a scale sufficient to change the outcome of the 2020 election.[68]

As President Trump was hearing from his campaign and his Justice Department that the allegations of widespread fraud were not supported by the evidence, his White House legal staff also reached the same conclusions, and agreed specifically with what Bill Barr told Trump. Both White House Counsel Pat Cipollone and White House Senior Advisor Eric Herschmann reinforced to President Trump that the Justice Department was doing its duty to investigate allegations of supposed voter fraud.[69]

Cipollone told the Select Committee that he "had seen no evidence of massive fraud in the election" and that he "forcefully" made this point "over and over again." For example, during a late-night group meeting with President Trump on December 18th, at which he and Herschmann urged Trump not to heed the advice of several election conspiracists at the meeting:

> Cipollone: They didn't think that we were, you know – they didn't think we believed this, you know, that there had been massive fraud in the election, and the reason they didn't think we believed it is because we didn't.
>
> Committee Staff: And you articulated that forcefully to them during the meeting?
>
> Cipollone: I did, yeah. I had seen no evidence of massive fraud in the election.... At some point, you have to deliver with the evidence. And I – again, I just to go back to what [Bill Barr] said, he had not seen and I was not aware of any evidence of fraud to the extent that it would change the results of the election. That was made clear to them, okay, over and over again.[70]

Similarly, White House Attorney Eric Herschmann was also very clear about his views:

> [T]hey never proved the allegations that they were making, and they were trying to develop.[71]

In short, President Trump was informed over and over again, by his senior appointees, campaign experts and those who had served him for years, that his election fraud allegations were nonsense.

How did President Trump continue to make false allegations despite all of this unequivocal information? Trump sought out those who were not scrupulous with the facts, and were willing to be dishonest. He found a new legal team to assert claims that his existing advisors and the Justice Department had specifically informed him were false. President Trump's new legal team, headed by Rudolph Giuliani, and their allies ultimately lost dozens of election lawsuits in Federal and State courts.

The testimony of Trump Campaign Manager Bill Stepien helps to put this series of events in perspective. Stepien described his interaction with Giuliani as an intentional "self-demotion," with Stepien stepping aside once it became clear that President Trump intended to spread falsehoods. Stepien knew the President's new team was relying on unsupportable accusations, and he refused to be associated with their approach:

> "There were two groups of family. We called them kind of my team and Rudy's team. I didn't mind being characterized as being part of 'team normal,' as reporters, you know, kind of started to do around that point in time."[72]

Having worked for Republican campaigns for over two decades, Stepien said, "I think along the way I've built up a pretty good -- I hope a good reputation for being honest and professional, and I didn't think what was happening was necessarily honest or professional at that point in time."[73]

As Giuliani visited Campaign headquarters to discuss election litigation, the Trump Campaign's professional staff began to view him as unhinged.[74] In addition, multiple law firms previously engaged to work for the Trump campaign decided that they could not participate in the strategy being instituted by Giuliani. They quit. Campaign General Counsel Matthew Morgan explained that he had conversations with "probably all of our counsel who [we]re signed up to assist on election day as they disengaged with the campaign."[75] The "general consensus was that the law firms were not comfortable making the arguments that Rudy Giuliani was making publicly."[76] When asked how many outside firms expressed this concern, Morgan recalled having "a similar conversation with most all of them."[77]

Stepien grew so wary of the new team that he locked Giuliani out of his office:

Committee Staff: Yeah. I'm getting the sense from listening to you here for a few hours that you sort of chose to pull back, that you were uncomfortable with what Mr. Giuliani and others were saying and doing and, therefore, you were purposefully stepping back from a day-to-day role as the leader of the campaign. Is that—I don't want to put words in your mouth. Is that accurate?

Stepien: That's accurate. That's accurate. You know, I had my assistant -- it was a big glass kind of wall office in our headquarters, and I had my assistant lock my door. I told her, don't let anyone in. You know, I'll be around when I need to be around. You know, tell me what I need to know. Tell me what's going on here, but, you know, you're going to see less of me.

And, you know, sure enough, you know, Mayor Giuliani tried to, you know, get in my office and ordered her to unlock the door, and she didn't do that, you know. She's, you know, smart about that. But your words are ones I agree with.[78]

Over the weeks that followed, dozens of judges across the country specifically rejected the allegations of fraud and irregularities being advanced by the Trump team and their allies. For example, courts described the arguments as "an amalgamation of theories, conjecture, and speculation," "allegations ... sorely wanting of relevant or reliable evidence," "strained legal arguments without merit," assertions that "did not prove by any standard of proof that any illegal votes were cast and counted," and even a "fundamental and obvious misreading of the Constitution."[79]

Reflecting back on this period, Trump Campaign Communications Director Tim Murtaugh texted colleagues in January 2021 about a news report that the New York State Bar was considering expelling Rudolph Giuliani over the Ellipse rally: "Why wouldn't they expel him based solely on the outrageous lies he told for 2 1/2 months?"[80]

This is exactly what ultimately came to pass. When suspending his license, a New York court said that Giuliani "communicated demonstrably false and misleading statements to courts, lawmakers and the public at large in his capacity as lawyer for former President Donald J. Trump and the Trump campaign in connection with Trump's failed effort at reelection in 2020."[81] The court added that "[t]he seriousness of [Giuliani's] uncontroverted misconduct cannot be overstated."[82]

Other Trump lawyers were sanctioned for making outlandish claims of election fraud without the evidence to back them up, including Sidney Powell, Lin Wood and seven other pro-Trump lawyers in a case that a Federal judge described as "a historic and profound abuse of the judicial process":

> It is one thing to take on the charge of vindicating rights associated with an allegedly fraudulent election. It is another to take on the charge of deceiving a federal court and the American people into believing that rights were infringed, without regard to whether any laws or rights were in fact violated. This is what happened here.[83]

A group of prominent Republicans have more recently issued a report – titled *Lost, Not Stolen* – examining "every count of every case brought in these six battleground states" by President Trump and his allies. The report concludes "that Donald Trump and his supporters had their day in court and failed to produce substantive evidence to make their case."[84] President Trump and his legal allies "failed because of a lack of evidence and not because of erroneous rulings or unfair judges.... In many cases, after making extravagant claims of wrongdoing, Trump's legal representatives showed up in court or state proceedings empty-handed, and then returned to their rallies and media campaigns to repeat the same unsupported claims."[85]

There is no reasonable basis for the allegation that these dozens of rulings by State and Federal courts were somehow politically motivated.[86] The outcome of these suits was uniform regardless of who appointed the judges. One of the authors of *Lost, Not Stolen*, longtime Republican election lawyer Benjamin Ginsberg, testified before the Select Committee that "in no instance did a court find that the charges of fraud were real," without variation based on the judges involved.[87] Indeed, eleven of the judges who ruled against Donald Trump and his supporters were appointed by Donald Trump himself.

One of those Trump nominees, Judge Stephanos Bibas of the U.S. Court of Appeals for the Third Circuit, rejected an appeal by the Trump Campaign claiming that Pennsylvania officials "did not undertake any meaningful effort" to fight illegal absentee ballots and uneven treatment of voters across counties.[88] Judge Bibas wrote in his decision that "calling an election unfair does not make it so. Charges require specific allegations and then proof. We have neither here."[89] Another Trump nominee, Judge Brett Ludwig of the Eastern District of Wisconsin, ruled against President Trump's lawsuit alleging that the result was skewed by illegal procedures that governed drop boxes, ballot address information, and individuals who claimed "indefinitely confined" status to vote from home.[90] Judge Ludwig wrote in his decision, that "[t]his Court has allowed plaintiff the chance to make his case and he has lost on the merits" because the procedures used "do not remotely rise to the level" of breaking Wisconsin's election rules.[91]

Nor is it true that these rulings focused solely on standing, or procedural issues. As Ginsberg confirmed in his testimony to the Select Committee, President Trump's team "did have their day in court."[92] Indeed, he and his co-authors determined in their report that 30 of these post-election cases were dismissed by a judge after an evidentiary hearing had been held, and many of these judges explicitly indicated in their decisions that the evidence presented by the plaintiffs was wholly insufficient on the merits.[93]

Ultimately, even Rudolph Giuliani and his legal team acknowledged that they had no definitive evidence of election fraud sufficient to change the election outcome. For example, although Giuliani repeatedly had claimed in public that Dominion voting machines stole the election, he admitted during his Select Committee deposition that "I do not think the machines stole the election."[94] An attorney representing his lead investigator, Bernard Kerik, declared in a letter to the Select Committee that "it was impossible for Kerik and his team to determine conclusively whether there was widespread fraud or whether that widespread fraud would have altered the outcome of the election."[95] Kerik also emailed President Trump's chief of staff on December 28, 2020, writing: "We can do all the investigations we want later, but if the president plans on winning, it's the legislators that have to be moved and this will do just that."[96] Other Trump lawyers and supporters, Jenna Ellis, John Eastman, Phil Waldron, and Michael Flynn, all invoked their Fifth Amendment privilege against self-incrimination when asked by the Select Committee what supposed proof they uncovered that the election was stolen.[97] Not a single witness--nor any combination of witnesses--provided the Select Committee with evidence demonstrating that fraud occurred on a scale even remotely close to changing the outcome in any State.[98]

By mid-December 2020, Donald Trump had come to what most of his staff believed was the end of the line. The Supreme Court rejected a lawsuit he supported filed by the State of Texas in the Supreme Court, and Donald Trump had this exchange, according to Special Assistant to the President Cassidy Hutchinson:

> The President was fired up about the Supreme Court decision. And so I was standing next to [Chief of Staff Mark] Meadows, but I had stepped back... The President [was] just raging about the decision and how it's wrong, and why didn't we make more calls, and just this typical anger outburst at this decision... And the President said I think - so he had said something to the effect of, "I don't want people to know we lost, Mark. This is embarrassing. Figure it out. We need to figure it out. I don't want people to know that we lost."[99]

On December 14, 2020, the Electoral College met to cast and certify each State's electoral votes. By this time, many of President Trump's senior staff, and certain members of his family, were urging him to concede that he had lost.

Labor Secretary Gene Scalia told the Committee that he called President Trump around this time and gave him such feedback quite directly:

> [S]o, I had put a call in to the President—I might have called on the 13th; we spoke, I believe, on the 14th—in which I conveyed to him that I thought that it was time for him to acknowledge that President Biden had prevailed in the election.... But I communicated to the President that when that legal process is exhausted and when the electors have voted, that's the point at which that outcome needs to be expected.... And I told him that I did believe, yes, that once those legal processes were run, if fraud had not been established that had affected the outcome of the election, that, unfortunately, I believed that what had to be done was concede the outcome.[100]

Deputy White House Press Secretary Judd Deere also told President Trump that he should concede. He recalled other staffers advising President Trump at some point to concede and that he "encouraged him to do it at least once after the electoral college met in mid-December."[101] White House Counsel Pat Cipollone also believed that President Trump should concede: "[I]f your question is did I believe he should concede the election at a point in time, yes, I did."[102]

Attorney General Barr told the Select Committee this: "And in my view, that [the December 14 electoral college vote] was the end of the matter. I didn't see - you know, I thought that this would lead inexorably to a new administration. I was not aware at that time of any theory, you know, why this could be reversed. And so I felt that the die was cast...."[103]

Barr also told the Committee that he suggested several weeks earlier that the President's efforts in this regard needed to come to an end soon, in conversation with several White House officials after his meeting with Trump on November 23rd:

> [A]s I walked out of the Oval Office, Jared was there with Dan Scavino, who ran the President's social media and who I thought was a reasonable guy and believe is a reasonable guy. And I said, how long is he going to carry on with this 'stolen election' stuff? Where is this going to go?
>
> And by that time, Meadows had caught up with me and – leaving the office, and caught up to me and said that – he said, look, I think that he's becoming more realistic and knows that there's a limit to how far he can take this. And then Jared said, you know, yeah, we're working on this, we're working on it.[104]

Despite all that Donald Trump was being told, he continued to purposely and maliciously make false claims. To understand the very stark differences between what he was being told and what he said publicly and in fundraising solicitations, the Committee has assembled the following examples.

Then-Deputy Attorney General Jeffrey Rosen (12/15/20):	*President Trump one week later (12/22/20):*
"And so he said, 'Well, what about this? I saw it on the videotape, somebody delivering a suitcase of ballots.' And we said, 'It wasn't a suitcase. It was a bin. That's what they use when they're counting ballots. It's benign.'"[105]	"There is even security camera footage from Georgia that shows officials telling poll watchers to leave the room before pulling suitcases of ballots out from under the tables and continuing to count for hours."[106]
Acting Deputy Attorney General Richard Donoghue (12/27 & 12/31/20):	*President Trump later that week (1/2/21):*
"I told the President myself that several times, in several conversations, that these allegations about ballots being smuggled in in a suitcase and run through the machine several times, it was not true, that we looked at it, we looked at the video, we interviewed the witnesses, that it was not true.... I believe it was in the phone call on December 27th. It was also in a meeting in the Oval Office on December 31st."[107]	"[S]he stuffed the machine. She stuffed the ballot. Each ballot went three times, they were showing: Here's ballot number one. Here it is a second time, third time, next ballot." [108]
GA Sec. State Brad Raffensperger (1/2/21):	*President Trump one day later (1/3/21):*
"You're talking about the State Farm video. And I think it's extremely unfortunate that Rudy Giuliani or his people, they sliced and diced that video and took it out of context." ... "[W]e did an audit of that and we proved conclusively that they were not scanned three times....	"I spoke to Secretary of State Brad Raffensperger yesterday about Fulton County and voter fraud in Georgia. He was unwilling, or unable, to answer questions such as the 'ballots under table' scam, ballot destruction, out of state 'voters', dead voters, and more. He has no clue!"[110]

Yes, Mr. President, we'll send you the link from WSB" [Trump]: "I don't care about a link. I don't need it."[109]	
Attorney General Bill Barr (12/1/20): "Then he raised the 'big vote dump,' as he called it, in Detroit. And, you know, he said, people saw boxes coming into the counting station at all hours of the morning and so forth.... I said, 'Mr. President, there are 630 precincts in Detroit, and unlike elsewhere in the State, they centralize the counting process, so they're not counted in each precinct, they're moved to counting stations, and so the normal process would involve boxes coming in at all different hours.' And I said, 'Did anyone point out to you -- did all the people complaining about it point out to you, you actually did better in Detroit than you did last time? I mean, there's no indication of fraud in Detroit.'"[111]	*President Trump one day later (12/2/20):* "I'll tell you what's wrong, voter fraud. Here's an example. This is Michigan. At 6:31 in the morning, a vote dump of 149,772 votes came in unexpectedly. We were winning by a lot. That batch was received in horror.... In Detroit everybody saw the tremendous conflict... there were more votes than there were voters."[112]
Acting Deputy Attorney General Richard Donoghue (12/27/20): "The President then continued, there are 'more votes than voters...'. But I was aware of that allegation, and I said, you know, that was just a matter of them 'comparing the 2020 votes cast to 2016 registration numbers.' That is 'not a valid complaint.'"[113]	*President Trump ten days later (1/6/21):* "More votes than they had voters. And many other States also."[114]
Acting Deputy Attorney General Richard Donoghue (1/3/21): "[W]e would say to him, you know, 'We checked that out, and there's nothing to it.... And we would cite to certain allegations. And so – like such as Pennsylvania, right. 'No, there were not 250,000 more votes reported than were actually cast. That's not true.' So we would say things like that."[115]	*President Trump three days later (1/6/21):* "In Pennsylvania, you had 205,000 more votes than you had voters. And the number is actually much greater than that now. That was as of a week ago. And this is a mathematical impossibility unless you want to say it's a total fraud."[116]
GA Sec. State Brad Raffensperger (1/2/21): [Trump]: "[I]t's 4,502 who voted, but they weren't on the voter registration roll, which they had to be. You had 18,325 vacant address voters. The address was vacant, and they're not allowed to be counted. That's 18,325." ...	*President Trump two days later (1/4/21):* "4,502 illegal ballots were cast by individuals who do not appear on the state's voter rolls. Well, that's sort of strange. 18,325 illegal ballots were cast by individuals who registered to vote using an address listed as vacant according to the postal service."[118]

[Raffensperger]: "Well, Mr. President, the challenge that you have is the data you have is wrong."[117]	
GA Sec. of State Brad Raffensperger (1/2/21): [Trump]: "So dead people voted, and I think the number is close to 5,000 people. And they went to obituaries. They went to all sorts of methods to come up with an accurate number, and a minimum is close to about 5,000 voters." ... [Raffensperger]: "The actual number were two. Two. Two people that were dead that voted. So that's wrong."[119]	*President Trump four days later (1/6/21):* "[T]he number of fraudulent ballots that we've identified across the state is staggering. Over 10,300 ballots in Georgia were cast by individuals whose names and dates of birth match Georgia residents who died in 2020 and prior to the election."[120]
GA Sec. State General Counsel Ryan Germany (1/2/21): [Trump]: "You had out-of-state voters. They voted in Georgia, but they were from out of state, of 4,925." ... [Germany]: "Every one we've been through are people that lived in Georgia, moved to a different state, but then moved back to Georgia legitimately." ... "They moved back in years ago. This was not like something just before the election. So there's something about that data that, it's just not accurate."[121]	*President Trump four days later (1/6/21):* "And at least 15,000 ballots were cast by individuals who moved out of the state prior to November 3rd election. They say they moved right back."[122]
White House Press Secretary Kayleigh McEnany (n.d.): "[T]he one specific I remember referencing was I don't agree with the Dominion track." ... "I specifically referenced waving him off of the Dominion theory earlier in my testimony." ... [Q] "Are you saying you think he still continued to tweet that after you waved him off of it?" [A] "Yeah..."[123]	*President Trump:* Between mid-November and January 5, 2021, President Trump tweeted or retweeted conspiracy theories about Dominion nearly three dozen times.[124]
Trump Campaign Senior Advisor Jason Miller: "...the international allegations for Dominion were not valid." [Q] "Okay. Did anybody communicate that to the President?" [A]: "I know that that was -- I know that was communicated. I know I communicated it"[125]	*President Trump:* "You have Dominion, which is very, very suspect to start off with. Nobody knows the ownership. People say the votes are counted in foreign countries and much worse..."[126]
Attorney General Bill Barr (11/23/20):	*President Trump three days later (11/26/20):*

"I specifically raised the Dominion voting machines, which I found to be one of the most disturbing allegations – 'disturbing' in the sense that I saw absolutely zero basis for the allegations ... I told him that it was crazy stuff and they were wasting their time on that and it was doing great, great disservice to the country."[127]	"[T]hose machines are fixed, they're rigged. You can press Trump and the vote goes to Biden…. All you have to do is play with a chip, and they played with a chip, especially in Wayne County and Detroit."[128]
Attorney General Bill Barr (12/1/20): "I explained, I said, look, if you have a machine and it counts 500 votes for Biden and 500 votes for Trump, and then you go back later and you have a -- you will have the 1,000 pieces of paper put through that machine, and you can see if there's any discrepancy… there has been no discrepancy."[129]	*President Trump one day later (12/2/20):* "In one Michigan County, as an example, that used Dominion systems, they found that nearly 6,000 votes had been wrongly switched from Trump to Biden, and this is just the tip of the iceberg. This is what we caught. How many didn't we catch?"[130]
Attorney General Bill Barr (12/14/20): "'I will, Mr. President. But there are a couple of things,' I responded. 'My understanding is that our experts have looked at the Antrim situation and are sure it was a human error that did not occur anywhere else. And, in any event, Antrim is doing a hand recount of the paper ballots, so we should know in a couple of days whether there is any real problem with the machines'."[131]	*President Trump one day later (12/15/20):* "This is BIG NEWS. Dominion Voting Machines are a disaster all over the Country. Changed the results of a landslide election. Can't let this happen…."[132]
Then-Deputy Attorney General Jeffrey Rosen (12/15/20): "[O]ther people were telling him there was fraud, you know, corruption in the election. The voting machines were no good. And we were telling him that is inconsistent, by 'we,' I mean Richard Donoghue and myself, that that was not what we were seeing." … "There was this open issue as to the Michigan report. And -- I think it was Mr. Cuccinelli, not certain, but had indicated that there was a hand recount. And I think he said, "That's the gold standard."[133]	*President Trump one day later (12/16/20):* "Study: Dominion Machines shifted 2-3% of Trump Votes to Biden. Far more votes than needed to sway election." Florida, Ohio, Texas and many other states were won by even greater margins than projected. Did just as well with Swing States, but bad things happened. @OANN"[134]
National Security Adviser Robert O'Brien (12/18/20): "I got a call from, I think, Molly Michael in outer oval, the President's assistant, and she said, 'I'm connecting you to the Oval'… somebody asked me, was there -- did I	*President Trump one day later (12/19/20):* "…There could also have been a hit on our ridiculous voting machines during the election, which is now obvious that I won big, making it an even more corrupted

have any evidence of election fraud in the voting machines or foreign interference in our voting machines. And I said, no, we've looked into that and there's no evidence of it."[135]	embarrassment for the USA. @DNI_Ratcliffe @SecPompeo".[136]
Acting Deputy AG Richard Donoghue (12/31/20): "We definitely talked about Antrim County again. That was sort of done at that point, because the hand recount had been done and all of that. But we cited back to that to say, you know, this is an example of what people are telling you and what's being filed in some of these court filings that are just not supported by the evidence."[137]	**_President Trump two days later (1/2/21):_** "Well, Brad. Not that there's not an issue, because we have a big issue with Dominion in other states and perhaps in yours…. in other states, we think we found tremendous corruption with Dominion machines, but we'll have to see." … "I won't give Dominion a pass because we found too many bad things."[138]
GA Sec. State Brad Raffensperger (1/2/21): "I don't believe that you're really questioning the Dominion machines. Because we did a hand re-tally, a 100 percent re-tally of all the ballots, and compared them to what the machines said and came up with virtually the same result. Then we did the recount, and we got virtually the same result."[139]	**_President Trump four days later (1/6/21):_** "In addition, there is the highly troubling matter of Dominion Voting Systems. In one Michigan county alone, 6,000 votes were switched from Trump to Biden and the same systems are used in the majority of states in our country." … "There is clear evidence that tens of thousands of votes were switched from President Trump to former Vice President Biden in several counties in Georgia."[140]

Evidence gathered by the Committee indicates that President Trump raised roughly one quarter of a billion dollars in fundraising efforts between the election and January 6th.[141] Those solicitations persistently claimed and referred to election fraud that did not exist. For example, the Trump Campaign, along with the Republican National Committee, sent millions of emails to their supporters, with messaging claiming that the election was "rigged," that their donations could stop Democrats from "trying to steal the election," and that Vice President Biden would be an "illegitimate president" if he took office.

Ultimately, Attorney General Bill Barr suggested that the Department of Justice's investigations disproving President Trump's fraud claims may have prevented an even more serious series of events:

> [F]rankly, I think the fact that I put myself in the position that I could say that we had looked at this and didn't think there was fraud was really important to moving things forward. And I sort of shudder to think what the situation would have been if the position of the Department was, "We're not even looking at this until after Biden's in office." I'm not sure we would've had a transition at all.[142]

RATHER THAN CONCEDE, DONALD TRUMP CHOOSES TO OBSTRUCT THE JANUARY 6TH PROCEEDING

President Trump disregarded the rulings of the courts and rejected the findings and conclusions and advice from his Justice Department, his campaign experts, and his White House and Cabinet advisors. He chose instead to try to overturn the election on January 6th and took a series of very specific steps to attempt to achieve that result.

A central element of Donald Trump's plan to overturn the election relied upon Vice President Mike Pence. As Vice President, Pence served as the President of the Senate, the presiding officer for the joint session of Congress on January 6th. Beginning in December, and with greater frequency as January 6th approached, Trump repeatedly and unlawfully pressured Pence in private and public to prevent Congress from counting lawful electoral votes from several States.

To understand the plan President Trump devised with attorney and law professor John Eastman, it is necessary to understand the constitutional structure for selecting our President.

At the Constitutional Convention 233 years ago, the framers considered but rejected multiple proposals that Congress itself vote to select the President of the United States.[143] Indeed the Framers voiced very specific concerns with Congress selecting the President. They viewed it as important that the electors, chosen for the specific purpose of selecting the President, should make the determination rather than Congress:

> It was desireable, that the sense of the people should operate in the choice of the person to whom so important a trust was to be confided. This end will be answered by committing the right of making it, not to any pre-established body, but to men, chosen by the people for the special purpose, and at the particular conjuncture.[144]

The Framers understood that a thoughtful structure for the appointment of the President was necessary to avoid certain evils: "Nothing was more to be desired, than that every practicable obstacle should be opposed to cabal, intrigue and corruption."[145] They were careful to ensure that "those who from situation might be suspected of too great devotion to the president in office" "were not among those that chose the president."[146] For that reason, "[n]o senator, representative, or other person holding a place of trust or profit under the United States, can be of the number of the electors."[147]

Article II of our Constitution, as modified by the Twelfth Amendment, governs election of the President. Article II created the electoral college, providing that the States would select electors in the manner provided by State legislatures, and those electors would in turn vote for the President. Today, every State selects Presidential electors by popular vote, and each State's laws provide for procedures to resolve election disputes, including through lawsuits if necessary. After any election issues are resolved in State or Federal court, each State's government transmits a certificate of the ascertainment of the appointed electors to Congress and the National Archives.

The electoral college meets in mid-December to cast their votes, and all of these electoral votes are then ultimately counted by Congress on January 6th. The Vice President, as President of the Senate, presides over the joint session of Congress to count votes. The Twelfth Amendment provides this straight-forward instruction: "The president of the Senate shall, in the presence of the Senate and House of Representatives, open all the certificates and the votes shall then be counted; The person having the greatest number of votes for President shall be the President..." The Vice President has only a ministerial role, opening the envelopes and ensuring that the votes are counted. Likewise, the Electoral Count Act of 1887 provides no substantive role for the Vice President in counting votes, reinforcing that he or she can only act in a ministerial fashion—the Vice President may not choose, for example, to decline to count particular votes. In most cases (*e.g.*, when one candidate has a majority of votes submitted by the States) Congress has only a ministerial role, as well. It simply counts electoral college votes provided by each State's governor. Congress is not a court and cannot overrule State and Federal court rulings in election challenges.

As January 6th approached, John Eastman and others devised a plan whereby Vice President Pence would, as the presiding officer, declare that certain electoral votes from certain States *could not* be counted at the joint session.[148] John Eastman knew before proposing this plan that it was not legal. Indeed, in a pre-election document discussing Congress's counting of electoral votes, Dr. Eastman specifically disagreed with a colleague's proposed argument that the Vice President had the power to choose which envelopes to "open" and which votes to "count." Dr. Eastman wrote:

> I don't agree with this. The 12th Amendment only says that the President of the Senate opens the ballots in the joint session then, in the passive voice, that the votes shall then be counted. 3 USC § 12 [of the Electoral Count Act] says merely that he is the presiding officer, and then it spells out specific procedures, presumptions, and default rules for which slates will be counted. Nowhere does it suggest that the president of the Senate gets to make the determination on his own. § 15 [of the Electoral Count Act] doesn't either.[149]

Despite recognizing prior to the 2020 election that the Vice President had no power to refuse to count certain electoral votes, Eastman nevertheless drafted memoranda 2 months later proposing that Pence could do exactly that on January 6th—refuse to count certified electoral votes from Arizona, Georgia, Michigan, Nevada, New Mexico, Pennsylvania and Wisconsin.[150] *Eastman v. Thompson et al.*

Eastman's theory was related to other efforts overseen by President Trump (described in detail below, *see infra* [])to create and transmit fake electoral slates to Congress and the National Archives, and to pressure States to change the election outcome and issue new electoral slates. Eastman supported these ideas despite writing two months earlier that:

> Article II [of the Constitution] says the electors are appointed "in such manner as the Legislature thereof may direct," but I don't think that entitles the Legislature to change the rules after the election and appoint a different slate of electors in a manner different than what was in place on election day. And 3 U.S.C. §15 [of the Electoral Count Act] gives dispositive weight to the slate of electors that was certified by the Governor in accord with 3 U.S.C. §5.[151]

Even after Eastman proposed the theories in his December and January memoranda, he acknowledged in conversations with Vice President Pence's counsel Greg Jacob that Pence could not lawfully do what his own memoranda proposed.[152] Eastman admitted that the U.S. Supreme Court would unanimously reject his legal theory. "He [Eastman] had acknowledged that he would lose 9-0 at the Supreme Court."[153] Moreover, Dr. Eastman acknowledged to Jacob that he didn't think Vice President Al Gore had that power in 2001, nor did he think Vice President Kamala Harris should have that power in 2025.[154]

In testimony before the Select Committee, Jacob described in detail why the Trump plan for Pence was illegal:

> [T]he Vice President's first instinct, when he heard this theory, was that there was no way that our Framers, who abhorred concentrated power, who had broken away from the tyranny of George III, would ever have put one person – particularly not a person who had a direct interest in the outcome because they were on the ticket for the election –in a role to have decisive impact on the outcome of the election. And our review of text, history, and, frankly, just common sense, all confirmed the Vice President's first instinct on that point. There is no justifiable basis to conclude that the Vice President has that kind of authority.[155]

This is how the Vice President later described his views in a public speech:

> I had no right to overturn the election. The Presidency belongs to the American people, and the American people alone. And frankly, there is no idea more un-American than the notion that any one person could choose the American President. Under the Constitution, I had no right to change the outcome of our election.[156]

But as January 6th approached, President Trump nevertheless embraced the new Eastman theories, and attempted to implement them. In a series of meetings and calls, President Trump attempted to pressure Pence to intervene on January 6th to prevent Congress from counting multiple States' electoral votes for Joe Biden. At several points in the days before January 6th, President Trump was told directly that Vice President Pence could not legally do what Trump was asking. For example, at a January 4th meeting in the Oval Office, Dr. Eastman acknowledged that any variation of his proposal – whether rejecting electoral votes outright or delaying certification to send them back to the States – would violate several provisions of the Electoral Count Act. According to Greg Jacob:

> In the conversation in the Oval Office on the 4th, I had raised the fact that . . . [Dr. Eastman's] preferred course had issues with the Electoral Count Act, which he had acknowledged was the case, that there would be an inconsistency with the Electoral Count Act[.][157]

Jacob recorded Eastman's admission in an internal memo he drafted for Vice President Pence on the evening of January 4th: "Professor Eastman acknowledges that his proposal violates several provisions of statutory law."[158] And, during a phone call with President Trump and Dr. Eastman on the evening of January 5, 2021, Dr. Eastman *again* acknowledged that his proposal also would violate several provisions of the Electoral Count Act.

> [W]e did have an in-depth discussion about [the Electoral Count Act] in the subsequent phone calls as I walked him through provision after provision on the recess and on the fact that . . . Congressmen and Senators are supposed to get to object and debate. And he acknowledged, one after another, that those provisions would -- in order for us to send it back to the States, we couldn't do those things as well. We can't do a 10-day, send it back to the States, and honor an Electoral Count Act provision that says you can't recess for more than one day and, once you get to the 5th, you have to stay continuously in session.[159]

As Pence's Chief of Staff, Marc Short, testified that the Vice President also repeatedly informed President Trump that the Vice President's role on January 6th was only ministerial.

> Committee Staff: But just to pick up on that, Mr. Short, was it your impression that the Vice President had directly conveyed his position on these issues to the President, not just to the world through a Dear Colleague Letter, but directly to President Trump?
>
> Marc Short: Many times.
>
> Committee Staff: And had been consistent in conveying his position to the President?
>
> Short: Very consistent.[160]

As the situation grew increasingly acrimonious, Vice President Pence's private counsel Richard Cullen contacted former Fourth Circuit Judge Michael Luttig, a renowned conservative judge for whom Dr. Eastman had previously clerked, and asked Luttig to make a public statement. On January 5th, Luttig wrote the following on Twitter: "The only responsibility and power of the Vice President under the Constitution is to faithfully count the electoral college votes as they have been cast."[161] As Judge Luttig testified in the Committee's hearings, "there was no basis in the Constitution or laws of the United States at all for the theory espoused by Dr. Eastman – at all. None."[162] Judge Luttig completely rejected Dr. Eastman's "blueprint to overturn the 2020 election" as "constitutional mischief" and 'the most reckless, insidious, and calamitous failure[] in both legal and political judgment in American history."[163]

Contemporaneous written correspondence also confirms both that: (1) Eastman himself recognized Pence could not lawfully refuse to count electoral votes, and (2) President Trump also knew this. While sheltering in a loading dock with the Vice President during the violent January 6th attack, Greg Jacob asked Dr. Eastman in an email, "Did you advise the President that in your professional judgment the Vice President DOES NOT have the power to decide things unilaterally?" Dr. Eastman's response stated that the President had "been so advised," but then indicated that President Trump continued to pressure the Vice President to act illegally: "But you know him – once he gets something in his head, it is hard to get him to change course."[164]

To be absolutely clear, no White House lawyer believed Pence could lawfully refuse to count electoral votes. White House Counsel Pat Cipollone told the Select Committee this:

> I thought that the Vice President did not have the authority to do what was being suggested under a proper reading of the law. I conveyed that, ok? I think I actually told somebody, you know, in the Vice President's – "Just blame me." You know this is – I'm not a politician, you know... but, you know, I just said, "I'm a lawyer. This is my legal opinion."[165]

Cipollone also testified that he was "sure [he] conveyed" his views.[166] Indeed, other testimony from Cipollone indicates that Trump knew of Cipollone's view and suggests that Trump purposely excluded Cipollone from the meeting with Pence and Pence's General Counsel on January 4th.[167] Indeed, at one point, Cipollone confronted Dr. Eastman in the hallway outside the Oval Office and expressed his disapproval of and anger with Dr. Eastman's position. According to Jason Miller, "Pat Cipollone thought the idea was nutty and had at one point confronted Eastman basically with the same sentiment" outside the Oval Office.[168] Pat

Cipollone did not deny having an angry confrontation with Dr. Eastman outside of the Oval Office – though he said he didn't have a specific recollection, he had no reason to contradict what Jason Miller said and, moreover, said that Dr. Eastman was aware of his views.[169]

Likewise, Eric Herschmann, another White House lawyer, expressed the same understanding that Dr. Eastman's plan "obviously made no sense" and "had no practical ability to work."[170] Herschmann also recounted telling Dr. Eastman directly that his plan was "completely crazy:"

> And I said to [Dr. Eastman], hold on a second, I want to understand what you're saying. You're saying you believe the Vice President, acting as President of the Senate, can be the sole decisionmaker as to, under your theory, who becomes the next President of the United States? And he said, yes. And I said, are you out of your F'ing mind, right. And that was pretty blunt. I said, you're completely crazy.[171]

Deputy White House Counsel Pat Philbin also had the same understanding.[172] Indeed, as Herschmann testified, even Rudolph Giuliani doubted that Vice President Mike Pence had any legal ability to do what Dr. Eastman had proposed.[173]

Despite all this opposition from all White House lawyers, Trump nevertheless continued to exert immense pressure on Pence to refuse to count electoral votes.

The pressure began before the January 4th Oval Office meeting with Pence, Dr. Eastman, Jacob, Short and Trump, but became even more intense thereafter. On the evening of January 5, 2021, the New York Times published an article reporting that "Vice President Mike Pence told President Trump on Tuesday that he did not believe he had the power to block congressional certification of Joseph R. Biden, Jr.'s victory in the Presidential election despite President Trump's baseless insistence that he did."[174] This reporting was correct – both as to the Vice President's power and as to Vice President Pence having informed President Trump that he did not have the authority to change the outcome of the election. But in response to that story, late in the evening before January 6th Joint Session, President Trump dictated to Jason Miller a statement falsely asserting, "The Vice President and I are in *total agreement* that the Vice President has the power to act."[175] This statement was released at President Trump's direction and was false.[176]

Thereafter Trump continued to apply public pressure in a series of tweets. At 1:00 a.m. on January 6th, "[i]f Vice President @Mike_Pence comes through for us, we will win the Presidency. Many States want to decertify the mistake they made in certifying incorrect & even fraudulent numbers in a process NOT approved by their State Legislatures (which it must be). Mike can send it back!"[177] At 8:17 a.m. on January 6th, he tweeted again: "States want to correct their votes, which they now know were based on irregularities and fraud, plus corrupt process never received legislative approval. All Mike Pence has to do is send them back to the States, AND WE WIN. Do it Mike, this is a time for extreme courage!"[178]

President Trump tried to reach the Vice President early in the morning of January 6th, but the Vice President did not take the call. The President finally reached the Vice President later that morning, shouting from the Oval Office to his assistants to "get the Vice President on the phone."[179] After again telling the Vice President that he had "the legal authority to send [electoral votes] back to the respective states," President Trump grew very heated.[180] Witnesses in the Oval Office during this call told the Select Committee that the President called Vice President Pence a "wimp,"[181] told him it would be "a political career killer" to certify the lawful electoral votes electing President Biden,[182] and accused him of "not [being] tough enough to make the call."[183] As Ivanka Trump would recount to her chief of staff moments later, her father called the Vice President "the p-word" for refusing to overturn the election.[184]

In response, Vice President Pence again refused to take any action other than counting the lawfully certified electoral votes of the States. But President Trump was angry and undeterred. After the conclusion of this call, he edited his speech for the Ellipse to insert language to which his lawyers objected – targeting Vice President Pence directly.[185]

Earlier that morning, Eric Herschmann had tried to remove the reference to Vice President Pence from the speech. As he told speechwriter Stephen Miller, he "didn't concur with the legal analysis" that John Eastman had advanced and believed it "wouldn't advance the ball" to discuss it publicly.[186] But after the call with Vice President Pence, speechwriters were instructed to reinsert the line. Although the final written draft of his speech referred to Pence just once – a line President Trump didn't end up reading[187] – the President went off-script five different times to pressure the Vice President:

"I hope Mike is going to do the right thing. I hope so. Because if Mike Pence does the right thing, we win the election," Trump first told the crowd.[188]

"Mike Pence is going to have to come through for us," Trump later said, "and if he doesn't, that will be a, a sad day for our country because you're sworn to uphold our Constitution."[189]

Addressing Pence directly, Trump told the assembled crowd: "Mike Pence, I hope you're going to stand up for the good of our Constitution and for the good of our country." Trump said at another point, "And if you're not, I'm going to be very disappointed in you. I will tell you right now. I'm not hearing good stories."[190]

"So I hope Mike has the courage to do what he has to do. And I hope he doesn't listen to the RINOs and the stupid people that he's listening to," Trump said.[191]

These statements to the assembled crowd at the Ellipse had Trump's intended effect – they produced substantial anger against Pence. When Pence released a statement confirming that he would not act to prevent Congress from counting electoral votes, the crowd's reaction was harshly negative:

I'm telling you what, I'm hearing that Pence — hearing the Pence just caved. No. Is that true? I didn't hear it. I'm hear — I'm hearing reports that Pence caved. No way. I'm telling you, if Pence caved, we're going to drag motherfuckers through the streets. You fucking politicians are going to get fucking drug through the streets.[192]

Pence voted against Trump. [Interviewer: "Ok. And that's when all this started?"] Yup. That's when we marched on the Capitol.[193]

We just heard that Mike Pence is not going to reject any fraudulent electoral votes. [Other speaker: "Boo. You're a traitor!"] That's right. You've heard it here first. Mike Pence has betrayed the United States of America. [Other speaker: "Fuck you, Mike Pence!"] Mike Pence has betrayed this President and he has betrayed the people of the United States and we will never, ever forget. [Cheers][194]

This woman cames [sic] up to the side of us and she says Pence folded. So it was kind of, like, Ok, well — in my mind I was thinking, well that's it. You know. Well, my son-in-law looks at me and he says I want to go in.[195]

[Q] What percentage of the crowd is going to the Capitol? [A] [Oath Keeper Jessica Watkins]: One hundred percent. It has, it has spread like wildfire that Pence has betrayed us, and everybody's marching on the Capitol. All million of us. It's insane.[196]

Bring him out. Bring out Pence. Bring him out. Bring out Pence. Bring him out. Bring out Pence. Bring him out. Bring out Pence.[197]

Hang Mike Pence. Hang Mike Pence. Hang Mike Pence. Hang Mike Pence. Hang Mike Pence.[198]

Once Trump returned to the White House, he was informed almost immediately that violence and lawlessness had broken out at the Capitol among his supporters.[199] At 2:24 p.m., President Trump applied yet further pressure to Pence (*see infra* []), posting a tweet accusing Vice President Mike Pence of cowardice for not using his role as President of the Senate to change the outcome of the election: "Mike Pence didn't have the courage to do what should have been done to protect our Country and our Constitution, giving States a chance to certify a corrected set of facts, not the fraudulent or inaccurate ones which they were asked to previously certify. USA demands the truth!"[200] Almost immediately thereafter, the crowd around the Capitol surged, and more individuals joined the effort to confront police and break further into the building.

The sentiment expressed in President Trump's 2:24 p.m. tweet, already present in the crowd, only grew more powerful as the President's words spread. Timothy Hale-Cusanelli - a white supremacist who expressed Nazi sympathies - heard about the tweet while in the Crypt around 2:25 p.m., and he, according to the Department of Justice, "knew what that meant." Vice President Pence had decided not to keep President Trump in power.[201] Other rioters described what happened next as follows:

Once we found out Pence turned on us and that they had stolen the election, like officially, the crowd went crazy. I mean, it became a mob. We crossed the gate.[202]

Then we heard the news on [P]ence...And lost it...So we stormed.[203]

They're making an announcement right now saying if Pence betrays us you better get your mind right because we're storming that building.[204]

Minutes after the tweet—at 2:35 p.m.—rioters continued their surge and broke a security line of the DC Metropolitan Police Department, resulting in the first fighting withdrawal in the history of the that force.[205]

President Trump issued this tweet after he had falsely claimed to the angry crowd that Vice President Mike Pence could "do the right thing" and ensure a second Trump term, after that angry crowd had turned into a violent mob assaulting the Capitol while chanting, "Hang Mike Pence!"[206] and after the U.S. Secret Service had evacuated the Vice President from the Senate floor.[207] One minute after the President's tweet, at 2:25 p.m., the Secret Service determined they could no longer protect the Vice President in his ceremonial office near the Senate Chamber, and evacuated the Vice President and his family to a secure location, missing the violent mob by a mere 40 feet.[208]

Further evidence presented at our hearing shows the violent reaction following President Trump's 2:24 p.m. tweet and the efforts to protect Vice President Pence in the time that followed.[209]

The day after the attack on the Capitol, Dr. Eastman called Eric Herschmann to talk about continuing litigation on behalf of the Trump Presidential campaign in Georgia. Herschmann described his reaction to Eastman this way:

> And I said to him, are you out of your F'ing mind? Right? I said, because I only want to hear two words coming out of your mouth from now on: Orderly transition. I said, I don't want to hear any other F'ing words coming out of your mouth, no matter what, other than orderly transition. Repeat those words to me."[210]

Herschmann concluded the call by telling Dr. Eastman: "Now I'm going to give you the best free legal advice you're ever getting in your life. Get a great F'ing criminal defense lawyer, you're going to need it," and hanging up the phone.[211]

In the course of investigating this series of facts, the Select Committee subpoenaed Dr. John Eastman's emails from his employer, Chapman University.[212] Dr. Eastman sued to prevent Chapman from producing the emails, arguing that the emails were attorney-client privileged. Federal District Court Judge David Carter reviewed Dr. Eastman's emails *in camera* to determine, among other things, whether the emails had to be produced because they likely furthered a crime committed by one of Dr. Eastman's clients or by Dr. Eastman himself. In addition to reviewing the emails themselves, Judge Carter reviewed substantial additional evidence presented by the Select Committee and by Dr. Eastman.

After reciting a series of factual findings regarding President Trump's multi-part plan to overturn the election, Judge Carter concluded that President Trump likely violated two criminal statutes: 18 U.S.C. § 1512(c) (corruptly obstructing, impeding or influencing Congress's official proceeding to count electoral votes); and 18 U.S.C. § 371 (conspiring to defraud the United States). The Court also concluded that John Eastman likely violated at least one of these criminal laws. As to §1512(c), Judge Carter explained:

> Taken together, this evidence demonstrates that President Trump likely knew the electoral count plan had no factual justification.
>
> The plan not only lacked factual basis but also legal justification. . . .
>
> The illegality of the plan was obvious. Our nation was founded on the peaceful transition of power, epitomized by George Washington laying down his sword to make way for democratic elections. Ignoring this history, President Trump

vigorously campaigned for the Vice President to single-handedly determine the results of the 2020 election. . . . Every American – and certainly the President of the United States – knows that in a democracy, leaders are elected, not installed. With a plan this "BOLD," President Trump knowingly tried to subvert this fundamental principle. Based on the evidence, the Court finds it more likely than not that President Trump corruptly attempted to obstruct the Joint Session of Congress on January 6, 2021.[213]

As to 18 U.S.C. § 371, Judge Carter identified evidence demonstrating that both President Trump and John Eastman knew their electoral count plan was illegal, and knew it could not "survive judicial scrutiny" in any of its iterations:

Dr. Eastman himself repeatedly recognized that his plan had no legal support. . . . Dr. Eastman likely acted deceitfully and dishonestly each time he pushed an outcome-driven plan that he knew was unsupported by the law.[214]

Finally, Judge Carter concluded:

Dr. Eastman and President Trump launched a campaign to overturn a democratic election, an action unprecedented in American history. Their campaign was not confined to the ivory tower – it was a coup in search of a legal theory. The plan spurred violent attacks on the seat of our nation's government, led to the deaths of several law enforcement officers, and deepened public distrust in our political process.[215]

Judge Luttig reached similar conclusions during his live hearing testimony: "I have written, as you said, Chairman Thompson, that, today, almost 2 years after that fateful day in January 2021, that, still, Donald Trump and his allies and supporters are a clear and present danger to American democracy."[216]

During the hearing, Judge Luttig took issue with certain of Greg Jacob's characterizations of the 12th Amendment's text, explaining that the applicable text was not ambiguous in any way. The Committee agrees with Judge Luttig: the application of the Twelfth Amendment's text is plain in this context; it does not authorize Congress to second-guess State and Federal courts and refuse to count State electoral votes based on concerns about fraud. *See infra* []. Although Jacob did not discuss his position in great detail during the hearing, his private testimony gives more insight on his actual views:

In my view, a lot has been said about the fact that the role of the Vice President in the electoral count on January 6th is purely ministerial, and that is a correct conclusion. But if you look at the constitutional text, the role of Congress is purely ministerial as well. You open the certificates and you count them. Those are the only things provided for in the Constitution.[217]

EFFORTS TO PRESSURE STATES TO CHANGE THE ELECTION OUTCOME, AND TO CREATE AND TRANSMIT FAKE ELECTION CERTIFICATES

Anticipating that the Eastman strategy for January 6th would be implemented, President Trump worked with a handful of others to prepare a series of false Trump electoral slates for seven States Biden actually won. President Trump personally conducted a teleconference with Eastman and Republican National Committee Chair Ronna McDaniel "a few days before December 14" and solicited the RNC's assistance with the scheme.[218] McDaniel agreed to provide that assistance.[219]

A series of contemporaneous documents demonstrate what President Trump and his allies, including attorney Kenneth Chesebro, were attempting to accomplish: they anticipated that the President of the Senate (which, under the Constitution, is the Vice President) could rely upon these false slates of electors on January 6th to justify refusing to count genuine electoral votes.[220]

The false slates were created by fake Republican electors on December 14th, at the same time the actual, certified electors in those States were meeting to cast their States' Electoral College votes for President Biden. By that point in time, election-related litigation was over in all or nearly all of the subject States, and Trump Campaign election lawyers realized that the fake slates could not be lawful or justifiable on any grounds. Justin Clark, the Trump Campaign Deputy Campaign Manager and Senior Counsel told the Select Committee that he "had real problems with the process."[221] Clark warned his colleagues, "unless we have litigation pending like in these States, like, I don't think this is appropriate or, you know, this isn't the right thing to do. I don't remember how I phrased it, but I got into a little bit of a back and forth and I think it was with Ken Chesebro, where I said, Alright, you know, you just get after it, like, I'm out."[222]

Matthew Morgan, the Trump Campaign General Counsel, told the Select Committee that without an official State certificate of ascertainment,[223] "the [fake] electors were, for lack of a better way of saying it, no good or not -- not valid."[224]

The Office of White House Counsel also appears to have expressed concerns with this fake elector plan. In his interview by the Select Committee White House Counsel Pat Cipollone acknowledged his view that by mid-December, the process was "done" and that his deputy, Pat Philbin, may have advised against the fake elector strategy.[225] In an informal Committee interview, Philbin described the fake elector scheme as one of the "bad theories" that were like "whack-a-mole" in the White House during this period.[226] Cipollone agreed with this characterization.[227]

In her testimony, Cassidy Hutchinson testified that she heard at least one member of the White House Counsel's Office say that the plan was not legal:

Committee Staff: ... to be clear, did you hear the White House Counsel's Office say that this plan to have alternate electors meet and cast votes for Donald Trump in States that he had lost was not legally sound?

Hutchinson: Yes, sir.[228]

Multiple Republicans who were persuaded to sign the fake certificates also testified that they felt misled or betrayed, and would not have done so had they known that the fake votes would be used on January 6th without an intervening court ruling One elector told the Select Committee that he thought his vote would be strictly contingent: "[I]t was a very consistent message that we were told throughout all of that, is this is the only reason why we're doing this, is to preserve the integrity of being able to have a challenge."[229]

The "Chairperson" of the Wisconsin fake electors, who was also at the time Chairman of the Wisconsin Republican Party, insisted in testimony to the Select Committee that he "was told that these would only count if a court ruled in our favor" and that he wouldn't have supported anyone using the Trump electors' votes without a court ruling.[230]

Despite the fact that all major election lawsuits thus far had failed, Trump and his co-conspirators in this effort, including John Eastman and Kenneth Chesebro, pressed forward with the fake elector scheme. Ultimately, these false electoral slates, five of which purported to represent the "duly elected" electoral college votes of their States, were transmitted to Executive Branch officials at the National Archives, and to the Legislative Branch, including to the Office of the President of the Senate, Vice President Mike Pence.[231]

The fake electors followed Chesebro's step-by-step instructions for completing and mailing the fake certificates to multiple officials in the U.S. Government,[232] complete with registered mail stickers and return address labels identifying senders like the "Arizona Republican Party" and the "Georgia Republican Party."[233] The Wisconsin Republican Party's fake certificates apparently weren't properly delivered, however, so the Trump campaign arranged to fly them to Washington just before the joint session on January 6th, and try to deliver them to the Vice President via Senator Ron Johnson and Representative Mike Kelly's offices.[234] Both Johnson and Kelly's offices attempted to do so, but Vice President Pence's aide refused the delivery.[235]

Despite pressure from President Trump, Vice President Pence and the Senate parliamentarian refused to recognize or count the unofficial fake electoral votes. Greg Jacob testified that he advised Vice President Pence on January 2nd that "none of the slates that had been sent in would qualify as an alternate slate" under the law and that the Senate Parliamentarian "was in agreement" with this conclusion.[236]

* * *

In addition to this plan to create and transmit fake electoral slates, Donald Trump was also personally and substantially involved in multiple efforts to pressure State election officials and State legislatures to alter official lawful election results. As U.S. District Judge Carter stated in his June 7, 2022, opinion:

> Dr. Eastman's actions in these few weeks [in December 2022] indicate that his and President Trump's pressure campaign to stop the electoral count did not end with Vice President Pence – it targeted every tier of federal and state elected officials. Convincing state legislatures to certify competing electors was essential to stop the count and ensure President Trump's reelection.[237]

Judge Carter also explained that "Dr. Eastman and President Trump's plan to disrupt the Joint Session was fully formed and actionable as early as December 7, 2020."[238]

Chapter 2 of this report provides substantial detail on many of President Trump's specific efforts to apply pressure to State officials and legislators. We provide a few examples here:

During a January 2, 2021, call, President Trump pressured Georgia's Republican Secretary of State Brad Raffensperger to "find 11,780 votes." During that call, President Trump asserted conspiracy theories about the election that Department of Justice officials had already debunked. Trump also made a thinly veiled threat to Raffensperger and his attorney about his failure to respond to Trump's demands: "That's a criminal, that's a criminal offense . . . That's a big risk to you and to Ryan, your lawyer . . . I'm notifying you that you're letting it happen."[239]

Judge Carter drew these conclusions:

> Mr. Raffensperger debunked the President's allegations "point by point" and explained that "the data you have is wrong;" however, President Trump still told him, "I just want to find 11,780 votes."[240]

*　　*　　*

> President Trump's repeated pleas for Georgia Secretary of State Raffensperger clearly demonstrate that his justification was not to investigate fraud, but to win the election. ... Taken together, this evidence demonstrates that President Trump likely knew the electoral count plan had no factual justification. The plan not only lacked factual basis but also legal justification.[241]

That call to Raffensperger came on the heels of Trump's repeated attacks on Raffensperger, election workers, and other public servants about Trump's loss in the election. A month earlier, the Georgia Secretary of State's Chief Operating Officer, Gabriel Sterling, had given this explicit public warning to Trump and his team, a warning that the Select Committee has determined President Trump apparently saw and disregarded:[242]

> [I]t has all gone too far. All of it....
>
> A 20-something tech in Gwinnett County today has death threats and a noose put out, saying he should be hung for treason because he was transferring a report on batches from an EMS to a county computer so he could read it.
>
> It has to stop.
>
> Mr. President, you have not condemned these actions or this language. Senators, you have not condemned this language or these actions. This has to stop. We need you to step up. And if you're going to take a position of leadership, show some.
>
> My boss, Secretary Raffensperger – his address is out there. They have people doing caravans in front of their house, they've had people come onto their property. Tricia, his wife of 40 years, is getting sexualized threats through her cellphone.
>
> It has to stop.
>
> This is elections, this is the backbone of democracy, and all of you who have not said a damn word are complicit in this. It's too much....
>
> What you don't have the ability to do – and you need to step up and say this – is stop inspiring people to commit potential acts of violence. Someone's going to get hurt. Someone's going to get shot. Someone's going to get killed.[243]

The stark warning was entirely appropriate, and prescient. In addition to the examples Sterling identified, Trump and his team were also fixated on Georgia election workers Ruby Freeman and Wandrea "Shaye" Moss. He and Giuliani mentioned Freeman repeatedly in meetings with State legislators, public rallies, and in the January 2nd call with Raffensperger. Referring to a video clip, Giuliani even accused Freeman and Moss of trading USB drives to affect votes "as if they [were] vials of heroin or cocaine."[244] This was completely bogus: it was not a USB drive; it was a ginger mint.[245]

After their contact information was published, Trump supporters sent hundreds of threats to the women and even showed up at Freeman's home.[246] As Freeman testified to the Select Committee, Trump and his followers' conduct had a profound impact on her life. She left her home based on advice from the FBI, and wouldn't move back for months.[247] And she explained, "I've lost my sense of security – all because a group of people, starting with Number 45 [Donald Trump] and his ally Rudy Giuliani, decided to scapegoat me and my daughter Shaye to push their own lies about how the Presidential election was stolen."[248] The treatment of Freeman and Moss was callous, inhumane, and inexcusable. Rudolph Giuliani and others with responsibility should be held accountable.

In Arizona, a primary target of Trump's pressure, and ire, was House Speaker Russell "Rusty" Bowers, a longtime Republican who had served 17 years in the State legislature. Throughout November and December, Bowers spoke to Trump, Giuliani, and members of Giuliani's legal team, in person or on the phone. During these calls, Trump and others alleged that the results in Arizona were affected by fraud and asked that Bowers consider replacing Presidential electors for Biden with electors for Trump.[249] Bowers demanded proof for the claims of fraud, but never got it. At one point, after Bowers pressed Giuliani on the claims of fraud, Giuliani responded, "we've got lots of theories, we just don't have the evidence."[250] Bowers explained to Giuliani: "You are asking me do something against my oath, and I will not break my oath."[251]

Trump and his supporters' intimidation tactics affected Bowers, too. Bowers's personal cell phone and home address were doxed,[252] leading demonstrators to show up at his home and shout insults until police arrived. One protestor who showed up at his home was armed and believed to be a member of an extremist militia.[253] Another hired a truck with a defamatory and profane allegation that Bowers, a deeply religious man, was a pedophile, and drove it through Bowers's neighborhood.[254] This, again, is the conduct of thugs and criminals, each of whom should be held accountable.

In Michigan, Trump focused on Republican Senate Majority Leader Mike Shirkey and Republican House Speaker Lee Chatfield. He invited them to the White House for a November 20, 2020, meeting during which Trump and Giuliani, who joined by phone, went through a "litany" of false allegations about supposed fraud in Michigan's election.[255] Chatfield recalled Trump's more generic directive for the group to "have some backbone and do the right thing," which he understood to mean overturning the election by naming Michigan's Electoral College electors for Trump.[256] Shirkey told Trump that he wouldn't do anything that would violate Michigan law,[257] and after the meeting ended, issued a joint statement with Chatfield: "We have not yet been made aware of any information that would change the outcome of the election in Michigan and as legislative leaders, we will follow the law and follow the normal process regarding Michigan's electors, just as we have said throughout this election."[258]

When Trump couldn't convince Shirkey and Chatfield to change the outcome of the election in Michigan during that meeting or in calls after, he or his team maliciously tweeted out Shirkey's personal cell phone number and a number for Chatfield that turned out to be wrong.[259] Shirkey received nearly 4,000 text messages after that, and another private citizen reported being inundated with calls and texts intended for Chatfield.[260]

None of Donald Trump's efforts ultimately succeeded in changing the official results in any State. That these efforts had failed was apparent to Donald Trump and his co-conspirators well before January 6th. By January 6th, there was no evidence at all that a majority of any State legislature would even attempt to change its electoral votes.[261]

This past October, Federal District Court Judge David Carter issued a further ruling relating to one of President Trump's lawsuits in Georgia. Judge Carter applied the crime-fraud exception to attorney-client privilege again, and identified potential criminal activity related to a knowingly false representation by Donald Trump to a Federal court. He wrote:

> The emails show that President Trump knew that the specific numbers of voter fraud were wrong but continued to tout those numbers, both in court and in public.[262]

As John Eastman wrote in an email on December 31, 2020, President Trump was "made aware that some of the allegations (and evidence proffered by the experts)" in a verified State court complaint was "inaccurate."[263] Dr. Eastman noted that "with that knowledge" President Trump could not accurately verify a Federal court complaint that incorporated by reference the "inaccurate" State court complaint: "I have no doubt that an aggressive DA or US Atty someplace will go after both the President and his lawyers once all the dust settles on this."[264] Despite this specific warning, "President Trump and his attorneys ultimately filed the complaint with the same inaccurate numbers without rectifying, clarifying, or otherwise changing them."[265] And President Trump personally "signed a verification swearing under oath that the incorporated, inaccurate numbers 'are true and correct' or 'believed to be true and correct' to the best of his knowledge and belief."[266] The numbers were not correct, and President Trump and his legal team knew it.

EFFORTS TO CORRUPT THE DEPARTMENT OF JUSTICE

In the weeks after the 2020 election, Attorney General Bill Barr advised President Trump that the Department of Justice had not seen any evidence to support Trump's theory that the election was stolen by fraud. Acting Attorney General Jeffrey Rosen and his Deputy repeatedly reinforced to President Trump that his claims of election fraud were false when they took over in mid-December. Also in mid-December 2020, Attorney General Barr announced his plans to resign. Between that time and January 6th, Trump spoke with Acting Attorney General Jeff Rosen and Acting Deputy Richard Donoghue repeatedly, attempting to persuade them and the Department of Justice to find factual support for his stolen election claims and thereby to assist his efforts to reverse election results.

As Rosen publicly testified, "… between December 23rd and January 3rd, the President either called me or met with me virtually every day, with one or two exceptions, like Christmas Day."[267] As discussed earlier, Justice Department investigations had demonstrated that these stolen election claims were false; both Rosen and Donoghue told Trump this comprehensively and repeatedly.

One of those conversations occurred on December 27th, when Trump called Rosen to go through a "stream of allegations" about the election.²⁶⁸ Donoghue described that call as an "escalation of the earlier conversations" they had.²⁶⁹ Initially, Trump called Rosen directly. When Donoghue joined the call, he sought to "make it clear to the President [that] these allegations were simply not true."²⁷⁰

> So [the President] went through [the allegations] – in what for me was a 90-minute conversation or so, and what for the former Acting AG was a 2-hour conversation – as the President went through them I went piece by piece to say "no, that's false, that is not true," and to correct him really in a serial fashion as he moved from one theory to another.²⁷¹

The President raised, among others, debunked claims about voting machines in Michigan, a truck driver who allegedly moved ballots from New York to Pennsylvania, and a purported election fraud at the State Farm Arena in Georgia.²⁷² None of the allegations were credible, and Rosen and Donoghue said so to the President.²⁷³

At one point during the December 27th call in which Donoghue refuted Trump's fraud allegations, Donoghue recorded in handwritten notes a request Trump made specifically to him and Acting Attorney General Rosen: "Just say the election was corrupt and leave the rest to me and the Republican Congressmen."²⁷⁴ Donoghue explained: "[T]he Department had zero involvement in anyone's political strategy," and "he wanted us to say that it was corrupt."²⁷⁵ "We told him we were not going to do that."²⁷⁶ At the time, neither Rosen nor Donoghue knew the full extent to which Republican Congressmen, including Representative Scott Perry, were attempting to assist Trump to overturn the election results.

The Committee's investigation has shown that Congressman Perry was working with one Department of Justice official, Jeffrey Clark, regarding the stolen election claims. Perry was working with Clark and with President Trump and Chief of Staff Mark Meadows with this goal: to enlist Clark to reverse the Department of Justice's findings regarding the election and help overturn the election outcome.²⁷⁷

After introducing Jeffrey Clark to the President, Perry sent multiple text messages to Meadows between December 26th and December 28th, pressing that Clark be elevated within the Department. Perry reminded Meadows that there are only "11 days to 1/6…We gotta get going!," and, as the days went on, one asking, "Did you call Jeff Clark?"²⁷⁸

Acting Attorney General Rosen first learned about Clark's contact with Trump in a call on Christmas Eve. On that call, President Trump mentioned Clark to Rosen, who was surprised to learn that Trump knew Clark and had met with him. Rosen later confronted Clark about the contact: "Jeff, anything going on that you think I should know about?"²⁷⁹ Clark didn't "immediately volunteer" the fact that he had met with the President, but ultimately "acknowledged that he had been at a meeting with the President in the Oval Office, not alone, with other people."²⁸⁰ Clark was "kind of defensive" and "somewhat apologetic," "casting it as that he had had a meeting with Congressman Perry from Pennsylvania and that, to his surprise, or, you know, he hadn't anticipated it, that they somehow wound up at a meeting in the Oval Office."²⁸¹ Clark's contact with Trump violated both Justice Department and White House policies designed to prevent political pressure on the Department.²⁸²

While Clark initially appeared apologetic and assured Rosen that "[i]t won't happen again,"²⁸³ he nevertheless continued to work and meet secretly with Trump and Congressman

Perry. Less than five days after assuring Rosen that he would comply with the Department's White House contacts policy, Clark told Rosen and Donoghue that he had again violated that policy. Donoghue confronted him: "I reminded him that I was his boss and that I had directed him to do otherwise."[284]

Around the same time, Representative Perry called Acting Deputy Attorney General Donoghue, criticized the FBI, and suggested that the Department hadn't been doing its job. Perry told Donoghue that Clark "would do something about this."[285]

On December 28th, Clark worked with a Department employee named Kenneth Klukowski – a political appointee who had earlier worked with John Eastman – to produce a draft letter from the Justice Department to the State legislature of Georgia.[286] That letter mirrored a number of the positions Trump and Eastman were taking at the time.[287] (Although both Clark and Eastman refused to answer questions by asserting their Fifth Amendment right against self-incrimination, evidence shows that Clark and Eastman were in communication in this period leading up to January 6th.[288] The draft letter to Georgia was intended to be one of several Department letters to State legislatures in swing States that had voted for Biden.[289]

The letter read: "The Department of Justice is investigating various irregularities in the 2020 election for President of the United States."[290] Clark continued: "The Department will update you as we are able on investigatory progress, but at this time we have identified significant concerns that may have impacted the outcome of the election in multiple States, including the State of Georgia."[291] This was *affirmatively untrue*. The Department had conducted many investigations of election fraud allegations by that point, but it absolutely did not have "significant concerns" that fraud "may have impacted the outcome of the election" in any State. Jeff Clark knew this; Donoghue confirmed it again in an email responding to Clark's letter: "[W]e simply do not currently have a basis to make such a statement. Despite dramatic claims to the contrary, we have not seen the type of fraud that calls into question the reported (and certified) results of the election."[292]

The letter also explicitly recommended that Georgia's State legislature should call a special session to evaluate potential election fraud. "In light of these developments, the Department recommends that the Georgia General Assembly should convene in special session so that its legislators are in a special position to take additional testimony, receive new evidence, and deliberate on the matter consistent with its duties under the U.S. Constitution."[293]

Clark's draft letter also referenced the fake electors that Trump and his campaign organized – arguing falsely that there were currently two competing slates of legitimate Presidential electors in Georgia:[294]

> The Department believes that in Georgia and several other States, both a slate of electors supporting Joseph R. Biden, Jr., and a separate slate of electors supporting Donald J. Trump, gathered on [December 14, 2020] at the proper location to cast their ballots, and that both sets of those ballots have been transmitted to Washington, D.C., to be opened by Vice President Pence.[295]

This, of course, was part of Donald Trump and John Eastman's plan for January 6th. This letter reflects an effort to use the Department of Justice to help overturn the election outcome in Georgia and elsewhere.

Rosen and Donoghue reacted immediately to this draft letter:

"[T]here's no chance that I would sign this letter or anything remotely like this," Donoghue wrote.[296] The plan set forth by Clark was "not even within the realm of possibility,"[297] and Donoghue warned that if they sent Clark's letter, it "would be a grave step for the Department to take and it could have tremendous Constitutional, political and social ramifications for the country."[298]

As Richard Donoghue testified when describing his response to Clark's proposed letter:

Well, I had to read both the email and the attached letter twice to make sure I really understood what he was proposing because it was so extreme to me I had a hard time getting my head around it initially.

But I read it, and I did understand it for what he intended, and I had to sit down and sort of compose what I thought was an appropriate response....

In my response I explained a number of reasons this is not the Department's role to suggest or dictate to State legislatures how they should select their electors. But more importantly, this was not based on fact. This was actually contrary to the facts as developed by Department investigations over the last several weeks and months.

So, I respond to that. And for the department to insert itself into the political process this way I think would have had grave consequences for the country. It may very well have spiraled us into a constitutional crisis.[299]

Rosen and Donoghue also met with Clark about the letter. Their conversation "was a very difficult and contentious" one, according to Donoghue.[300] "What you're proposing is nothing less than the United States Justice Department meddling in the outcome of a Presidential election," Donoghue admonished Clark, to which Clark indignantly responded, "I think a lot of people have meddled in this election."[301]

Both Rosen and Donoghue refused to sign the letter, and confronted Clark with the actual results of the Department's investigations.[302] They also permitted Clark access to a classified briefing from the Office of the Director of National Intelligence ("ODNI") showing Clark that allegations he made to Rosen and Donoghue about foreign interference with voting machines were not true. According to Rosen, the decision to give Clark the briefing at that point "was a difficult question because, if he's going to brief the President, I reluctantly think it's probably better that he's heard from Director Ratcliffe than that he not, even if – I don't think he should brief the President. But, at this point, he's telling me that this is happening whether I agree with it or not. So, so I let him have that briefing."[303]

After Clark received the ODNI briefing, "he acknowledged [to Donoghue] that there was nothing in that briefing that would have supported his earlier suspicion about foreign involvement."[304] While Clark then dropped his claims about foreign interference, he continued to press to send the letter to Georgia and other States, despite being told that the Department of Justice investigations had found no fraud sufficient to overturn the election outcome in Georgia or any other States. This was an intentional choice by Jeff Clark to contradict specific Department findings on election fraud, and purposely insert the

Department into the Presidential election on President Trump's behalf and risk creating or exacerbating a constitutional crisis.

By this point, President Trump recognized that neither Rosen nor Donoghue would sign the letter or support his false election claims. Trump and his team then communicated further with Clark and offered him the job of Acting Attorney General. On January 2nd, Clark told Rosen that he "… would turn down the President's offer if [Rosen] reversed [his] position and signed the letter" that he and Klukowski had drafted.[305] The next day, Clark decided to accept and informed Rosen, who then called White House Counsel to seek a meeting directly with Trump. As Rosen put it, "… I wasn't going to accept being fired by my subordinate, so I wanted to talk to the President directly."[306]

On January 3rd, that meeting was convened. Although contemporaneous White House documents suggest that Clark had *already* been appointed as the Acting Attorney General,[307] all the participants in the meeting other than Clark and President Trump aggressively opposed Clark's appointment.

At that point, Rosen decided to "broaden the circle" and ask that his subordinates inform all the other Assistant Attorneys General (AAGs) what was afoot.[308] Rosen wanted to know how the AAGs would respond if Jeff Clark was installed as the Acting Attorney General. Pat Hovakimian, who worked for Rosen, then set up a conference call. The AAGs almost immediately agreed that they would resign if Rosen was removed from office.[309]

Rosen, Donoghue, and Steve Engel, the Assistant Attorney General for the Office of Legal Counsel, attended the meeting. White House lawyers Pat Cipollone, Eric Herschmann and Pat Philbin joined as well.

When the meeting started, Clark attempted to defend his appointment. Clark declared that this was the "last opportunity to sort of set things straight with this defective election," and he had the "intelligence," the "will," and "desire" to "pursue these matters in the way that the President thought most appropriate."[310] Everyone else present disagreed that Clark could conceivably accomplish these things.

White House Counsel Pat Cipollone threatened to resign as well, describing Clark's letter as a "murder-suicide pact."[311] Cipollone warned that the letter would "damage everyone who touches it" and no one should have anything to do with it.[312]

Trump asked Donoghue and Engel what they would do if Clark took office. Both confirmed they would resign.[313] Steve Engel recalled that the President next asked if he would resign:

> At some point, [] I believe Rich Donoghue said that senior Department officials would all resign if Mr. Clark were put in, and the President turned to me and said, 'Steve, you wouldn't resign, would you?' I said, 'Well, Mr. President, I've been with you through four Attorneys General, including two Acting Attorneys General, and I just couldn't be part of this if Mr. Clark were here.' And I said, 'And I believe that the other senior Department officials would resign as well. And Mr. Clark would be here by himself with a hostile building, those folks who remained, and nothing would get done.'[314]

Donoghue added that they would not be the only ones to resign. "You should understand that your entire Department leadership will resign," Donoghue recalled saying. This included every Assistant Attorney General. "Mr. President, these aren't bureaucratic leftovers from another administration," Donoghue reminded Trump, "You picked them. This is your leadership team." Donoghue added, "And what happens if, within 48 hours, we have hundreds of resignations from your Justice Department because of your actions? What does that say about your leadership?"[315] Steve Engel then reinforced Donoghue's point, saying that Clark would be leading a "graveyard."

Faced with mass resignations and recognizing that the "breakage" could be too severe, Donald Trump decided to rescind his offer to Clark and drop his plans to use the Justice Department to aid in his efforts to overturn the election outcome.[316] The President looked at Clark and said, "I appreciate your willingness to do it. I appreciate you being willing to suffer the abuse. But the reality is, you're not going to get anything done. These guys are going to quit. Everyone else is going to resign. It's going to be a disaster. The bureaucracy will eat you alive. And no matter how much you want to get things done in the next few weeks, you won't be able to get it done, and it's not going to be worth the breakage."[317]

* * *

Evidence gathered by the Committee also suggests that President Trump offered Sidney Powell the position of Special Counsel for election related matters during a highly charged White House meeting on December 18, 2020.[318] White House lawyers vehemently opposed Powell's appointment, and it also was not ultimately made formal.

SUMMONING A MOB TO WASHINGTON, AND KNOWING THEY WERE ANGRY AND ARMED, INSTRUCTING THEM TO MARCH TO THE CAPITOL

In the early morning hours of December 19th, shortly after the contentious December 18th White House meeting with Sidney Powell and others, Donald Trump sent a tweet urging his supporters to travel to Washington for January 6th. In that tweet, Trump attached false allegations that the election was stolen and promised a "wild" time on January 6th.[319] This Twitter invitation was followed by over a dozen other instances in which he used Twitter to encourage supporters to rally for him in Washington, DC on January 6th.[320]

The Committee has assembled detailed material demonstrating the effects of these communications from members of far-right extremist groups, like the Proud Boys, Oath Keepers, Three Percenters, and others, and from individuals looking to respond to their president's call to action. President Trump's supporters believed the election was stolen because they listened to his words,[321] and they knew what he had called them to do; stop the certification of the electoral count.[322]

For example, one supporter, Charles Bradford Smith, noted on December 22, 2020 that "Trump is asking everyone to go" to Washington, DC on January 6th "to fill the streets" on the "day Pence counts up the votes."[323] Derek Sulenta posted to Facebook on December 23, 2020 that "I'll be there Jan 6th to support the president no matter what happens" because "That's the day he called for patriots to show up."[324] By December 31, 2020, Robert Morss believed January 6th stood for the moment when "1776 Will Commence Again" because President Trump asked them to "Be there, Will be Wild."[325] Kenneth Grayson predicted what would eventually happen on January 6th, when on December 23, 2020, he wrote on Facebook that President Trump called people to Washington, DC through his December 19th tweet and then added "IF TRUMP TELLS US TO STORM THE FUKIN CAPITAL IMA DO THAT THEN!"[326] Some demonstrated their inspiration for January 6th by circulating flyers, which proclaimed "#OccupyCongress" over images of the United States Capitol.[327] Robert Gieswein, a Coloradan affiliated with Three Percenters who was among the first to breach the Capitol, said that he came to Washington, DC "to keep President Trump in."[328]

Chapter 8 of this report documents how the Proud Boys led the attack, penetrated the Capitol, and led hundreds of others inside. Multiple Proud Boys reacted immediately to President Trump's December 19th tweet and began their planning. Immediately, Proud Boys leaders reorganized their hierarchy, with Enrique Tarrio, Joseph Biggs, and Ethan Nordean messaging groups of Proud Boys about what to expect on January 6th.[329] Tarrio created a group chat known as the Ministry of Self-Defense for hand-selected Proud Boys whom he wanted to "organize and direct" plans for January 6th.[330] On social media, Tarrio referenced "revolt" and "[r]evolution," and conspicuously asked "What if we invade it?" on Telegram.[331] As of December 29, 2020, Tarrio told the group the events on January 6th would be "centered around the Capitol."[332]

At the time of publication of this report, prosecutions of certain Proud Boys are ongoing. To date, one Proud Boy has pled guilty to seditious conspiracy and other Proud Boys have pled guilty to other crimes, including conspiracy to obstruct Congress.[333] Jeremy Bertino, a Proud Boy who pled guilty to seditious conspiracy, admitted that he:

> understood from internal discussions among the Proud Boys that in the leadup to January 6, the willingness to resort to unlawful conduct increasingly included a willingness to use and promote violence to achieve political objectives.[334]

Moreover,

> Bertino believed that the 2020 election had been "stolen" and, as January 6, 2021, approached, believed that drastic measures, including violence, were necessary to prevent Congress from certifying the Electoral College Vote on January 6, 2021. Bertino made his views in this regard known publicly, as well as in private discussions with MOSD leadership. Bertino understood from his discussions with MOSD leadership that they agreed that the election had been stolen, that the purpose of traveling to Washington, D.C., on January 6, 2021, was to stop the certification of the Electoral College Vote, and that the MOSD leaders were willing to do whatever it would take, including using force against police and others, to achieve that objective.[335]

As set out in Bertino's plea agreement, members of MOSD:

> openly discussed plans for potential violence at the Capitol [... and] members of MOSD leadership were discussing the possibility of storming the Capitol. Bertino believed that storming the Capitol would achieve the group's goal of stopping Congress from certifying the Electoral College Vote. Bertino understood that storming the Capitol or its grounds would be illegal and would require using force against police or other government officials.[336]

Another Proud Boy who has pled guilty to conspiracy and assault charges, Charles Donohoe, understood that the Proud Boys planned to storm the Capitol. Donohoe, a Proud Boys local chapter leader from North Carolina:

> was aware [as early as January 4, 2021] that members of MOSD leadership were discussing the possibility of storming the Capitol. Donohoe believed that storming the Capitol would achieve the group's goal of stopping the government from carrying out the transfer of presidential power.[337]

The Department of Justice has charged a number of Oath Keepers with seditious conspiracy. Specifically, the government alleges that "[a]fter the Presidential Election, Elmer Stewart Rhodes III conspired with his co-defendants, introduced below, and other co-conspirators, known and unknown to the Grand Jury, to oppose by force the lawful transfer of presidential power."[338] A jury agreed, convicting Stewart Rhodes and Kelly Meggs – the leader of the Florida Oath Keepers chapter – of seditious conspiracy. The jury also convicted Rhodes and Meggs, as well as fellow Oath Keepers Jessica Watkins, Kenneth Harrelson, and Thomas Caldwell,[339] of other serious felonies for their actions on January 6th.[340]

Meggs celebrated the December 19th tweet, sending an encrypted Signal message to Florida Oath Keepers that President Trump "wants us to make it WILD that's what he's saying. He called us all to the Capitol and wants us to make it wild!!! … Gentlemen we are heading to DC pack your shit!!"[341] Similarly, Oath Keeper Joshua James – who pleaded guilty to seditious conspiracy – told Oath Keepers that there was now a "NATIONAL CALL TO ACTION FOR DC JAN 6TH" following President Trump's words.[342]

Stewart Rhodes, the Oath Keepers' founder, felt that "the time for peaceful protest is over" after December 19th and, according to the government, "urged President Trump to use military force to stop the lawful transfer of presidential power, describing January 6, 2021, as "a hard constitutional deadline" to do so.[343] Rhodes created a "an invitation-only Signal group chat titled, 'DC OP: Jan 6 21'" on December 30, 2020, which he and other Oath Keepers, like Meggs and James, used to plan for January 6th, including by creating a "quick reaction force" of firearms to be stashed in Virginia.[344]

Multiple members of the Oath Keepers have pleaded guilty to seditious conspiracy. Brian Ulrich started planning for January 6th right after President Trump sent out his December 19th tweet. The Department of Justice summarized Ulrich's communications, as follows:

> Ulrich messaged the "Oath Keepers of Georgia" Signal group chat, "Trump acts now maybe a few hundred radicals die trying to burn down cities … Trump sits on his hands Biden wins … millions die resisting the death of the 1st and 2nd amendment." On December 20, 2020, an individual in the "Oath Keepers of Georgia" Signal group chat, who later traveled with Ulrich to Washington, D.C., and breached the Capitol grounds with Ulrich on January 6, 2021, messaged, "January 6th. The great reset. America or not."[345]

The Justice Department's Statement of Offense for Oath Keeper Joshua James provided these details:

> In advance of and on January 6, 2021, James and others agreed to take part in the plan developed by Rhodes to use any means necessary, up to and including

the use of force, to stop the lawful transfer of presidential power. In the weeks leading up to January 6, 2021, Rhodes instructed James and other coconspirators to be prepared, if called upon, to report to the White House grounds to secure the perimeter and use lethal force if necessary against anyone who tried to remove President Trump from the White House, including the National Guard or other government actors who might be sent to remove President Trump as a result of the Presidential Election.[346]

The former President's call also galvanized Three Percenters to act. A group known as The Three Percenters Original sent a message to its members on December 16, 2020, noting they "stand ready and are standing by to answer the call from our President should the need arise" to combat the "pure evil that is conspiring to steal our country away from the american people" through the "2020 presidential election."[347] After President Trump's tweet, the group put out another letter instructing "any member who can attend ... to participate" on January 6th because "[t]he President of the United States has put out a general call for the patriots of this Nation to gather" in Washington, DC.[348]

Other Three Percenter groups also responded. Alan Hostetter and Russell Taylor led a group of Three Percenters calling themselves the California Patriots – DC Brigade, who have been charged with conspiracy to obstruct Congress because they organized to fight to keep President Trump in power on January 6th after President Trump's December 19th tweet inspired them to come to Washington, DC.[349] On December 19th, Hostetter posted on Instagram:

President Trump tweeted that all patriots should descend on Washington DC on Wednesday 1/6/2021. This is the date of the Joint Session of Congress in which they will either accept or reject the fake/phony/stolen electoral college votes.[350]

Between December 19th and January 6th, Hostetter, Taylor, and other members of the California Patriots – DC Brigade exchanged messages and posted to social media about bringing gear, including "weaponry," like "hatchet[s]," "bat[s]," or "[l]arge metal flashlights," and possibly "firearms," and, about being "ready and willing to fight" like it was "1776." Taylor even spoke in front of the Supreme Court on January 5, 2021, explaining that "[p]atriots" would "not return to our peaceful way of life until this election is made right ... ."[351] On December 29, 2020, Taylor exclaimed "I personally want to be on the front steps and be one of the first ones to breach the doors!"[352]

Similarly, members of the Florida Guardians of Freedom, Three Percent sent around a flyer on December 24, 2020, saying they were "responding to the call from President Donald J. Trump to assist in the security, protection, and support of the people as we all protest the fraudulent election and re-establish liberty for our nation."[353] Their leader, Jeremy Liggett, posted a meme to Facebook stating that "3% Will Show In Record Numbers In DC"[354] and put out a "safety video" instructing people that they could bring "an expandable metal baton, a walking cane and a folding knife"[355] to Washington, DC on January 6th. Several have been arrested for participating in the violence around the tunnel on January 6th.[356]

When interviewed by the FBI on March 31, 2021, Danny Rodriguez – a Three Percenter from California who tased Officer Michael Fanone in the neck as rioters tried to break through a door on the west side of the Capitol – reflected on his decision to go to Washington, DC[357]:

Trump called us to D.C. ... and he's calling for help -- I thought he was calling for help. I thought he was -- I thought we were doing the right thing. ... [W]e thought we were going to hit it like a civil war. There was going to be a big battle. ... I thought that the main fight, the main battle, was going to be in D.C. because Trump called everyone there.[358]

These groups were not operating in silos. Meggs bragged on Facebook that following President Trump's December 19th tweet he had formed an alliance between the Oath Keepers, the Florida Three Percenters, and the Proud Boys "to work together to shut this shit down."[359] On December 19th, Meggs called Enrique Tarrio and they spoke for more than three minutes.[360] Three days later, Meggs messaged Liggett, echoing his excitement about the December 19th tweet and specifically referencing the seat of Congress: "He called us all to the Capitol and wants us to make it wild!!!"[361] Liggett said "I will have a ton of men with me" and Meggs replied that "we have made Contact [sic] with PB [Proud Boys] and they always have a big group. Force multiplier. ... I figure we could splinter off the main group of PB and come up behind them. Fucking crush them for good."[362] Aside from Meggs, Stewart Rhodes brought in at least one local militia leader[363] and Three Percenters into the Oath Keepers January 6th planning chats that came about following President Trump's tweet.[364]

Even on January 6th, rioters referenced the tweet. An unknown rioter was caught on video as they ascended the Capitol steps saying "He said it was gonna be wild. He didn't lie."[365] MPD body-worn cameras captured Cale Clayton around 3:15 p.m. as he taunted officers from under the scaffolding: "Your fucking president told us to be here. You should be on this side, right here, going with us. You are an American citizen. Your fucking President told you to do that. You too. You too. You. All of you guys. That Tweet was for you guys. For us. For you."[366]

As January 6th neared, intelligence emerged indicating that January 6th was likely to be violent, and specifically that the Capitol was a target. On January 3rd, an intelligence summary informed Department of Justice officials of plans to "occupy the Capitol" and "invade" the Capitol on January 6th. This summarized a "SITE Intelligence Group" report about the "online rhetoric focused on the 6 Jan event." Some of the reporting includes: "Calls to occupy federal buildings." "intimidating Congress and invading the capitol building." The email also quoted WUSA9 local reporting: "one of the websites used for organizing the event was encouraging attendees to bring guns."[367]

Acting Deputy Attorney General Richard Donoghue testified:

And we knew that if you have tens of thousands of very upset people showing up in Washington, DC, that there was potential for violence.[368]

At the same time, a Defense Department official predicted on a White House National Security Council call that violence could be targeted at the Capitol on January 6th. According to Chairman of the Joint Chiefs of Staff Gen. Mark Milley:

So during these calls, I — I only remember in hindsight because he was almost like clairvoyant. [Deputy Secretary of Defense David] Norquist says during one of these calls, the greatest threat is a direct assault on the Capitol. I'll never forget it.[369]

Likewise, documentation received by the Committee from the Secret Service demonstrates a growing number of warnings both that January 6th was likely to be violent, and specifically that the Capitol would likely be the target, including intelligence directly regarding the Proud Boys and Oath Keepers militia groups.

Even two weeks ahead of January 6th, the intelligence started to show what could happen. On December 22, 2020, the FBI received a screenshot of an online chat among Oath Keepers, seemingly referring to the State capitols besieged by protesters across the country earlier that year: "if they were going to go in, then they should have went all the way."[370] "There is only one way. It is not signs. It's not rallies. It's fucking bullets," one user replied.[371]

A public source emailed the Secret Service a document titled "Armed and Ready, Mr. President," on December 24th, which summarized online comments responding to President Trump's December 19th tweet.[372] Protestors should "start marching into the chambers," one user wrote.[373] Trump "can't exactly openly tell you to revolt," another replied. "This is the closest he'll ever get."[374] "I read [the President's tweet] as armed," someone said.[375] "[T]here is not enough cops in DC to stop what is coming," replied yet another.[376] "[B]e already in place when Congress tries to get to their meeting," the comments continued, and "make sure they know who to fear.'"[377] "[W]aiting for Trump to say the word," a person said, and "this is what Trump expects," exclaimed another.[378] Capitol Police's head of intelligence, Jack Donohue, got the same compilation from a former colleague at the New York Police Department on December 28, 2020.[379]

On December 26, 2020, the Secret Service received a tip about the Proud Boys detailing plans to have "a large enough group to march into DC armed [that] will outnumber the police so they can't be stopped."[380] "Their plan is to literally kill people," the informant stated. "Please please take this tip seriously ...."[381] On December 29, 2020, Secret Service forwarded related warnings to Capitol Police that pro-Trump demonstrators were being urged to "occupy federal building[s]," including "march[ing] into the capital building and mak[ing] them quake in their shoes by our mere presence."[382]

Civilians also tipped off Capitol Police about bringing weapons to besiege the Capitol. One tipster, who had "track[ed] online far right extremism for years," emailed Capitol Police warning "I've seen countless tweets from Trump supporters saying they will be armed," and "I[']ve also seen tweets from people organizing to 'storm the Capitol' on January 6th."[383]

On December 29, 2020, Secret Service forwarded related warnings to Capitol Police that pro-Trump demonstrators were being urged to "occupy federal building," including "march[ing] into the capital building and mak[ing] them quake in their shoes by our mere presence."[384] Indeed, a Secret Service intelligence briefing on December 30th entitled "March for Trump," highlighted the President's "Will be wild!" tweet alongside hashtags #WeAreTheStorm, #1776Rebel, and #OccupyCapitols, writing "President Trump supporters have proposed a movement to occupy Capitol Hill."[385]

On January 1, 2021, a lieutenant in the intelligence branch at DC Police forwarded a civilian tip about "a website planning terroristic behavior on Jan 6th, during the rally" to Capitol Police intelligence.[386] "There are detailed plans to storm federal buildings," including "the capitol in DC on Jan 6th," the tipster reported, linking to thedonald.win.[387]

On January 2, 2021, the FBI discovered a social media posting that read, "This is not a rally and it's no longer a protest. This is a final stand . . . many are ready to die to take back #USA . . . . And don't be surprised if we take the #capital building."[388]

On January 3, 2021, a Parler user's post – under the name 1776(2.0) Minuteman – noting "after weds we are going to need a new congress" and "Jan 6 may actually be their [Members of Congress] last day in office" reached the FBI and Capitol Police.[389]

The FBI field office in Norfolk, Virginia issued an alert to law enforcement agencies on January 5th tiled "Potential for Violence in Washington, D.C. Area in Connection with Planned 'StopTheSteal' Protest on 6 January 2021," which noted:

> An online thread discussed specific calls for violence to include stating 'Be ready to fight. Congress needs to hear glass breaking, doors being kicked in, and blood... being spilled. Get violent...stop calling this a march, or rally, or a protest. Go there ready for war. We get our President or we die. NOTHING else will achieve this goal.'[390]

In addition, the alert copied "perimeter maps [of the Capitol] and caravan pictures [that] were posted" on thedonald.win, particularly worrying that the "caravans ... had the same colors as the sections of the perimeter" of the Capitol.[391] Secret Service also knew about caravans planning to come to DC to "Occupy the Capitol."[392]

That same day, representatives from DHS, FBI, DC's Homeland Security and Emergency Management Agency, Secret Service, DC Police, and Capitol Police shared a website, Red State Secession, which had a post titled "Why the Second American Revolution Starts Jan 6." A user asked visitors to post where they could find the home addresses of Democratic congressmen and "political enemies" and asked if "any of our enemies [will] be working in offices in DC that afternoon."[393] "What are their routes to and from the event?" the post continued.[394] "[T]he crowd will be looking for enemies."[395]

A Secret Service open-source unit flagged an account on thedonald.win that threatened to bring a sniper rifle to a rally on January 6th. The user also posted a picture of a handgun and rifle with the caption, "Sunday Gun Day Providing Overwatch January 6th Will be Wild."[396]

The Secret Service learned from the FBI on January 5th about right-wing groups establishing armed quick reaction forces in Virginia, where they could amass firearms illegal in DC.[397] Trump supporters staged there waiting across the river "to respond to 'calls for help.'"[398] The Oath Keepers were such a group.[399]

President Trump's closest aides knew about the political power of sites like thedonald.win, which is where much of this violent rhetoric and planning happened. On December 30, 2020, Jason Miller – a senior adviser to and former spokesman for the former President – texted Chief of Staff Mark Meadows a link to the thedonald.win, adding "I got the base FIRED UP."[400] The link connected to a page with comments like "Gallows don't require electricity," "if the filthy commie maggots try to push their fraud through, there will be hell to pay," and Congress can certify Trump the winner or leave "in a bodybag."[401] Symbolic gallows were constructed on January 6th at the foot of the Capitol.[402] [consider adding photo here]

After President Trump's signal, his supporters did not hide their plans for violence at the Capitol, and those threats made their way to national and local law enforcement agencies. As described in this report, the intelligence agencies did detect this planning, and they shared it with the White House and with the U.S. Secret Service.

Testimony from White House staff also suggests real concerns about the risk of violence as January 6th approached. Cassidy Hutchinson, for example, testified about a conversation she had with her boss, Mark Meadows, on January 2nd:

> I went into Mark's office, and he was still on his phone. . . . . I said to Mark, "Rudy [Giuliani] said these things to me. What's going on here? Anything I should know about?"
>
> This was – he was, like, looking at his phone. He was like, "Oh, it's all about the rally on Wednesday. Isn't that what he was talking to you about?"
>
> I said, "Yeah. Yeah, sounds like we're going to the Capitol."
>
> He said, "Yeah. Are you talking with Tony?"
>
> "I'm having a conversation, sir."
>
> He said – still looking at his phone. I remember he was scrolling. He was like, "Yeah. You know, things might get real, real bad on the 6th."
>
> And I remember saying to him, "What do you mean?"
>
> He was like, "I don't know. There's just going to be a lot of people here, and there's a lot of different ideas right now. I'm not really sure of everything that's going on. Let's just make sure we keep tabs on it."[403]

Hutchinson also testified about a conversation she had with Director of National Intelligence, Ratcliffe:

> He had expressed to me that he was concerned that it could spiral out of control and potentially be dangerous, either for our democracy or the way that things were going for the 6th.[404]

Hope Hicks texted Trump Campaign spokesperson Hogan Gidley in the midst of the January 6th violence, explaining that she had "suggested ... several times" on the preceding days (January 4th and January 5th) that President Trump publicly state that January 6th must remain peaceful and that he had refused her advice to do so.[405] Her recollection was that Herschmann earlier advised President Trump to make a preemptive public statement in advance of January 6th calling for no violence that day.[406] No such statement was made.

The District of Columbia Homeland Security office explicitly warned that groups were planning to "occupy the [Capitol] to halt the vote."[407]

> [W]e got derogatory information from OSINT suggesting that some very, very violent individuals were organizing to come to DC, and not only were they

organized to come to DC, but they were — these groups, these nonaligned groups were aligning. And so all the red flags went up at that point, you know, when you have armed militia, you know, collaborating with White supremacy groups, collaborating with conspiracy theory groups online all toward a common goal, you start seeing what we call in, you know, terrorism, a blended ideology, and that's a very, very bad sign. ... [T]hen when they were clearly across — not just across one platform but across multiple platforms of these groups coordinating, not just like chatting, "Hey, how's it going, what's the weather like where you're at," but like, "what are you bringing, what are you wearing, you know, where do we meet up, do you have plans for the Capitol." That's operational – that's like preoperational intelligence, right, and that is something that's clearly alarming.[408]

Again, this type of intelligence was shared, including obvious warnings about potential violence prior to January 6th.[409] What was not shared, and was not fully understood by intelligence and law enforcement entities, is what role President Trump would play on January 6th in exacerbating the violence, and later refusing for multiple hours to instruct his supporters to stand down and leave the Capitol. No intelligence collection was apparently performed on President Trump's plans for January 6th, nor was there any analysis performed on what he might do to exacerbate potential violence. Certain Republican members of Congress who were working with Trump and the Giuliani team may have had insight on this particular risk, but none appear to have alerted the Capitol Police or any other law enforcement authority.

On January 2, 2021, Katrina Pierson wrote in an email to fellow rally organizers, "POTUS expectations are to have something intimate at the [E]llipse, and call on everyone to march to the Capitol."[410] And, on January 4, 2021, another rally organizer texted Mike Lindell, the MyPillow CEO, that President Trump would "unexpectedly" call on his supporters to march to the Capitol:

This stays only between us ... . It can also not get out about the march because I will be in trouble with the national park service and all the agencies but POTUS is going to just call for it "unexpectedly."[411]

Testimony obtained by the Committee also indicates that President Trump was specifically aware that the crowd he had called to Washington was fired up and angry on the evening of January 5th. Judd Deere, a deputy White House press secretary recalled a conversation with President Trump in the Oval Office on the evening of January 5th:

Judd Deere: "I said he should focus on policy accomplishments. I didn't mention the 2020 election."

Committee Staff: "Okay. What was his response?"

Deere: "He acknowledged that and said, 'We've had a lot,' something along those lines, but didn't – he fairly quickly moved to how fired up the crowd is, or was going to be."

Committee Staff: "Okay. What did he say about it?"

Deere: "Just that they were – they were fired up. They were angry. They feel like the election's been stolen, that the election was rigged, that – he went on and on about that for a little bit."[412]

Testimony indicated that President Trump was briefed on the risk of violence on the morning of the 6th before he left the White House. Cassidy Hutchinson provided this testimony:

Vice Chair Cheney: So, Ms. Hutchinson, is it your understanding that Mr. Ornato told the President about weapons at the rally on the morning of January 6th?

Hutchinson: That is what Mr. Ornato relayed to me.[413]

The head of President Trump's security detail, Bobby Engel, told the Select Committee that he when he shared critical information with White House Deputy Chief of Staff Anthony Ornato, it was a means of conveying that information with the Oval Office: "So, when it came to passing information to Mr. Ornato, I – my assumption was that it would get to the chief [of staff, Mark Meadows], or that he was sharing the information with the chief. I don't – and the filtering process, or if the chief thinks it needs to get to the President, then he would share it with the President."[414] Also, Engel confirmed that if "information would come to my attention, whether it was a protective intelligence issue or a concern or – primarily, I would – I would make sure that the information got filtered up through the appropriate chain usually through Mr. Ornato. So if I received a report on something that was happening in the DC area, I'd either forward that information to Mr. Ornato, or call him about that information or communicate in some way."[415]

The Select Committee also queried Deputy Chief of Staff Ornato this November about what he generally would have done in this sort of situation, asking him the following: "Generally you receive information about things like the groups that are coming, the stuff that we talked earlier. You would bring that to Mr. Meadows and likely did here, although you don't have a specific recollection?"[416] Ornato responded: "That is correct, sir."[417] Ornato also explained to the Committee that "... in my normal daily functions, in my general functions as my job, I would've had a conversation with him about all the groups coming in and what was expected from the secret service."[418] As for the morning of January 6th itself, he had the following answer:

Committee Staff: Do you remember talking to Chief of Staff Mark Meadows about any of your concerns about the threat landscape going into January 6th?

Ornato: I don't recall; however, in my position I would've made sure he was tracking the demos, which he received a daily brief, Presidential briefing. So he most likely was getting all this in his daily brief as well. I wouldn't know what was in his intelligence brief that day, but I would've made sure that he was tracking these things and just mentioned, "Hey, are you tracking the demos?" If he gave me a "yeah", I don't recall it today, but I'm sure that was something that took place.[419]

Ornato had access to intelligence that suggested violence at the Capitol on January 6th, and it was his job to inform Meadows and Trump of that. Although Ornato told us that he did not recall doing so, the Select Committee found multiple parts of Ornato's testimony questionable. The Select Committee finds it difficult to believe that neither Meadows nor

Ornato told Trump, as was their job, about the intelligence that was emerging as the January 6th rally approached.

Hours before the Ellipse rally on January 6th, the fact that the assembled crowd was prepared for potential violence was widely known. In addition to intelligence reports indicating potential violence at the Capitol, weapons and other prohibited items were being seized by police on the streets and by Secret Service at the magnetometers for the Ellipse speech. Secret Service confiscated a haul of weapons from the 28,000 spectators who did pass through the magnetometers: 242 cannisters of pepper spray, 269 knives or blades, 18 brass knuckles, 18 tasers, 6 pieces of body armor, 3 gas masks, 30 batons or blunt instruments, and 17 miscellaneous items like scissors, needles, or screwdrivers.[420] And thousands of others purposely remained outside the magnetometers, or left their packs outside.[421]

Others brought firearms. Three men in fatigues from Broward County, Florida brandished AR-15s in front of Metropolitan police officers on 14th Street and Independence Avenue on the morning of January 6th.[422] MPD advised over the radio that one individual was possibly armed with a "Glock" at 14th and Constitution Avenue, and another was possibly armed with a "rifle" at 15th and Constitution Avenue around 11:23 a.m.[423] The National Park Service detained an individual with a rifle between 12 and 1 p.m.[424] Almost all of this was known before Donald Trump took the stage at the Ellipse.

By the time President Trump was preparing to give his speech, he and his advisors knew enough to cancel the rally. And he certainly knew enough to cancel any plans for a march to the Capitol. According to testimony obtained by the Select Committee, Trump knew that elements of the crowd were armed, and had prohibited items, and that many thousands would not pass through the magnetometers for that reason. Testimony indicates that the President had received an earlier security briefing, and testimony indicates that the Secret Service mentioned the prohibited items again as they drove President Trump to the Ellipse.

Cassidy Hutchinson was with the President backstage. Her contemporaneous text messages indicate that President Trump was "effing furious" about the fact that a large number of his supporters would not go through the magnetometers:

Cassidy Hutchinson: But the crowd looks good from this vanish [sic] point. As long as we get the shot. He was fucking furious

Tony Ornato: He doesn't get it that the people on the monument side don't want to come in. They can see from there and don't want to come in. They can see from there and don't have to go through mags. With 30k magged inside.

Cassidy Hutchinson: That's what was relayed several times and in different iterations

Cassidy Hutchinson: Poor max got chewed out

Cassidy Hutchinson: He also kept mentioning [an off the record trip] to Capitol before he took the stage

Tony Ornato: Bobby will tell him no. It's not safe to do. No assets available to safely do it.[425]

And Hutchinson described what President Trump said as he prepared to take the stage:

> When we were in the off-stage announce area tent behind the stage, he was very concerned about the shot. Meaning the photograph that we would get because the rally space wasn't full. One of the reasons, which I've previously stated, was because he wanted it to be full and for people to not feel excluded because they had come far to watch him at the rally. And he felt the mags were at fault for not letting everybody in, but another leading reason and likely the primary reasons is because he wanted it full and he was angry that we weren't letting people through the mags with weapons—what the Secret Service deemed as weapons, and are, are weapons. But when we were in the off-stage announce tent, I was a part of a conversation, I was in the vicinity of a conversation where I overheard the President say something to the effect of, "I don't F'ing care that they have weapons. They're not here to hurt me. Take the F'ing mags away. Let my people in. They can march to the Capitol from here. Let the people in. Take the F'ing mags away."[426]

The Secret Service special agent who drove the President after his speech told the Select Committee that Trump made a similar remark in the vehicle when his demand to go to the Capitol was refused—essentially that Trump did not believe his supporters posed a security risk to him personally.[427]

Minutes after the exchange that Hutchinson described—when President Trump took the stage—he pointedly expressed his concern about the thousands of attendees who would not enter the rally area and instructed Secret Service to allow that part of the crowd to enter anyway:

> ... I'd love to have if those tens of thousands of people would be allowed. The military, the secret service. And we want to thank you and the police law enforcement. Great. You're doing a great job. But I'd love it if they could be allowed to come up here with us. Is that possible? Can you just let [them] come up, please?[428]

Although President Trump and his advisors knew of the risk of violence, and knew specifically that elements of the crowd were angry and some were armed, from intelligence and law enforcement reports that morning, President Trump nevertheless went forward with the rally, and then specifically instructed the crowd to march to the Capitol: "Because you'll never take back our country with weakness. You have to show strength and you have to be strong. We have come to demand that Congress do the right thing and only count the electors who have been lawfully slated, lawfully slated."[429] Much of President Trump's speech was improvised. Even before his improvisation, during the review of President Trump's prepared remarks, White House lawyer Eric Herschmann specifically requested that "if there were any factual allegations, someone needed to independently validate or verify the statements."[430] And in the days just before January 6th, Herschmann "chewed out" John Eastman and told him he was "out of [his] F'ing mind" to argue that the Vice President could be the sole decision-maker as to who becomes the next President.[431] Herschmann told us, "I so berated him that I believed that theory would not go forward."[432] But President Trump made that very argument during his speech at the Ellipse and made many false statements. Herschmann attended that speech, but walked out during the middle of it.[433]

President Trump's speech to the crowd that day lasted more than an hour. The speech walked through dozens of known falsehoods about purported election fraud. And Trump again made false and malicious claims about Dominion voting systems.[434] As discussed earlier, he again pressured Vice President Mike Pence to refuse to count lawful electoral votes, going off script repeatedly, leading the crowd to believe falsely that Pence could and would alter the election outcome:

> And I actually, I just spoke to Mike. I said: "Mike, that doesn't take courage. What takes courage is to do nothing. That takes courage." And then we're stuck with a president who lost the election by a lot and we have to live with that for four more years. We're just not going to let that happen....
>
> When you catch somebody in a fraud, you're allowed to go by very different rules.
> So I hope Mike has the courage to do what he has to do. And I hope he doesn't listen to the RINOs and the stupid people that he's listening to."[435]

This characterization of Vice President Pence's decision had a direct impact on those who marched to and approached the Capitol, as illustrated by this testimony from a person convicted of crimes committed on January 6th:

> So this woman came up to the side of us, and she, says, Pence folded. So it was kind of, like, okay. Well, in my mind I was thinking, Well, that's it, you know. Well, my son-in-law looks at me, and he says, I want to go in.[436]

Trump used the word "peacefully," written by speech writers, one time. But he delivered many other scripted and unscripted comments that conveyed a very different message:

> Because you'll never take back our country with weakness. You have to show strength and you have to be strong. We have come to demand that Congress do the right thing and only count the electors who have been lawfully slated, lawfully slated. . . .
>
> And we fight. We fight like hell. And if you don't fight like hell, you're not going to have a country anymore....[437]

Trump also was not the only rally speaker to do these things. Mayor Giuliani for instance also said that "Let's have trial by combat."[438] Likewise, John Eastman used his two minutes on the Ellipse stage to make a claim already known to be false – that corrupted voted machines stole the election.[439]

The best indication of the impact of Trump's words, both during the Ellipse speech and beforehand, are the comments from those supporters who attended the Ellipse rally and their conduct immediately thereafter. Videoclips show several of the attendees on their way to the Capitol or shortly after they arrived:

I'm telling you what, I'm hearing that Pence — hearing the Pence just caved. No. Is that true? I didn't hear it. I'm hear — I'm hearing reports that Pence caved. No way. I'm telling you, if Pence caved, we're going to drag motherfuckers through the streets. You fucking politicians are going to get fucking drug through the streets.[440]

Yes. I guess the hope is that there's such a show of force here that Pence will decide do the right thing, according to Trump.[441]

Pence voted against Trump. [Interviewer: "Ok. And that's when all this started?"] Yup. That's when we marched on the Capitol." [442]

We just heard that Mike Pence is not going to reject any fraudulent electoral votes. [Other speaker: "Boo. You're a traitor! Boo!"] That's right. You've heard it here first. Mike Pence has betrayed the United States of America. [Other speaker: "Boo! Fuck you, Mike Pence!"] Mike Pence has betrayed this President and he has betrayed the people of the United States and we will never, ever forget. [Cheers][443]

[Q] What percentage of the crowd is going to the Capitol? [A] [Oath Keeper Jessica Watkins]: One hundred percent. It has, it has spread like wildfire that Pence has betrayed us, and everybody's marching on the Capitol. All million of us. It's insane.[444]

Another criminal defendant—charged with assaulting an officer with a flagpole and other crimes—explained in an interview why he went to the Capitol and fought:

Dale Huttle: We were not there illegally, we were invited there by the President himself. . . . Trump's backers had been told that the election had been stolen.

. . .

Reporter Megan Hickey: But do you think he encouraged violence?

Dale Huttle: Well, I sat there, or stood there, with half a million people listening to his speech. And in that speech, both Giuliani and [Trump] said we were going to have to fight like hell to save our country. Now, whether it was a figure of speech or not—it wasn't taken that way.

Reporter Megan Hickey: You didn't take it as a figure of speech?

Dale Huttle: No.[445]

President Trump concluded his speech at 1:10 p.m.

Among other statements from the Ellipse podium, President Trump informed the crowd that he would be marching to the Capitol with them:

Now, it is up to Congress to confront this egregious assault on our democracy. And after this, we're going to walk down, **and I'll be there with you**, we're going to walk down, we're going to walk down. Anyone you want, but I think right here, **we're going to walk down to the Capitol**, and we're going to cheer on our brave senators and congressmen and women, and we're probably not going to be cheering so much for some of them.[446]

Hutchinson testified that she first became aware of President Trump's plans to attend Congress's session to count votes on or about January 2nd. She learned this from a conversation with Giuliani: "It's going to be great. The President's going to be there. He's going to look powerful. He's – he's going to be with the members. He's going to be with the Senators."[447] Evidence also indicates that multiple members of the White House staff, including White House lawyers, were concerned about the President's apparent intentions to go to the Capitol. [448]

After he exited the stage, President Trump entered the Presidential SUV and forcefully expressed his intention that Bobby Engel, the head of his Secret Service detail, direct the motorcade to the Capitol. The Committee has now obtained evidence from several sources about a "furious interaction" in the SUV. The vast majority of witnesses who have testified before the Select Committee about this topic, including multiple members of the Secret Service, a member of the Metropolitan police, and national security officials in the White House, described President Trump's behavior as "irate," "furious," "insistent," "profane" and "heated." Hutchinson heard about the exchange second-hand and related what she heard in our June 28, 2022, hearing from Ornato (as did another witness, a White House employee with national security responsibilities, who shared that Ornato also recounted to him President Trump's "irate" behavior in the Presidential vehicle.) Other members of the White House staff and Secret Service also heard about the exchange after the fact. The White House employee with national security responsibilities gave this testimony:

> Committee Staff: But it sounds like you recall some rumor or some discussion around the West Wing about the President's anger about being told that he couldn't go to the Capitol. Is that right?
>
> Employee: So Mr. Ornato said that he was angry that he couldn't go right away. In the days following that, I do remember, you know, again, hearing again how angry the President was when, you know, they were in the limo. But beyond specifics of that, that's pretty much the extent of the cooler talk.[449]

The Committee has regarded both Hutchinson and the corroborating testimony by the White House employee with national security responsibilities as earnest and has no reason to conclude that either had a reason to invent their accounts. A Secret Service agent who worked on one of the details in the White House and was present in the Ellipse motorcade had this comment:

> Committee Staff: Ms. Hutchinson has suggested to the committee that you sympathized with her after her testimony, and believed her account. Is that accurate?
>
> Special Agent: I have no – yeah, that's accurate. I have no reason – I mean, we – we became friends. We worked – I worked every day with her for 6 months. Yeah, she became a friend of mine. We had a good working relationship. I have no reason – she's never done me wrong. She's never lied that I know of.[450]

The Committee's principal concern was that the President actually intended to participate personally in the January 6th efforts at the Capitol, leading the attempt to overturn the election either from inside the House Chamber, from a stage outside the Capitol, or otherwise. The Committee regarded those facts as important because they are relevant to President Trump's intent on January 6th. There is no question from all the evidence assembled that President Trump *did have that intent.*[451]

As it became clear that Donald Trump desired to travel to the Capitol on January 6th, a White House Security Official in the White House complex became very concerned about his intentions:

> To be completely honest, we were all in a state of shock. . . . it just – one, I think the actual physical feasibility of doing it, and then also we all knew what that implicated and what that meant, that this was no longer a rally, that this was going to move to something else if he physically walked to the Capitol. I – I don't know if you want to use the word "insurrection," "coup," whatever. We all knew that this would move from a normal, democratic, you know, public event into something else.[452]

President Trump continued to push to travel to the Capitol even after his return to the White House, despite knowing that a riot was underway. Kayleigh McEnany, the White House press secretary, spoke with President Trump about his desire to go to the Capitol after he returned to the White House from the Ellipse. "So to the best of my recollection, I recall him being – wanting to – saying that he wanted to physically walk and be a part of the march and then saying that he would ride the Beast if he needed to, ride in the Presidential limo."[453]

Later in the afternoon, Mark Meadows relayed to Cassidy Hutchinson that President Trump was still upset that he would not be able to go to the Capitol that day. As he told Hutchinson, "the President wasn't happy that Bobby [Engel] didn't pull it off for him and that Mark didn't work hard enough to get the movement on the books."[454]

187 MINUTES: TRUMP'S DERELICTION OF DUTY

Just after 1:00 p.m., Vice President Pence, serving as President of the Senate under Article I of the Constitution, gaveled the Congress into its Joint Session. President Trump was giving a speech at the Ellipse, which he concluded at 1:10 pm. For the next few hours, an attack on our Capitol occurred, perpetrated by Trump supporters many of whom were present at the Ellipse for President Trump's speech. More than 140 Capitol and Metropolitan police were injured, some very seriously.[455] A perimeter security line of Metropolitan Police intended to secure the Capitol against intrusion broke in the face of thousands of armed rioters – more than two thousand of whom gained access to the interior of the Capitol building.[456] A woman who attempted to forcibly enter the Chamber of the House of Representatives through a broken window while the House was in session was shot and killed by police guarding the chamber. Vice President Pence and his family were at risk, as were those Secret Service professionals protecting him. Congressional proceedings were halted, and legislators were rushed to secure locations.

From the outset of the violence and for several hours that followed, people at the Capitol, people inside President Trump's Administration, elected officials of both parties, members of President Trump's family, and Fox News commentators sympathetic to President Trump all tried to contact him to urge him to do one singular thing – one thing that all of these people immediately understood was required: Instruct his supporters to stand down and disperse – to leave the Capitol.

As the evidence overwhelmingly demonstrates, President Trump specifically and repeatedly refused to do so – for multiple hours – while the mayhem ensued. Chapter 8 of this report explains in meticulous detail the horrific nature of the violence taking place, that was directed at law enforcement officers at the Capitol and that put the lives of American lawmakers at risk. Yet in spite of this, President Trump watched the violence on television from a dining room adjacent to the Oval Office, calling Senators to urge them to help him delay the electoral count, but refusing to supply the specific help that everyone knew was unequivocally required. As this report shows, when Trump finally did make such a statement at 4:17 p.m. – after hours of violence – the statement immediately had the expected effect; the rioters began to disperse immediately and leave the Capitol.[457]

To fully understand the President's behavior during those hours – now commonly known as the "187 minutes" – it is important to understand the context in which it occurred. As outlined in this report, by the afternoon of January 6th, virtually all of President Trump's efforts to overturn the outcome of the 2020 election had failed. Virtually all the lawsuits had already been lost. Vice President Mike Pence had refused Trump's pressure to stop the count of certain electoral votes. State officials and legislators had refused to reverse the election outcomes in every State where Trump and his team applied pressure. The Justice Department's investigations of alleged election fraud had all contradicted Trump's allegations.

The only factor working in Trump's favor that might succeed in materially delaying the counting of electoral votes for President-elect Biden was the violent crowd at the Capitol. And for much of the afternoon of January 6th, it appeared that the crowd had accomplished that purpose. Congressional leaders were advised by Capitol Police at one or more points during the attack that it would likely take several days before the Capitol could safely be reopened.[458]

By the time the President's speech concluded, the lawlessness at the United States Capitol had already begun, but the situation was about to get much worse.

By 1:25 p.m., President Trump was informed that the Capitol was under attack.

Minutes after arriving back at the White House, the President ran into a member of the White House staff and asked if they had watched his speech on television. "Sir, they cut it off because they're rioting down at the Capitol," the employee said. The President asked what they meant by that. "[T]hey're rioting down there at the Capitol," the employee repeated. "Oh really?" the President asked. "All right, let's go see."[459] A photograph taken by the White House photographer—the last one permitted until later in the day—captures the moment the President was made aware of the violent uprising at the Capitol.[460]

Not long thereafter, as thousands of Trump supporters from the Ellipse speech continued to arrive at the Capitol, the DC Metropolitan Police Department declared a riot at the Capitol at 1:49 p.m., the same time Capitol Police Chief Steven Sund informed the DC National Guard "that there was a dire emergency on Capitol Hill and requested the immediate assistance" of as many national guard troops as possible.[461]

No photographs exist of the President for the remainder of the afternoon until after 4 p.m. President Trump appears to have instructed that the White House photographer was not to take any photographs.[462] The Select Committee also was unable to locate any official records of President Trump's telephone calls that afternoon.[463] And the President's official Daily Diary contains no information for this afternoon between the hours of 1:19 p.m. and 4:03 p.m., at the height of the worst attack on the seat of the United States Congress in over two centuries.[464]

The Select Committee did, however, obtain records from non-official sources that contained data of some phone calls President Trump made that afternoon. Even though "he was placing lots of calls" that afternoon, according to his personal assistant,[465] the Select Committee was given no records of any calls from the President to security or law enforcement officials that afternoon, and that absence of data is consistent with testimony of witnesses who would have knowledge of any such calls, who said that he did not do so.[466] Based on testimony from President Trump's close aides, we know that President Trump remained in the Dining Room adjacent to the Oval Office for the rest of the afternoon until after 4:03 p.m.[467]

In fact, from cellular telephone records, it appears that at 1:39 p.m. and 2:03 p.m., after being informed of the riot at the Capitol, President Trump called his lawyer, Rudolph Giuliani. These calls lasted approximately four minutes and eight minutes, respectively.[468] And Press Secretary Kayleigh McEnany testified that President Trump also called a number of Senators.[469] The number or names of all such Members of Congress is unknown, although Senator Mike Lee (R-UT) received one such outgoing call from the President within the hour that followed.[470]

At 1:49 p.m., just as the DC Metropolitan Police officially declared a riot and the Capitol Police were calling for help from the National Guard to address the crisis, President Trump sent a tweet with a link to a recording of his speech at the Ellipse.[471]

At about that point, White House Counsel Pat Cipollone became aware of the Capitol riot. The Committee collected sworn testimony from several White House officials, each with similar accounts. The President's White House Counsel Pat Cipollone testified that he raced downstairs, and went to the Oval Office Dining Room as soon as he learned about the violence at the Capitol—likely just around or just after 2 p.m. Cipollone knew immediately that the President had to deliver a message to the rioters—asking them to leave the Capitol.

Here is how he described this series of events:

... the first time I remember going downstairs was when people had breached the Capitol... But I went down with [Deputy White House Counsel] Pat [Philbin], and I remember we were both very upset about what was happening. And we both wanted, you know, action to be taken related to that... But we went down to the Oval Office, we went through the Oval office, and we went to the back where the President was.... I think he was already in the dining room... I can't talk about conversations [with the

President]. I think I was pretty clear there needed to be an immediate and forceful response, statement, public statement, that people need to leave the Capitol now.[472]

Cipollone also left little doubt that virtually everyone among senior White House staff had the same view:

There were a lot of people in the White House that day . . . Senior people who, you know, felt the same way that I did and who were working very hard to achieve that result. There were – I think Ivanka was one of them. And Eric Herschmann was there, Pat Philbin was there, and a number of other people.... many people suggested it. ... Many people felt the same way. I'm sure I had conversations with Mark [Meadows] about this during the course of the day and expressed my opinion very forcefully that this needs to be done.[473]

Likewise, senior staff cooperated to produce a message for the President on a notecard, which read:

"ANYONE WHO ENTERED THE CAPITOL ~~ILLEGALLY~~ WITHOUT PROPER AUTHORITY SHOULD LEAVE IMMEDIATELY."[474]

The President declined to make the statement. Cipollone also made it clear that the advice they were giving to the President never changed throughout this three-hour period. Trump refused to do what was necessary.

Committee Staff: ... [I]t sounds like you from the very onset of violence at the Capitol right around 2 o'clock were pushing for a strong statement that people should leave the Capitol. Is that right?

Cipollone: I was, and others were as well.[475]

Cassidy Hutchinson, who worked closely with Mark Meadows and sat directly outside his office, confirmed this account and described several additional details:

I see Pat Cipollone barreling down the hallway towards our office. And he rushed right in, looked at me, said, "Is Mark in his office?" And I said, "Yes." And on a normal day he would've said, "Can I pop in," or, "Is he talking to anyone," or, "Is it an appropriate time for me to go chat with him," and myself or Eliza would go let him in or tell him no. But after I had said yes, he just looked at me and started shaking his head and went over, opened Mark's office door, stood there with the door propped open, and said something to the – Mark was still sitting on his phone. I remember, like, glancing in. He was still sitting on his phone.

And I remember Pat saying to him something to the effect of, "The rioters have gotten to the Capitol, Mark. We need to go down and see the President now." And Mark looked up at him and said, "He doesn't want to do anything, Pat." And Pat said something to the effect of – and very clearly said this to Mark – something to the effect of, "Mark, something needs to be done, or people are going to die and the blood's gonna be on your F'ing hands. This is getting out of control. I'm going down there.[476]

The Select Committee believes that the entire White House senior staff was in favor of a Presidential statement specifically instructing the violent rioters to leave. But President Trump refused. White House Counsel Pat Cipollone answered certain questions from the Select Committee on this subject as follows:

Vice Chair Cheney: And when you talk about others on the staff thinking more should be done, or thinking that the President needed to tell people to go home, who would you put in that category?

Cipollone: Well, I would put ... Pat Philbin, Eric Herschmann. Overall, Mark Meadows, Ivanka. Once Jared go there, Jared, General Kellogg. I'm probably missing some, but those are – Kayleigh I think was there. But I don't – Dan Scavino.

Vice Chair Cheney: And who on the staff did not want people to leave the Capitol?"

Cipollone: On the staff?

Vice Chair Cheney: In the White House?

Cipollone: I can't think of anybody on that day who didn't want people to get out of the Capitol once the – particularly once the violence started. No. I mean –

Mr. Schiff: What about the President?

Vice Chair Cheney: Yeah.
...
[Consultation between Mr. Cipollone and his counsel.]

Cipollone: Yeah. I can't reveal communications. But obviously I think, you know – yeah.[477]

The testimony of a White House employee with national security responsibilities also corroborated these facts. This employee testified about a conversation between Pat Cipollone and Eric Herschmann in which Herschmann indicated that the President does not want to do anything to halt the violence. That employee told the Select Committee that he overheard Herschmann saying something to the effect of "the President didn't want anything done."[478]

Deputy Press Secretary Judd Deere also testified to the Select Committee that as soon as it was clear that the Capitol's outer perimeter had been breached, he urged that the President make a statement telling the rioters to go home:

Committee Staff:	And so what did you do at that point?
Judd Deere:	If I recall, I went back up to [Press Secretary] Kayleigh [McEnany]'s office and indicated that we now likely needed to say something.
Committee Staff:	Okay. And why did you think it was necessary to say something?
Deere:	Well, I mean, it appears that individuals are storming the U.S. Capitol building. They also appear to be supporters of Donald Trump, who may have been in attendance at the rally. We're going to need to say something.
Committee Staff:	And did you have a view as to what should be said by the White House?
Deere:	If I recall, I told Kayleigh that I thought that we needed to encourage individuals to stop, to respect law enforcement, and to go home…. And it was – it was incumbent upon us to encourage those individuals, should they be supporters of ours, to stop.[479]

Testimony from both Deputy Press Secretary Matthews and White House Counsel Cipollone indicated that it would have been easy, and nearly instantaneous, for Trump to make a public statement insisting that the crowd disperse. As Deputy Press Secretary Sarah Matthews explained, he could have done so in under a minute:

> … it would take probably less than 60 seconds from the Oval Office dining room over to the Press Briefing Room. And, for folks that might not know, the Briefing Room is the room that you see the White House Press Secretary do briefings from with the podium and the blue backdrop. And there is a camera that is on in there at all times. And so, if the President had wanted to make a statement and address the American people, he could have been on camera almost instantly.[480]

Cipollone also shared that assessment:

Committee Staff:	Would it have been possible at any moment for the President to walk down to the podium in the briefing room and talk to the nation at any time between when you first gave him that advice at 2 o'clock and 4:17 when the video statement went out? Would that have been possible?
Cipollone:	Would it have been possible?"
Committee Staff:	Yes.
Cipollone:	Yes, it would have been possible.[481]

At 2:13 p.m., rioters broke into the Capitol and flooded the building.[482]

As the violence began to escalate, many Trump supporters and others outside the White House began urgently seeking his intervention. Mark Meadows's phone was flooded with text messages. These are just some of them:

2:32 p.m. from Fox News anchor Laura Ingraham: "Hey Mark, The president needs to tell people in the Capitol to go home."[483]

2:35 p.m. from Mick Mulvaney: "Mark: he needs to stop this, now. Can I do anything to help?"[484]

2:46 p.m. from Rep. William Timmons (R-SC): "The president needs to stop this ASAP"[485]

2:53 p.m. from Donald Trump, Jr.: "He's got to condem [sic] this shit. Asap. The captiol [sic] police tweet is not enough."[486]

3:04 p.m. from Rep. Jeff Duncan (R-SC): "POTUS needs to calm this shit down"[487]

3:09 p.m. from former White House Chief of Staff Reince Priebus: "TELL THEM TO GO HOME !!!"[488]

3:13 p.m. from Alyssa Farah Griffin: "Potus has to come out firmly and tell protestors to dissipate. Someone is going to get killed."[489]

3:15 p.m. from Rep. Chip Roy (R-TX): "Fix this now."[490]

3:31 p.m. from Fox News anchor Sean Hannity: "Can he make a statement. I saw the tweet. Ask people to peacefully leave the capital [sic]"[491]

3:58 p.m. from Fox News anchor Brian Kilmeade: "Please get him on tv. Destroying every thing you guys have accomplished"[492]

Others on Capitol Hill appeared in the media, or otherwise appeared via internet. Representative Mike Gallagher (R-WI) issued a video appealing directly to the President:

Mr. President, you have got to stop this. You are the only person who can call this off. Call it off. The election is over. Call it off![493]

Some Members of Congress sent texts to President Trump's immediate staff or took to Twitter, where they knew the President spent time:

Sen. Bill Cassidy (R-LA) issued a tweet: @realDonaldTrump please appear on TV, condemn the violence and tell people to disband.[494]

Rep. Jaime Herrera Beutler (R-WA) sent a text to Mark Meadows: We need to hear from the president. On TV. I hate that Biden jumped him on it.[495]

Republican Leader Kevin McCarthy tried repeatedly to reach President Trump, and did at least once. He also reached out for help to multiple members of President Trump's family, including Ivanka Trump and Jared Kushner.[496] Kushner characterized Leader McCarthy's demeanor on the call as "scared":

Kushner:	I could hear in his voice that he really was nervous, and so, obviously, I took that seriously. And, you know, I didn't know if I'd be able to have any impact, but I said, you know, it's better to at least try. And so I – like I said, I turned the shower off, threw on a suit, and, you know, and rushed into the White House as quickly as I could.
Committee Staff:	Yeah. What did he ask you to do? When you say have an impact, what is it specifically that he needed your help with?
Kushner:	I don't recall a specific ask, just anything you could do. Again, I got the sense that, you know, they were – they were – you know, they were scared.
Committee Staff:	"They" meaning Leader McCarthy and people on the Hill because of the violence?
Kushner:	That he was scared, yes.[497]

Kevin McCarthy told Fox News at 3:09 p.m. about his call with the President[498] and elaborated about its contents in a conversation with CBS News's Norah O'Donnell at around 3:30 p.m.:

O'Donnell: Have you spoken with the President and asked him to perhaps come to the Capitol and tell his supporters it's time to leave?

Leader McCarthy: I have spoken to the President. I asked him to talk to the nation and tell them to stop this....

* * *

O'Donnell: The President invited tens of thousands of people to quote unquote stop the steal. I don't know if you heard his more-than-hour-long remarks or the remarks of his son, who was the wind-up. It was some heated stuff, Leader McCarthy. I just wonder whether someone is going to accurately call a spade a spade, and I am giving you the opportunity right now that your precious and beloved United States Capitol and our democracy is witnessing this. Call a spade a spade.

Leader McCarthy: I was very clear with the President when I called him. This has to stop. And he has to, he's gotta go to the American public and tell them to stop this.

* * *

O'Donnell: Leader McCarthy, the President of the United States has a briefing room steps from the Oval Office. It is, the cameras are hot 24/7, as you know. Why hasn't he walked down and said that, now?

Leader McCarthy: I conveyed to the President what I think is best to do, and I'm hopeful the President will do it.[499]

The Committee has evidence from multiple sources regarding the content of Kevin McCarthy's direct conversation with Donald Trump during the violence.

Rep. Jaime Herrera Beutler (R-WA), to whom McCarthy spoke soon after, relayed more of the conversation between McCarthy and President Trump:

And he said [to President Trump], "You have got to get on TV. You've got to get on Twitter. You've got to call these people off." You know what the President said to him? This is as it's happening. He said, "Well Kevin, these aren't my people. You know, these are Antifa." And Kevin responded and said, "No, they're your people. They literally just came through my office windows and my staff are running for cover. I mean they're running for their lives. You need to call them off." And the President's response to Kevin to me was chilling. He said, "Well Kevin, I guess they're just more upset about the election, you know, theft than you are".[500]

Rep. Herrera Beutler's account of the incident was also corroborated by former Acting White House Chief of Staff Mick Mulvaney, who testified that Leader McCarthy told him several days later that President Trump had said during their call: "Kevin, maybe these people are just more angry about this than you are. Maybe they're more upset."[501]

Mulvaney was also trying to reach administration officials to urge President Trump to instruct his supporters to leave the Capitol.[502] As were many elected officials in both parties, including Nancy Pelosi and Chuck Schumer, and several Republican Members of Congress.[503]

As already noted, Pat Cipollone and others in the White House repeatedly urged President Trump to tell his supporters to leave the Capitol. Cipollone described his conversations with Mark Meadows after they failed to convince President Trump to deliver the necessary message:

Committee Staff: Do you remember any discussion with Mark Meadows with respect to his view that the President didn't want to do anything or was somehow resistant to wanting to say something along the lines that you suggested.

Pat Cipollone:	Not just – just to be clear, many people suggested it."
Committee Staff:	Yeah.
Cipollone:	Not just me. Many people felt the same way. I'm sure I had conversations with Mark about this during the course of the day and expressed my opinion very forcefully that this needs to be done.[504]

* * *

Committee Staff:	So your advice was tell people to leave the Capitol, and that took over 2 hours when there were subsequent statements made, tweets put forth, that in your view were insufficient. Did you continue, Mr. Cipollone, throughout the period of time up until 4:17, continue, you and others, to push for a stronger statement?
Cipollone:	Yes.[505]

* * *

Committee Staff:	... at the onset of the violence when you first notice on television or wherever that rioters have actually breached the Capitol, did you have a conversation with Mark Meadows in which Meadows indicated he doesn't want to do anything, "he" meaning the President?
Cipollone:	I don't – I had a conversation I'm sure with Mark Meadows, I'm sure with other people, of what I thought should be done. Did Mark say that to me? I don't have a recollection of him saying that to me, but he may have said something along the lines.[506]

At 2:16 p.m., security records indicate that the Vice President was "being pulled" to a safer location.[507]

In an interview with the Select Committee, a White House Security Official on duty at the White House explained his observations as he listened to Secret Service communications and made contemporaneous entries into a security log. In particular, he explained an entry he made at 2:24 p.m.:

Committee Staff: Ok. That last entry on this page is: "Service at the Capitol does not sound good right now.

Official: Correct.

Committee Staff: What does that mean?

Official: The members of the VP detail at this time were starting to fear for their own lives. There were a lot of -- there was a lot of yelling, a lot of – I don't know – a lot [of] very personal calls over the radio. So – it was disturbing. I don't like talking about it, but there were calls to say good-bye to family members, so on and so forth. It was getting -- for whatever the reason was on the ground, the VP detail thought that this was about to get very ugly.

Committee Staff: And did you hear that over the radio?

Official: Correct.

...

Committee Staff: ... obviously, you've conveyed that's disturbing, but what prompted you to put it into an entry as it states there, Service at the Capitol –

Official: That they're running out of options, and they're getting nervous. It sounds like that we came very close to either Service having to use lethal options or worse. At that point, I don't know. Is the VP compromised? Is the detail – like, I don't know. like, we didn't have visibility, but it doesn't – if they're screaming and saying things, like, say good-bye to the family, like, the floor needs to know this is going to a whole another level soon.[508]

Also at 2:24 p.m., knowing the riot was underway and that Vice President Pence was at the Capitol, President Trump sent this tweet:

Mike Pence didn't have the courage to do what should have been done to protect our Country and our Constitution, giving States a chance to certify a corrected set of facts, not the fraudulent or inaccurate ones which they were asked to previously certify. USA demands the truth![509]

Evidence shows that the 2:24 p.m. tweet immediately precipitated further violence at the Capitol. Immediately after this tweet, the crowds both inside and outside of the Capitol building violently surged forward.[510] Outside the building, within ten minutes thousands of rioters overran the line on the west side of the Capitol that was being held by the Metropolitan Police Force's Civil Disturbance Unit, the first time in history of the DC Metro Police that such a security line had ever been broken.[511]

Virtually everyone in the White House staff the Select Committee interviewed condemned the 2:24 p.m. tweet in the strongest terms.

Deputy National Security Adviser Matthew Pottinger told the Select Committee that the 2:24 p.m. tweet was so destructive that it convinced him to resign as soon as possible:

One of my aides handed me a sheet of paper that contained the tweet that you just read. I read it and was quite disturbed by it. I was disturbed and worried to see that the President was attacking Vice President Pence for doing his constitutional duty.

So the tweet looked to me like the opposite of what we really needed at that moment, which was a de-escalation. And that is why I had said earlier that it looked like fuel being poured on the fire.

So that was the moment that I decided that I was going to resign, that that would be my last day at the White House. I simply didn't want to be associated with the events with the events that were unfolding at the Capitol.[512]

Deputy Press Secretary Sarah Matthews had a similar reaction:

So it was obvious that the situation at the Capitol was violent and escalating quickly. And so I thought that the tweet about the Vice President was the last thing that was needed in that moment.

And I remember thinking that this was going to be bad for him to tweet this, because it was essentially him giving the green light to these people, telling them that what they were doing at the steps of the Capitol and entering the Capitol was okay, that they were justified in their anger.

And he shouldn't have been doing that. He should have been telling these people to go home and to leave and to condemn the violence that we were seeing.

And I am someone who has worked with him, you know, I worked on the campaign, traveled all around the country, going to countless rallies with him, and I have seen the impact that his words have on his supporters. They truly latch onto every word and every tweet that he says.

And so, I think that in that moment for him to tweet out the message about Mike Pence, it was him pouring gasoline on the fire and making it much worse.[513]

Deputy Press Secretary Judd Deere stated the following:

Committee Staff: What was your reaction when you saw that tweet?

Deere: Extremely unhelpful.

Committee Staff: Why?

Deere: It wasn't the message that we needed at that time. It wasn't going to – the scenes at the U.S. Capitol were only getting worse at that point. This was not going to help that.[514]

White House Counsel Pat Cipollone told the Select Committee, "I don't remember when exactly I heard about that tweet, but my reaction to it is that's a terrible tweet, and I disagreed with the sentiment. And I thought it was wrong."[515]

Likewise, Counselor to the President Hope Hicks texted a colleague that evening: "Attacking the VP? Wtf is wrong with him".[516]

At 2:26 p.m., Vice President Pence was again moved to a different location.[517]

President Trump had the TV on in the dining room.[518] At 2:38 p.m., Fox News was showing video of the chaos and attack, with tear gas filling the air in the Capitol Rotunda. And a newscaster reported, "[T]his is a very dangerous situation."[519] This is the context in which Trump sent the tweet.

Testimony obtained by the Committee indicates that President Trump knew about the rioters' anger at Vice President Mike Pence, and indicated something to the effect that "Mike [Pence] deserves it."[520] As Cassidy Hutchinson explained:

> I remember Pat saying something to the effect of, "Mark, we need to do something more. They're literally calling for the Vice President to be f'ing hung." And Mark had responded something to the effect of, "You heard him, Pat. He thinks Mike deserves it. He doesn't think they're doing anything wrong." To which Pat said something, "[t]his is f'ing crazy, we need to be doing something more," briefly stepped into Mark's office, and when Mark had said something – when Mark had said something to the effect of, "He doesn't think they're doing anything wrong," knowing what I had heard briefly in the dining room coupled with Pat discussing the hanging Mike Pence chants in the lobby of our office and then Mark's response, I understood "they're" to be the rioters in the Capitol that were chanting for the Vice President to be hung.[521]

Although White House Counsel Pat Cipollone was limited in what he would discuss because of privilege concerns, he stated the following:

Committee Staff: Do you remember any discussion at any point during the day about rioters at the Capitol chanting "hang Mike Pence?"

Cipollone: Yes. I remember – I remember hearing that – about that. Yes.

Committee Staff: Yeah. And –

Cipollone: I don't know if I observed that myself on TV. I don't remember.

Committee Staff: I'm just curious, I understand the privilege line you've drawn, but do you remember what you can share with us about the discussion about those chants, the 'hang Mike Pence' chants?

Cipollone: I could tell you my view of that.

Committee Staff: Yeah. Please.

Cipollone: My view of that is that is outrageous.

Committee Staff: Uh-huh.

Cipollone: And for anyone to suggest such a thing as the Vice President of the United States, for people in that crowd to be chanting that I thought was terrible. I thought it was outrageous and wrong. And I expressed that very clearly to people.[522]

Almost immediately after the 2:24 p.m. tweet, Eric Herschmann went upstairs in the West Wing to try to enlist Ivanka Trump's assistance to persuade her father to do the right thing.[523] Ivanka rushed down to the Oval Office dining room. Although no one could convince President Trump to call for the violent rioters to leave the Capitol, Ivanka persuaded President Trump that a tweet could be issued to discourage violence against the police.

At 2:38 p.m., President Trump sent this tweet:

"Please support our Capitol Police and Law Enforcement. They are truly on the side of our Country. Stay peaceful!"[524]

While some in the meeting invoked executive privilege, or failed to recall the specifics, others told us what happened at that point. Sarah Matthews, the White House Deputy Press Secretary, had urged her boss, Kayleigh McEnany, to have the President make a stronger statement. But she informed us that President Trump resisted using the word "peaceful" in his message:

[Q]: Ms. Matthews, Ms. McEnany told us she came right back to the press office after meeting with the President about this particular tweet. What did she tell you about what happened in that dining room?

[A]: When she got back, she told me that a tweet had been sent out. And I told her that I thought the tweet did not go far enough, that I thought there needed to be a call to action and he needed to condemn the violence. And we were in a room full of people, but people weren't paying attention. And so, she looked directly at me and in a hushed tone shared with me that the President did not want to include any sort of mention of peace in that tweet and that it took some convincing on their part, those who were in the room. And she said that there was a back and forth going over different phrases to find something that he was comfortable with. And it wasn't until Ivanka Trump suggested the phrase 'stay peaceful' that he finally agreed to include it."[525]

At 3:13 p.m., President Trump sent another tweet, but again declined to tell people to go home:

"I am asking for everyone at the U.S. Capitol to remain peaceful. No violence! Remember, WE are the Party of Law & Order – respect the Law and our great men and women in Blue. Thank you!"[526]

Almost everyone, including staff in the White House also found the President's 2:38 p.m. and 3:13 p.m. tweets to be insufficient because they did not instruct the rioters to leave the Capitol. As mentioned, President Trump's son, Donald Trump Jr., texted Meadows:

He's got to condem [sic] this shit. Asap. The captiol [sic] police tweet is not enough.[527]

Sean Hannity also texted Mark Meadows:

Can he make a statement. I saw the tweet. Ask people to peacefully leave the capital [sic].[528]

None of these efforts resulted in President Trump immediately issuing the message that was needed. White House staff had these comments:

Pottinger: Yeah. It was insufficient. I think what – you you could count me among those who was hoping to see an unequivocal strong statement clearing out the Capitol, telling people to stand down, leave, go home. I think that's what we were hoping for.[529]

...

Matthews: Yeah. So a conversation started in the press office after the President sent out those two tweets that I deemed were insufficient.... I thought that we should condemn the violence and condemn it unequivocally. And I thought that he needed to include a call to action and to tell these people to go home.[530]

And they were right. Evidence showed that neither of these tweets had any appreciable impact on the violent rioters. Unlike the video-message tweet that did not come until 4:17 finally instructing rioters to leave, neither the 2:38 nor the 3:13 tweets made any difference.

At some point after 3:05 p.m. that afternoon, President Trump's Chief of Staff – and President Trump himself – were informed that someone was shot.[531] That person was Ashli Babbitt, who was fatally shot at 2:44 p.m. as she and other rioters tried to gain access to the House chamber.[532] There is no indication that this affected the President's state of mind that day, and we found no evidence that the President expressed any remorse that day.

Meanwhile, leaders in Congress – including Speaker Pelosi, Senator Schumer, Senator McConnell – and the Vice President, were taking action. They called the Secretary of Defense, the Attorney General, governors and officials in Virginia, Maryland, and the District of Columbia, begging for assistance.[533]

President-elect Biden also broadcast a video calling on President Trump to take action:
I call on President Trump to go on national television now to fulfill his oath and defend the Constitution and demand an end to this siege.[534]

President Trump could have done this, of course, anytime after he learned of the violence at the Capitol. At 4:17 p.m., 187 minutes after finishing his speech (and even longer after the attack began), President Trump finally broadcast a video message in which he asked those attacking the Capitol to leave:

> I know your pain. I know you're hurt. We had an election that was stolen from us. It was a landslide election, and everyone knows it, especially the other side, but you have to go home now. We have to have peace.[535]

President Trump's Deputy Press Secretary, Sarah Matthews testified about her reaction to this video message:

> [H]e told the people who we had just watched storm our nation's Capitol with the intent on overthrowing our democracy, violently attack police officers, and chant heinous things like, "Hang Mike Pence," "We love you. You're very special." As a spokesperson for him, I knew that I would be asked to defend that. And to me, his refusal to act and call off the mob that day and his refusal to condemn the violence was indefensible. And so, I knew that I would be resigning that evening.[536]

By this time, the National Guard and other additional law enforcement had begun to arrive in force and started to turn the tide of the violence. Many of those attackers in the Capitol saw or received word of President Trump's 4:17 p.m. message, and they understood this message as an instruction to leave:[537]

- Stephen Ayres testified in front of the Select Committee that: "Well, we were there. As soon as that come out, everybody started talking about it, and it seemed like it started to disperse, you know, some of the crowd. Obviously, you know, once we got back to the hotel room, we seen that it was still going on, but it definitely dispersed a lot of the crowd."[538]

- Jacob Chansley, also known as the QAnon-Shaman answered Trump's directive: "I'm here delivering the President's message. Donald Trump has asked everybody to go home." Another responded to Chansley: "That's our order."[539]

- Other unknown individuals also listened to President Trump's message while outside the Capitol, and responded: "He says, go home. He says, go home." And "Yeah. Here. He said to go home."[540]

At 6:01 p.m., President Trump sent his last tweet of the day, not condemning the violence, but instead attempting to justify it:

> These are the things and events that happen when a sacred election landslide victory is so unceremoniously & viciously stripped away from great patriots who have been badly & unfairly treated for so long. Go home with love & in peace. Remember this day forever![541]

Staff in President Trump's own White House and campaign had a strong reaction to this message:

> Sarah Matthews: At that point I had already made the decision to resign and this tweet just further cemented my decision. I thought that January 6, 2021, was one of the darkest days in our Nation's history and President Trump was

treating it as a celebratory occasion with that tweet. And so, it just further cemented my decision to resign.[542]

Tim Murtaugh: I don't think it's a patriotic act to attack the Capitol. But I have no idea how to characterize the people other than they trespassed, destroyed property, and assaulted the U.S. Capitol. I think calling them patriots is a, let's say, a stretch, to say the least. . . . I don't think it's a patriotic act to attack the U.S. Capitol.[543]

Pat Cipollone: [W]hat happened at the Capitol cannot be justified in any form or fashion. It was wrong, and it was tragic. And a lot – and it was a terrible day. It was a terrible day for this country.[544]

Greg Jacob: I thought it was inappropriate. . . . To my mind, it was a day that should live in infamy.[545]

At 6:27 p.m., President Trump retired to his residence for the night. As he did, he had one final comment to an employee who accompanied him to the residence. The one takeaway that the President expressed in that moment, following a horrific afternoon of violence and the worst attack against the U.S. Capitol building in over two centuries, was this: "Mike Pence let me down."[546]

President Trump's inner circle was still trying to delay the counting of electoral votes into the evening, even after the violence had been quelled. Rudolph Giuliani tried calling numerous Members of Congress in the hour before the joint session resumed, including Rep. Jim Jordan (R-OH) and Senators Marsha Blackburn (R-TN), Tommy Tuberville (R-AL), Bill Hagerty (R-TN), Lindsey Graham (R-SC), Josh Hawley (R-MO), and Ted Cruz (R-TX).[547] His voicemail intended for Senator Tuberville at 7:02 p.m. that evening eventually was made public:

Sen. Tuberville? Or I should say Coach Tuberville. This is Rudy Giuliani, the President's lawyer. I'm calling you because I want to discuss with you how they're trying to rush this hearing and how we need you, our Republican friends, to try to just slow it down so we can get these legislatures to get more information to you.[548]

Reflecting on President Trump's conduct that day, Vice President Pence noted that President Trump "had made no effort to contact me in the midst of the rioting or any point afterward."[549] He wrote that President Trump's "reckless words had endangered my family and all those serving at the Capitol."[550]

President Trump did not contact a single top national security official during the day. Not at the Pentagon, nor at the Department of Homeland Security, the Department of Justice, the F.B.I., the Capitol Police Department, or the D.C. Mayor's office.[551] As Vice President Pence has confirmed, President Trump didn't even try to reach his own Vice President to make sure that Pence was safe.[552] President Trump did not order any of his staff to facilitate a law enforcement response of any sort.[553] His Chairman of the Joint Chiefs of Staff—who is by statute the primary military advisor to the President—had this reaction:

General Milley: "You know, you're the Commander in Chief. You've got an assault going on on the Capitol of the United States of America. And there's nothing? No call? Nothing? Zero?"[554]

General Milley did, however, receive a call from President Trump's Chief of Staff Mark Meadows that day. Here is how he described that call:

He said, "We have to kill the narrative that the Vice President is making all the decisions. We need to establish the narrative, you know, that the President is still in charge and that things are steady or stable, or words to that effect. I immediately interpreted that as politics, politics, politics. Red flag for me, personally. No action. But I remember it distinctly. And I don't do political narratives."[555]

Some have suggested that President Trump gave an order to have 10,000 troops ready for January 6th.[556] The Select Committee found no evidence of this. In fact, President Trump's Acting Secretary of Defense Christopher Miller directly refuted this when he testified under oath:

Committee Staff: To be crystal clear, there was no direct order from President Trump to put 10,000 troops to be on the ready for January 6th, correct?

Miller: No. Yeah. That's correct. There was no direct—there was no order from the President.[557]

Later, on the evening of January 6th, President Trump's former campaign manager, Brad Parscale, texted Katrina Pierson, one of President Trump's rally organizers, that the events of the day were the result of a "sitting president asking for civil war" and that "This week I feel guilty for helping him win" now that "… a woman is dead." Pierson answered: "You do realize this was going to happen." Parscale replied: "Yeah. If I was Trump and knew my rhetoric killed someone." "It wasn't the rhetoric," Pierson suggested. But Parscale insisted: "Yes it was."[558]

THE IMMEDIATE AFTERMATH OF JANUARY 6TH

In days following January 6th, President Trump's family and staff attempted repeatedly to persuade him not to repeat his election fraud allegations, to concede defeat, and to allow the transition to President Biden to proceed. Trump did make two video recordings, which initially appeared contrite. But evidence suggests that these statements were designed at least in part to ward off other potential consequences of January 6th, such as invocation of the 25th Amendment or impeachment.

In fact, Minority Leader Kevin McCarthy indicated after the attack, in a discussion with House Republican leaders that he would ask President Trump to resign:

Rep. Cheney: I guess there's a question when we were talking about the 25th Amendment resolution, and you asked what would happen after he's gone? Is there any chance? Are you hearing that he might resign? Is there any reason to think that might happen?

Leader McCarthy: I've had a few discussions. My gut tells me no. I'm seriously thinking of having that discussion with him tonight. I haven't talked to him in a couple of days. From what I know of him, I mean, you guys all know him too, do you think he'd ever back away? But what I think I'm going to do is I'm going to call him. This is what I think. We know [the 25th Amendment resolution] will pass the House. I think there's a chance it will pass the Senate, even when he's gone. And I think there's a lot of different ramifications for that. . . . Again, the only discussion I would have with him is that I think this will pass, and it would be my recommendation you should resign.[559]

Before January 6th, Fox News personality Sean Hannity warned that January 6th could be disastrous:

Dec. 31, 2020 text from Sean Hannity to Mark Meadows:

We can't lose the entire WH counsels office. I do NOT see January 6 happening the way he is being told. After the 6 th. He should announce will lead the nationwide effort to reform voting integrity. Go to Fl and watch Joe mess up daily. Stay engaged. When he speaks people will listen.[560]

January 5, 2021 texts from Sean Hannity to Mark Meadows:

Im very worried about the next 48 hours

Pence pressure. WH counsel will leave.

Sorry, I can't talk right now.

On with boss[561]

A member of the Republican Freedom caucus also warned, on December 31, 2020, and on January 1, 2021:

The President should call everyone off. It's the only path. If we substitute the will of states through electors with a vote by Congress every 4 years... we have destroyed the electoral college... Respectfully.[562] If POTUS allows this to occur... we're driving a stake in the heart of the federal republic...[563]

After January 6th, Sean Hannity of Fox News worked to persuade President Trump to stop talking about election fraud, proposed that Trump pardon Hunter Biden, and discussed attending the Inauguration:

1- No more stolen election talk.

2- Yes, impeachment and 25 th amendment are real, and many people will quit.
3- He was intrigued by the Pardon idea!! (Hunter)
4- Resistant but listened to Pence thoughts, to make it right.
5- Seemed to like attending Inauguration talk.[564]

Ultimately, President Trump took little of the advice from Hannity and his White House staff. A few days later, Hannity wrote again to Meadows and Jim Jordan:

> Guys, we have a clear path to land the plane in 9 days. He can't mention the election again. Ever. I did not have a good call with him today. And worse, I'm not sure what is left to do or say, and I don t like not knowing if it's truly understood. Ideas?[565]

Likewise, despite her many contrary public statements, Republican Congresswoman Marjorie Taylor Greene privately texted her concerns on January 6th about a continuing and real threat of violence:

> Mark I was just told there is an active shooter on the first floor of the Capitol Please tell the President to calm people This isn't the way to solve anything[566]

Donald Trump was impeached on January 13th. In a speech that day, Republican Leader Kevin McCarthy made this statement from the House floor, but voted against impeachment:

> The President bears responsibility for Wednesday's attack on Congress by mob rioters. He should have immediately denounced the mob when he saw what was unfolding. These facts require immediate action by President Trump, accept his share of responsibility, quell the brewing unrest and ensure President-elect Biden is able to successfully begin his term. The President's immediate action also deserves congressional action, which is why I think a fact-finding commission and a censure resolution would be prudent.[567]

Later, McCarthy told members of the House Republican conference that Trump had acknowledged that he was at least partially responsible for the January 6th attack.

> I asked him personally today, does he hold responsibility for what happened? Does he feel bad about what happened? He told me he does have some responsibility for what happened. And he need to acknowledge that.[568]

Since January 6th, President Trump has continued to claim falsely that the 2020 Presidential election was stolen. Not only that, he has urged other politicians to push this argument as well. Representative Mo Brooks has issued a public statement appearing to represent Trump's private views and intentions:

> President Trump asked me to rescind the 2020 elections, immediately remove Joe Biden from the White House, immediately put President Trump back in the White House, and hold a new special election for the presidency.[569]

REFERRALS TO THE U.S. DEPARTMENT OF JUSTICE SPECIAL COUNSEL AND HOUSE ETHICS COMMITTEE

The Committee's work has produced a substantial body of new information. We know far more about the President's plans and actions to overturn the election than almost all Members of Congress did when President Trump was impeached on January 13, 2021, or when he was tried by the Senate in February of that year. Fifty-seven of 100 Senators voted to convict President Trump at that time, and more than 20 others condemned the President's conduct and said they were voting against conviction because the President's term had already expired.[570] At the time, the Republican Leader of the U.S. Senate said this about Donald Trump: "A mob was assaulting the Capitol in his name. These criminals were carrying his banners, hanging his flags, and screaming their loyalty to him. It was obvious that only President Trump could end this. He was the only one who could."[571] House Republican Leader Kevin McCarthy, who spoke directly with President Trump during the violence of January 6th, expressed similar views both in private and in public. Privately, McCarthy stated: "But let me be very clear to you and I have been very clear to the President. He bears responsibility for his words and actions. No if, ands or buts."[572] In public, Rep. McCarthy concluded: "The President bears responsibility for Wednesday's attack on Congress by mob rioters."[573]

Today we know that the planning to overturn the election on January 6th was substantially more extensive, and involved many other players, and many other efforts over a longer time period. Indeed, the violent attack and invasion of the Capitol, and what provoked it, are only a part of the story.

From the outset of its hearings, the Committee has explained that President Trump and a number of other individuals made a series of very specific plans, ultimately with multiple separate elements, but all with one overriding objective: to corruptly obstruct, impede, or influence the counting of electoral votes on January 6th, and thereby overturn the lawful results of the election. The underlying and fundamental feature of that planning was the effort to get one man, Vice President Mike Pence, to assert and then exercise unprecedented and lawless powers to unilaterally alter the actual election outcome on January 6th. Evidence obtained by the Committee demonstrates that John Eastman, who worked with President Trump to put that and other elements of the plan in place, knew even before the 2020 Presidential election that Vice President Pence could not lawfully refuse to count official, certified electoral slates submitted by the governors of the States.[574] Testimony and contemporaneous documentary evidence also indicate that President Trump knew that the plan was unlawful before January 6th.[575] When the Vice President's Counsel wrote to Eastman on January 6th to ask whether the latter had informed the President that the Vice President did not have authority to decide the election unilaterally, Eastman responded: "He's been so advised," and added "[b]ut you know him – once he gets something in his head, it is hard to get him to change course."[576]

Many of the other elements of President Trump's plans were specifically designed to create a set of circumstances on January 6th to assist President Trump in overturning the lawful election outcome during Congress's Joint Session that day. For example, President Trump pressured State legislatures to adopt new electoral slates that Vice President Pence could, unlawfully, count. Trump solicited State officials to "find" a sufficient number of votes to alter the final count, and instructed the Department of Justice to "just say that the election was was [sic] corrupt + leave the rest to me and the R[epublican] Congressmen."[577] President Trump offered the job of Acting Attorney General to Jeffrey Clark: as our evidence has unequivocally demonstrated, Clark intended to use that position to send a series of letters from the Department of Justice to multiple States falsely asserting that the Department had found fraud and urging those States to convene their legislatures to alter their official electoral slates[578]. And President Trump, with the help of the Republican National Committee and others, oversaw an effort to create and transmit to Government officials a series of intentionally false electoral slates for Vice President Pence to utilize on January 6th to alter or delay the count of lawful votes.[579]

Of course, other elements of the plan complemented these efforts too. As this Report documents, President Trump was advised by his own experts and the Justice Department that his election fraud allegations were false, and he knew he had lost virtually all the legal challenges to the election, but he nevertheless engaged in a successful but fraudulent effort to persuade tens of millions of Americans that the election was stolen from him. This effort was designed to convince Americans that President Trump's actions to overturn the election were justified. President Trump then urged his supporters to travel to Washington on January 6th to apply pressure to Congress to halt the count and change the election outcome, explaining to those who were coming to Washington that they needed to "take back" their country and "stop the steal."[580]

It is helpful in understanding these facts to focus on specific moments in time when President Trump made corrupt, dishonest and unlawful choices to pursue his plans. For example, by December 14th when the Electoral College met and certified Joe Biden's victory, President Trump knew that he had failed in all the relevant litigation; he had been advised by his own experts and the Justice Department that his election fraud claims were false; and he had been told by numerous advisors that he had lost and should concede. But despite his duty as President to take care that the laws are faithfully executed, he chose instead to ignore all of the judicial rulings and the facts before him and push forward to overturn the election. Likewise, in the days and hours before the violence of January 6th, President Trump knew that no State had issued any changed electoral slate. Indeed, neither President Trump nor his co-conspirators had any evidence that any majority of any State legislature was willing to do so. President Trump also knew that Vice President Pence could not lawfully refuse to count legitimate votes. Despite all of these facts, President Trump nevertheless proceeded to instruct Vice President Pence to execute a plan he already knew was illegal. And then knowing that a violent riot was underway, President Trump breached his oath of office; our Commander in Chief refused for hours to take the one simple step that his advisors were begging him to take—to instruct his supports to disperse, stand down, and leave the Capitol. Instead, fully understanding what had unfolded at the Capitol, President Trump exacerbated the violence with a tweet attacking Vice President Pence.[581] Any rational person who had watched the events that day knew that President Trump's 2:24 p.m. tweet would lead to further violence. It did. And, at almost exactly the same time, President Trump continued to lobby Congress to delay the electoral count.

As the evidence demonstrates, the rioters at the Capitol had invaded the building and halted the electoral count. They did not begin to relent until President Trump finally issued a video statement instructing his supporters to leave the Capitol at 4:17 p.m., which had an immediate and helpful effect: rioters began to disperse[582] – but not before the Capitol was invaded, the election count was halted, feces were smeared in the Capitol, the Vice President and his family and many others were put in danger, and more than 140 law enforcement officers were attacked and seriously injured by mob rioters. Even if it were true that President Trump genuinely believed the election was stolen, *this is no defense*. No President can ignore the courts and purposely violate the law no matter what supposed "justification" he or she presents.

These conclusions are not the Committee's alone. In the course of its investigation, the Committee had occasion to present evidence to Federal District Court Judge David Carter, who weighed that evidence against submissions from President Trump's lawyer, John Eastman. Judge Carter considered this evidence in the context of a discovery dispute – specifically whether the Committee could obtain certain of Eastman's documents pursuant to the "crime-fraud" exception to the attorney-client privilege. That exception provides that otherwise privileged documents may lose their privilege if they were part of an effort to commit a crime or a fraud, in this case by President Trump. Judge Carter set out his factual findings, discussing multiple elements of President Trump's multi-part plan to overturn the election,[583] and then addressed whether the evidence, including Eastman's email communications, demonstrated that Trump and Eastman committed crimes. "Based on the evidence," Judge Carter explained, "the Court finds it more likely than not" that President Trump corruptly attempted to obstruct the Joint Session of Congress on January 6, 2021," and "more likely than not that President Trump and Dr. Eastman dishonestly conspired to obstruct the Joint Session of Congress on January 6th."[584] Judge Carter also concluded that President Trump's and Eastman's "pressure campaign to stop the electoral count did not end with Vice President Pence—it targeted every tier of federal and state elected officials"[585] and was "a coup in search of a legal theory."[586] "The plan spurred violent attacks on the seat of our nation's government," Judge Carter wrote, and it threatened to "permanently end[] the peaceful transition of power. . . ."[587]

The U.S. Department of Justice has been investigating and prosecuting persons who invaded the Capitol, engaged in violence, and planned violence on that day. The Department has charged more than 900 individuals, and nearly 500 have already been convicted or pleaded guilty as we write.[588] As the Committee's investigation progressed through its hearings, public reporting emerged suggesting that the Department of Justice had also begun to investigate several others specifically involved in the events being examined by the Committee. Such reports indicated that search warrants had been issued, based on findings of probable cause, for the cell phones of John Eastman, Jeffrey Clark, and Representative Scott Perry.[589] Other reports suggested that the Department had empaneled one or more grand juries and was pursuing a ruling compelling several of this Committee's witnesses, including Pat Cipollone and Greg Jacob, to give testimony on topics for which President Trump had apparently asserted executive privilege. Recent reporting suggests that a Federal District Court judge has now rejected President Trump's executive privilege claims in that context.[590]

Criminal referrals from a Congressional committee are often made in circumstances where prosecutors are not yet known to be pursuing some of the same facts and evidence. That is not the case here. During the course of our investigation, both the U.S.

Department of Justice and at least one local prosecutor's office (Fulton County, Georgia) have been actively conducting criminal investigations concurrently with this Congressional investigation.[591] In fact, the U.S. Department of Justice has recently taken the extraordinary step of appointing a Special Counsel to investigate the former President's conduct.[592]

The Committee recognizes that the Department of Justice and other prosecutorial authorities may be in a position to utilize investigative tools, including search warrants and grand juries, superior to the means the Committee has for obtaining relevant information and testimony. Indeed, both the Department of Justice and the Fulton County District Attorney may now have access to witness testimony and records that have been unavailable to the Committee, including testimony from President Trump's Chief of Staff Mark Meadows, and others who either asserted privileges or invoked their Fifth Amendment rights.[593] The Department may also be able to access, via grand jury subpoena or otherwise, the testimony of Republican Leader Kevin McCarthy, Representative Scott Perry, Representative Jim Jordan and others, each of whom appears to have had materially relevant communications with Donald Trump or others in the White House but who failed to comply with the Select Committee's subpoenas.

Taking all of these facts into account, and based on the breadth of the evidence it has accumulated, the Committee makes the following criminal referrals to the Department of Justice's Special Counsel.

I. *Obstruction of an Official Proceeding (18 U.S.C. § 1512(c))*

Section 1512(c)(2) of Title 18 of the United States Code makes it a crime to "corruptly" "obstruct[], influence[], or impede[] any official proceeding, or attempt[] to do so."[594] Sufficient evidence exists of one or more potential violations of this statute for a criminal referral of President Trump and others.[595]

First, there should be no question that Congress's Joint Session to count electoral votes on January 6th was an "official proceeding" under Section 1512(c). Many Federal judges have already reached that specific conclusion.[596]

Second, there should be no doubt that President Trump knew that his actions were likely to "obstruct, influence or impede" that proceeding. Based on the evidence developed, President Trump was attempting to prevent or delay the counting of lawful certified Electoral College votes from multiple States.[597] President Trump was directly and personally involved in this effort, personally pressuring Vice President Pence relentlessly as the Joint Session on January 6th approached.[598]

Third, President Trump acted with a "corrupt" purpose. Vice President Pence, Greg Jacob and others repeatedly told the President that the Vice President had no unilateral authority to prevent certification of the election.[599] Indeed, in an email exchange during the violence of January 6th, Eastman *admitted* that President Trump had been "advised" that Vice President Pence could not lawfully refuse to count votes under the Electoral Count Act, but "once he gets something in his head, it's hard to get him to change course."[600] In addition, President Trump knew that he had lost dozens of State and Federal lawsuits, and that the Justice Department, his campaign and his other advisors concluded that there was insufficient fraud to alter the outcome. President Trump also knew that no majority of any State legislature had taken or manifested any intention to take any official action that could change a State's electoral college votes.[601] But President Trump pushed forward anyway. As Judge Carter explained, "[b]ecause President Trump likely knew that the plan to disrupt the electoral count was wrongful, his mindset exceeds the threshold for acting 'corruptly' under § 1512(c)."[602]

Sufficient evidence exists of one or more potential violations of 18 U.S.C. § 1512(c) for a criminal referral of President Trump based solely on his plan to get Vice President Pence to prevent certification of the election at the Joint Session of Congress. Those facts standing alone are sufficient. But such a charge under that statute can also be based on the plan to create and transmit to the Executive and Legislative branches fraudulent electoral slates, which were ultimately intended to facilitate an unlawful action by Vice President Pence –to refuse to count legitimate, certified electoral votes during Congress's official January 6th proceeding.[603] Additionally, evidence developed about the many other elements of President Trump's plans to overturn the election, including soliciting State legislatures, State officials, and others to alter official electoral outcomes, provides further evidence that President Trump was attempting through multiple means to corruptly obstruct, impede or influence the counting of electoral votes on January 6th. This is also true of President Trump's personal directive to the Department of Justice to "just say that the election was was [sic] corrupt + leave the rest to me and the R[epublican] Congressmen."[604]

We also stress in particular the draft letter to the Georgia legislature authored by Jeffrey Clark and another Trump political appointee at the Department of Justice. The draft letter embraces many of the same theories that John Eastman and others were asserting in President Trump's effort to lobby State legislatures. White House Counsel Pat Cipollone described that letter as "a murder-suicide pact," and other White House and Justice Department officials offered similar descriptions.[605] As described herein, that draft letter was intended to help persuade a State legislature to change its certified slate of Electoral College electors based on false allegations of fraud, so Vice President Pence could unilaterally and unlawfully decide to count a different slate on January 6th.[606] The letter was transparently false, improper, and illegal. President Trump had multiple communications with Clark in the days before January 6th, and there is no basis to doubt that President Trump offered Clark the position of Acting Attorney General knowing that Clark would send the letter and others like it.[607]

Of course, President Trump is also responsible for recruiting tens of thousands of his supporters to Washington for January 6th, and knowing they were angry and some were armed, instructing them to march to the Capitol and "fight like hell."[608] And then, while knowing a violent riot was underway, he refused for multiple hours to take the single step his advisors and supporters were begging him to take to halt the violence: to make a public statement instructing his supporters to disperse and leave the Capitol.[609] Through action and inaction, President Trump corruptly obstructed, delayed and impeded the vote count.

In addition, the Committee believes sufficient evidence exists for a criminal referral of John Eastman and certain other Trump associates under 18 U.S.C. §1512(c). The evidence shows that Eastman knew in advance of the 2020 election that Vice President Pence could not refuse to count electoral votes on January 6th.[610] In the days before January 6th, Eastman was warned repeatedly that his plan was illegal and "completely crazy," and would "cause riots in the streets."[611] Nonetheless, Eastman continued to assist President Trump's pressure campaign in public and in private, including in meetings with the Vice President and in his own speech at the Ellipse on January 6th. And even as the violence was playing out at the Capitol, Eastman admitted in writing that his plan violated the law but pressed for Pence to do it anyway.[612] In the immediate aftermath of January 6th, White House lawyer Eric Herschmann told Eastman that he should "[g]et a great F'ing criminal defense lawyer, you're going to need it."[613] Others working with Eastman likely share in Eastman's culpability. For example, Kenneth Chesebro was a central player in the scheme to submit fake electors to the Congress and the National Archives.

The Committee notes that multiple Republican Members of Congress, including Representative Scott Perry, likely have material facts regarding President Trump's plans to overturn the election. For example, many Members of Congress attended a White House meeting on December 21, 2020, in which the plan to have the Vice President affect the outcome of the election was disclosed and discussed. Evidence indicates that certain of those Members unsuccessfully sought Presidential pardons from President Trump after January 6th,[614] as did Eastman,[615] revealing their own clear consciousness of guilt.

II. Conspiracy to Defraud the United States (18 U.S.C. § 371)

Section 371 of Title 18 of the U.S. Code provides that "[i]f two or more persons conspire either to commit any offense against the United States, or to defraud the United States, or any agency thereof in any manner or for any purpose, and one or more of such persons do any act to effect the object of the conspiracy, each shall be fined under this title or imprisoned not more than five years, or both." The Committee believes sufficient evidence exists for a criminal referral of President Trump and others under this statute.[616]

First, President Trump entered into an agreement with individuals to obstruct a lawful function of the government (the certification of the election). The evidence of this element overlaps greatly with the evidence of the Section 1512(c)(2) violations, so we will not repeat it at length here. President Trump engaged in a multi-part plan described in this Report to obstruct a lawful certification of the election. Judge Carter focused his opinions largely on John Eastman's role, as Eastman's documents were at issue in that case, concluding that "the evidence shows that an agreement to enact the electoral count plan likely existed between President Trump and Dr. Eastman."[617] But President Trump entered into agreements – whether formal or informal[618] – with several other individuals who assisted with the multi-part plan. With regard to the Department of Justice, Jeffrey Clark stands out as a participant in the conspiracy, as the evidence suggests that Clark entered into an agreement with President Trump that if appointed Acting Attorney General, he would send a letter to State officials falsely stating that the Department of Justice believed that State legislatures had a sufficient factual basis to convene to select new electors. This was false – the Department of Justice had reached the conclusion that there was no factual basis to contend that the election was stolen. Again, as with Section 1512(c), the conspiracy under Section 371 appears to have also included other individuals such as Chesebro, Rudolph Giuliani, and Mark Meadows, but this Committee does not attempt to determine all of the participants of the conspiracy, many of whom refused to answer this Committee's questions.

Second, there are several bases for finding that the conspirators used "deceitful or dishonest means." For example, President Trump repeatedly lied about the election, after he had been told by his advisors that there was no evidence of fraud sufficient to change the results of the election.[619] In addition, the plot to get the Vice President to unilaterally prevent certification of the election was manifestly (and admittedly) illegal, as discussed above. Eastman and others told President Trump that it would violate the Electoral Count Act if the Vice President unilaterally rejected electors. Thus Judge Carter once again had little trouble finding that the intent requirement ("deceitful or dishonest means") was met, stating that "President Trump continuing to push that plan despite being aware of its illegality constituted obstruction by 'dishonest' means under § 371."[620] Judge Carter rejected the notion that Eastman's plan – which the President adopted and actualized – was a "good faith interpretation" of the law, finding instead that it was "a partisan distortion of the democratic process."[621] Similarly, both President Trump and Clark had been told repeatedly that the Department of Justice had found no evidence of significant fraud in any of its investigations, but they nonetheless pushed the Department of Justice to send a letter to State officials stating that the Department had found such fraud. And Georgia Secretary of State Brad Raffensperger and others made clear to President Trump that they had no authority to "find" him 11,780 votes, but the President relentlessly insisted that they do exactly that, even to the point of suggesting there could be criminal consequences if they refused.[622]

Third, there were numerous overt acts in furtherance of the agreement, including each of the parts of the President's effort to overturn the election. As Judge Carter concluded, President Trump and Dr. Eastman participated in "numerous overt acts in furtherance of their shared plan."[623] These included, but certainly were not limited to, direct pleas to the Vice President to reject electors or delay certification, including in Oval Office meetings and the President's vulgar comments to the Vice President on the morning of January 6. Judge Carter also addressed evidence that President Trump knowingly made false representations to a court. Judge Carter concluded that Dr. Eastman's emails showed "that President Trump knew that the specific numbers of voter fraud" cited in a complaint on behalf of President Trump "were wrong but continued to tout those numbers, both in court and to the public." Judge Carter found that the emails in question were related to and in furtherance of a conspiracy to defraud the United States.[624]

In finding that President Trump, Eastman, and others engaged in conspiracy to defraud the United States under Section 371, Judge Carter relied on the documents at issue (largely consisting of Eastman's own emails) and evidence presented to the court by this Committee. This Committee's investigation has progressed significantly since Judge Carter issued his first crime-fraud ruling in March 2022. The evidence found by this Committee and discussed in detail in this Report further document that the conspiracy to defraud the United States under Section 371 extended far beyond the effort to pressure the Vice President to prevent certification of the election. The Committee believes there is sufficient evidence for a criminal referral of the multi-part plan described in this Report under Section 371, as the very purpose of the plan was to prevent the lawful certification of Joe Biden's election as President.

III. Conspiracy to Make a False Statement (18 U.S.C. §§ 371, 1001)

President Trump, through others acting at his behest, submitted slates of fake electors to Congress and the National Archives. Section 1001 of Title 18 of the United States Code applies, in relevant part, to "whoever, in any matter within the jurisdiction of the executive, legislative, or judicial branch of the Government of the United States, knowingly and willfully—

(1) falsifies, conceals, or covers up by any trick, scheme, or device a material fact;
(2) makes any materially false, fictitious, or fraudulent statement or representation; or
(3) makes or uses any false writing or document knowing the same to contain any materially false, fictitious, or fraudulent statement or entry."

According to the Department of Justice, whether a false statement is criminal under Section 1001 "depends on whether there is an affirmative response to each of the following questions:

1. Was the act or statement material?
2. Was the act within the jurisdiction of a department or agency of the United States?
3. Was the act done knowingly and willfully?"[625]

In addition, and as explained above, 18 U.S.C. § 371 makes it a crime to conspire to "commit any offense against the United States."[626]

The evidence suggests President Trump conspired with others to submit slates of fake electors to Congress and the National Archives. Sufficient evidence exists of a violation of 18 U.S.C. §§ 371 and 1001 for a criminal referral of President Trump and others.

As explained earlier and in Chapter 3 of this Report, the certifications signed by Trump electors in multiple States were patently false. Vice President Biden won each of those States, and the relevant State authorities had so certified. It can hardly be disputed that the false slates of electors were material, as nothing can be more material to the Joint Session of Congress to certify the election than the question of which candidate won which States. Indeed, evidence obtained by the Committee suggests that those attempting to submit certain of the electoral votes regarded the need to provide that material to Vice President Pence as urgent.[627]

There should be no question that Section 1001 applies here. The false electoral slates were provided both to the Executive Branch (the National Archives) and the Legislative Branch.[628] The statute applies to "any matter within the jurisdiction of the executive, legislative, or judicial branch of the Government of the United States."[629] It is well established that false statements to Congress can constitute violations of Section 1001.[630]

Finally, the false statement was made knowingly and willfully. There is some evidence suggesting that some signatories of the fake certificates believed that the certificates were contingent, to be used only in the event that President Trump prevailed in litigation challenging the election results in their States. That may be relevant to the question whether those electors knowingly and willfully signed a false statement at the time they signed the certificates. But it is of no moment to President Trump's conduct, as President Trump (including acting through co-conspirators such as John Eastman and Kenneth Chesebro) relied on the existence of those fake electors as a basis for asserting that the Vice President could reject or delay certification of the Biden electors. In fact, as explained earlier and in Chapter 5 of this Report, Eastman's memorandum setting out a six-step plan for overturning the election on January 6th begins by stating that "7 states have transmitted dual slates of electors to the President of the Senate."

The remaining question is who engaged in this conspiracy to make the false statement to Congress under Section 1001. The evidence is clear that President Trump personally participated in a scheme to have the Trump electors meet, cast votes, and send their votes to the Joint Session of Congress in several States that Vice President Biden won, and then his supporters relied on the existence of these fake electors as part of their effort to obstruct the Joint Session. Republican National Committee (RNC) Chairwoman Ronna McDaniel testified before this Committee that President Trump and Eastman directly requested that the RNC organize the effort to have these fake (i.e. Trump) electors meet and cast their votes.[631] Thus, the Committee believes that sufficient evidence exists for a criminal referral of President Trump for illegally engaging in a conspiracy to violate Section 1001; the evidence indicates that he entered into an agreement with Eastman and others to make the false statement (the fake electoral certificates), by deceitful or dishonest means, and at least one member of the conspiracy engaged in at least one overt act in furtherance of the conspiracy (*e.g.* President Trump and Eastman's call to Ronna McDaniel).

IV. "Incite," "Assist" or "Aid and Comfort" an Insurrection (18 U.S.C. § 2383)

Section 2383 of Title 18 of the United States Code applies to anyone who "incites, sets on foot, assists, or engages in any rebellion or insurrection against the authority of the United States or the laws thereof, or gives aid or comfort thereto."[632] The Committee recognizes that §2383 does not require evidence of an "agreement" between President Trump and the violent rioters to establish a violation of that provision; instead, the President need only have incited, assisted or aided and comforted those engaged in violence or other lawless activity in an effort to prevent the peaceful transition of the Presidency under our Constitution. A Federal court has already concluded that President Trump's statements during his Ellipse speech were "plausibly words of incitement not protected by the First Amendment."[633] Moreover, President Trump was impeached for "Incitement of Insurrection," and a majority of the Senate voted to convict, with many more suggesting they might have voted to convict had President Trump still been in office at the time.[634]

As explained throughout this Report and in this Committee's hearings, President Trump was directly responsible for summoning what became a violent mob to Washington, DC, urging them to march to the Capitol, and then further provoking the already violent and lawless crowd with his 2:24p.m. tweet about the Vice President. Even though President Trump had repeatedly been told that Vice President Pence had no legal authority to stop the certification of the election, he asserted in his speech on January 6 that if the Vice President "comes through for us" that he could deliver victory to Trump: "if Mike Pence does the right thing, we win the election." This created a desperate and false expectation in President Trump's mob that ended up putting the Vice President and his entourage and many others at the Capitol in physical danger. When President Trump tweeted at 2:24 p.m., he knew violence was underway. His tweet exacerbated that violence.[635]

During the ensuing riot, the President refused to condemn the violence or encourage the crowd to disperse despite repeated pleas from his staff and family that he do so. The Committee has evidence from multiple sources establishing these facts, including testimony from former White House Counsel Pat Cipollone. Although Cipollone's testimony did not disclose a number of direct communications with President Trump in light of concerns about Executive Privilege, the Department now appears to have obtained a ruling that Cipollone can testify before a grand jury about these communications. Based on the information it has obtained, the Committee believes that Cipollone and others can provide direct testimony establishing that President Trump refused repeatedly, for multiple hours, to make a public statement directing his violent and lawless supporters to leave the Capitol. President Trump did not want his supporters (who had effectively halted the vote counting) to disperse. Evidence obtained by the Committee also indicates that President Trump did not want to provide security assistance to the Capitol during that violent period.[636] This appalling behavior by our Commander in Chief occurred despite his affirmative Constitutional duty to act, to ensure that the laws are faithfully executed.[637]

The Committee believes that sufficient evidence exists for a criminal referral of President Trump for "assist[ing]" or "ai[ding] and comfort[ing]" those at the Capitol who engaged in a violent attack on the United States. The Committee has developed significant evidence that President Trump intended to disrupt the peaceful transition of power and believes that the Department of Justice can likely elicit testimony relevant to an investigation under Section 2383.

For example, Chief of Staff Mark Meadows told White House Counsel Pat Cipollone that the President "doesn't want to do anything" to stop the violence.[638] Worse, at 2:24 p.m., the President inflamed and exacerbated the mob violence by sending a tweet stating that the Vice President "didn't have the courage to do what should have been done."[639] The President threw gasoline on the fire despite knowing that there was a violent riot underway at the Capitol. Indeed, video and audio footage from the attack shows that many of the rioters specifically mentioned Vice President Pence.[640] And immediately after President Trump sent his tweet, the violence escalated. Between 2:25p.m. and 2:28 p.m., rioters breached the East Rotunda doors, other rioters breached the police line in the Capitol Crypt, Vice President Pence had to be evacuated from his Senate office, and Rep. McCarthy was evacuated from his Capitol office.[641]

Evidence developed in the Committee's investigation showed that the President, when told that the crowd was chanting "Hang Mike Pence," responded that perhaps the Vice President deserved to be hanged.[642] And President Trump rebuffed pleas from Rep. Kevin McCarthy to ask that his supporters leave the Capitol, stating "Well, Kevin, I guess these people are more upset about the election than you are." After hours of deadly riot, President Trump eventually released a videotaped statement encouraging the crowd to disperse, though openly professing his "love" for the members of the mob and empathizing with their frustration at the "stolen" election. President Trump has since expressed a desire to pardon those involved in the attack.[643]

Both the purpose and the effect of the President's actions were to mobilize a large crowd to descend on the Capitol. Several defendants in pending criminal cases identified the President's allegations about the "stolen election" as the key motivation for their activities at the Capitol. Many of them specifically cited the President's tweets asking his supporters to come to Washington, DC on January 6. For example, one defendant who later pleaded guilty to threatening House Speaker Nancy Pelosi texted a family member on January 6th to say: "[Trump] wants heads and I'm going to deliver."[644] Another defendant released a statement through his attorney, stating: "I was in Washington, DC on January 6, 2021, because I believed I was following the instructions of former President Trump and he was my President and the commander-in-chief. His statements also had me believing the election was stolen from him."[645]

As the violence began to subside and law enforcement continued to secure the Capitol, President Trump tweeted again, at 6:01 pm to justify the actions of the rioters: "These are the things and events that happen," he wrote, when his so-called victory was "so unceremoniously & viciously stripped away. . . ."[646] When he wrote those words, he knew exactly what he was doing. Before President Trump issued the tweet, a White House staffer cautioned him that the statement would imply that he "had something to do with the events that happened at the Capitol"—but he tweeted it anyway.[647] The final words of that tweet leave little doubt about President Trump's sentiments toward those who invaded the Capitol: "Remember this day forever!"[648]

V. Other Conspiracy Statutes (18 U.S.C. §§ 372 and 2384)

Depending on evidence developed by the Department of Justice, the President's actions with the knowledge of the risk of violence could also constitute a violation of 18 U.S.C. § 372 and § 2384, both of which require proof of a conspiracy. Section 372 prohibits a conspiracy between two or more persons "to prevent, by force, intimidation, or threat, any person from accepting or holding any office, trust, or place of confidence under the United States, or from discharging any duties thereof, or to induce by like means any officer of the United States to leave the place, where his duties as an officer are required to be performed, or to injure him in the discharge of his official duties."[649] Oath Keepers Kelly Meggs, Kenneth Harrelson, and Jessica Watkins were convicted of violating 18 U.S.C. 372 in connection with the January 6 attack on the Capitol.[650] The Committee believes that former Chief of Staff, Mark Meadows (who refused to testify and was held in contempt of Congress) could have specific evidence relevant to such charges, as may witnesses who invoked their Fifth Amendment rights against self-incrimination before this Committee.

Section 2384, the seditious conspiracy statute, prohibits "conspir[acy] to overthrow, put down, or to destroy by force the Government of the United States . . . or to oppose by force the authority thereof, or by force to prevent, hinder or delay the execution of any law of the United States . . . ."[651] A jury has already determined beyond a reasonable doubt that a conspiracy existed under Section 2384, as the leader of the Oath Keepers and at least one other individual were convicted of seditious conspiracy under Section 2384 for their actions related to the attack on the Capitol.[652] A trial regarding a series of other "Proud Boy" defendants may also address similar issues.[653]

The Department of Justice, through its investigative tools that exceed those of this Committee, may have evidence sufficient to prosecute President Trump under Sections 372 and 2384. Accordingly, we believe sufficient evidence exists for a criminal referral of President Trump under these two statutes.

VI. The Committee's Concerns Regarding Possible Obstruction of its Investigation

The Committee has substantial concerns regarding potential efforts to obstruct its investigation, including by certain counsel (some paid by groups connected to the former President) who may have advised clients to provide false or misleading testimony to the Committee.[654] Such actions could violate 18 U.S.C. §§ 1505, 1512. The Committee is aware that both the U.S. Department of Justice and the Fulton County District Attorney's Office have already obtained information relevant to these matters, including from the Committee directly. We urge the Department of Justice to examine the facts to discern whether prosecution is warranted. The Committee's broad concerns regarding obstruction and witness credibility are addressed in the Executive Summary to this Report.

VII. Accountability for Those Who Plotted Unlawfully to Overturn the Election is Critical.

To date, the Justice Department has pursued prosecution of hundreds of individuals who planned and participated in the January 6th invasion of and attack on our Capitol. But the Department has not yet charged individuals who engaged in the broader plan to overturn the election through the means discussed in this Report. The Committee has concluded that it is critical to hold those individuals accountable as well, including those who worked with President Trump to create and effectuate these plans.

In his speech from the Ellipse on January 6th, President Trump recited a host of election fraud allegations he knew to be false, and then told tens of thousands of his angry supporters this:

> And fraud breaks up everything, doesn't it? When you catch somebody in a fraud, you're allowed to go by very different rules. So I hope Mike has the courage to do what he has to do. And I hope he doesn't listen to the RINOs and the stupid people that he's listening to. [655]

The meaning of President Trump's comments was sufficiently clear then, but he recently gave America an even more detailed understanding of his state of mind. Trump wrote that allegations of "massive fraud" related to the 2020 election "allow[] for the termination of all rules, regulations and articles, even those found in the Constitution."[656] And President Trump considered pardoning those involved in the attack and has since expressed a desire to pardon them – and even give them an apology – if he returns to the Oval Office.[657]

In the Committee's judgment, based on all the evidence developed, President Trump believed then, and continues to believe now, that he is above the law, not bound by our Constitution and its explicit checks on Presidential authority. This recent Trump statement only heightens our concern about accountability. If President Trump and the associates who assisted him in an effort to overturn the lawful outcome of the 2020 election are not ultimately held accountable under the law, their behavior may become a precedent and invitation to danger for future elections. A failure to hold them accountable now may ultimately lead to future unlawful efforts to overturn our elections, thereby threatening the security and viability of our Republic.

VIII. Referral of Members to the House Ethics Committee for Failure to Comply with Subpoenas

During the course of the Select Committee's investigation of President Trump's efforts to subvert the election, the Committee learned that various Members of Congress had information relevant to the investigation. Accordingly, the Committee wrote letters to a number of Members involved in that activity inviting them to participate voluntarily in the Select Committee's investigation. None of the members was willing to provide information, which forced the Select Committee to consider alternative means of securing evidence about the conduct of these Members and the information they might have. On May 12, 2022, the Select Committee subpoenaed several members of Congress—including House Minority Leader Kevin McCarthy, Representative Jim Jordan, Representative Scott Perry, and Representative Andy Biggs—to obtain information related to the Committee's investigation.

This was a significant step, but it was one that was warranted by the certain volume of information these Members possessed that was relevant to the Select Committee's investigation, as well as the centrality of their efforts to President Trump's multi-part plan to remain in power.

Representative McCarthy, among other things, had multiple communications with President Trump, Vice President Pence, and others on and related to January 6th. For example, during the attack on the Capitol, Representative McCarthy urgently requested that the former President issue a statement calling off the rioters, to which President Trump responded by "push[ing] back" and said: "Well, Kevin, I guess these people are more upset about the election than you are."[658] And, after the attack, Representative McCarthy spoke on the House floor and said that, "[t]here is absolutely no evidence" that antifa caused the attack on the Capitol and instead called on President Trump to "accept his share of responsibility" for the violence.[659] As noted above, Representative McCarthy privately confided in colleagues that President Trump accepted some responsibility for the attack on the Capitol.[660]

Representative Jordan was a significant player in President Trump's efforts. He participated in numerous post-election meetings in which senior White House officials, Rudolph Giuliani, and others, discussed strategies for challenging the election, chief among them claims that the election had been tainted by fraud. On January 2, 2021, Representative Jordan led a conference call in which he, President Trump, and other Members of Congress discussed strategies for delaying the January 6th joint session. During that call, the group also discussed issuing social media posts encouraging President Trump's supporters to "march to the Capitol" on the 6th.[661] An hour and a half later, President Trump and Representative Jordan spoke by phone for 18 minutes.[662] The day before January 6th, Representative Jordan texted Mark Meadows, passing along advice that Vice President Pence should "call out all the electoral votes that he believes are unconstitutional as no electoral votes at all."[663] He spoke with President Trump by phone at least twice on January 6th, though he has provided inconsistent public statements about how many times they spoke and what they discussed.[664] He also received five calls from Rudolph Giuliani that evening, and the two connected at least twice, at 7:33 p.m. and 7:49 p.m.[665] During that time, Giuliani has testified, he was attempting to reach Members of Congress after the joint session resumed to encourage them to continue objecting to Joe Biden's electoral votes.[666] And, in the days following January 6th, Representative Jordan spoke with White House staff about the prospect of Presidential pardons for Members of Congress.[667]

Like Representative Jordan, Representative Perry was also involved in early post-election messaging strategy. Both Representative Jordan and Representative Perry were involved in discussions with White House officials about Vice President Pence's role on January 6th as early as November 2020.[668] Representative Perry was present for conversations in which the White House Counsel's Office informed him and others that President Trump's efforts to submit fake electoral votes were not legally sound.[669] But perhaps most pivotally, he was involved in President Trump's efforts to install Jeffrey Clark as the Acting Attorney General in December 2020 and January 2021. Beginning in early December 2020, Representative Perry suggested Clark as a candidate to Mark Meadows,[670] then introduced Clark to President Trump.[671] In the days before January 6th, Representative Perry advocated for President Trump to speak at the Capitol during the joint session, speaking to Mark Meadows on at least one occasion about it.[672] He was also a participant in the January 2, 2021 call in which Representative Jordan, President Trump, and others discussed issuing social media posts to encourage Trump supporters to march to the Capitol on January 6th.[673] After January 6th, Representative Perry reached out to White House staff asking to receive a Presidential pardon.[674]

Representative Biggs was involved in numerous elements of President Trump's efforts to contest the election results. As early as November 6, 2020, Representative Biggs texted Mark Meadows, urging him to "encourage the state legislatures to appoint [electors]."[675] In the following days, Representative Biggs told Meadows not to let President Trump concede his loss.[676] Between then and January 6th, Representative Biggs coordinated with Arizona State Representative Mark Finchem to gather signatures from Arizona lawmakers endorsing fake Trump electors.[677] He also contacted fake Trump electors in at least one State seeking evidence related to voter fraud.[678]

To date, none of the subpoenaed Members has complied with either voluntary or compulsory requests for participation.

Representative McCarthy initially responded to the Select Committee's subpoena in two letters on May 27 and May 30, 2022, in which he objected to the Select Committee's composition and validity of the subpoena and offered to submit written interrogatories in lieu of deposition testimony. Although the Select Committee did not release Representative

McCarthy from his subpoena obligations, Representative McCarthy failed to appear for his scheduled deposition on May 31, 2022. The Select Committee responded to Representative McCarthy's letters this same day, rejecting his proposal to participate via written interrogatories and compelling his appearance for deposition testimony no later than June 11, 2022. Although Representative McCarthy again responded via letter on June 9, 2022, he did not appear for deposition testimony on or before the specified June 11, 2022, deadline.

Representative Jordan also responded to the Select Committee's subpoena just before his scheduled deposition in a letter on May 25, 2022, containing a variety of objections. Representative Jordan also requested material from the Select Committee, including all materials referencing him in the Select Committee's possession and all internal legal analysis related to the constitutionality of Member subpoenas. Although the Select Committee did not release Representative Jordan from his subpoena obligations, Representative Jordan failed to appear for his scheduled deposition on May 27, 2022. On May 31, 2022, the Select Committee responded to the substance of Representative Jordan's May 25th letter and indicated that Representative Jordan should appear for deposition testimony no later than June 11, 2022. On June 9, 2022, Representative Jordan again wrote to reiterate the points from his May 25th letter. That same day, Representative Jordan sent out a fundraising email with the subject line: "I'VE BEEN SUBPOENED."[679] Representative Jordan did not appear before the Select Committee on or before the June 11, 2022, deadline.

Representative Perry likewise responded to the Select Committee's subpoena on May 24, 2022, in a letter, "declin[ing] to appear for deposition" and requesting that the subpoena be "immediately withdrawn."[680] Although the Select Committee did not release Representative Perry from his subpoena obligations, Representative Perry failed to appear on May 26, 2022, for his scheduled deposition. Representative Perry sent a second letter to the Select Committee on May 31, 2022, with additional objections. That same day, the Select Committee responded to Representative Perry's letters and stated that he should appear before the Select Committee no later than June 11, 2022, for deposition testimony. Representative Perry responded via letter on June 10, 2022, maintaining his objections. He did not appear before the June 11, 2022, deadline.

Representative Biggs issued a press release on the day the Select Committee issued its subpoena, calling the subpoena "illegitimate" and "pure political theater." The day before his scheduled deposition, Representative Biggs sent a letter to the Select Committee with a series of objections and an invocation of Speech or Debate immunity. Although the Select Committee did not release Representative Biggs from his subpoena obligations, Representative Biggs did not appear for his scheduled deposition on May 26, 2022. On May 31, 2022, the Select Committee responded to the substance of Representative Biggs's May 25th letter and indicated that Representative Biggs should appear for deposition testimony no later than June 11, 2022. Although Representative Biggs responded with another letter on June 9th, he did not appear before the June 11, 2022, deadline.

Despite the Select Committee's repeated attempts to obtain information from these Members and the issuance of subpoenas, each has refused to cooperate and failed to comply with a lawfully issued subpoena. Accordingly, the Select Committee is referring their failure to comply with the subpoenas issued to them to the Ethics Committee for further action. To be clear, this referral is only for failure to comply with lawfully issued subpoenas.

The Rules of the House of Representatives make clear that their willful noncompliance violates multiple standards of conduct and subjects them to discipline. Willful noncompliance with compulsory congressional committee subpoenas by House Members violates the spirit and letter of House Rule XXIII, Clause 1, which requires House Members to conduct themselves "at all times in a manner that shall reflect creditably on the House." As a previous version of the House Ethics Manual explained, this catchall provision encompasses "'flagrant' violations of the law that reflect on 'Congress as a whole,' and that might otherwise go unpunished."[681] The subpoenaed House Members' refusal to comply with their subpoena obligations satisfies these criteria. A House Member's willful failure to comply with a congressional subpoena also reflects discredit on Congress. If left unpunished, such behavior undermines Congress's longstanding power to investigate in support of its lawmaking authority and suggests that Members of Congress may disregard legal obligations that apply to ordinary citizens.

For these reasons, the Select Committee refers Leader McCarthy and Representatives Jordan, Perry, and Biggs for sanction by the House Ethics Committee for failure to comply with subpoenas. The Committee also believes that each of these individuals, along with other Members who attended the December 21st planning meeting with President Trump at the White House,[682] should be questioned in a public forum about their advance knowledge of and role in President Trump's plan to prevent the peaceful transition of power.

EFFORTS TO AVOID TESTIFYING, EVIDENCE OF OBSTRUCTION, AND ASSESSMENTS OF WITNESS CREDIBILITY

More than 30 witnesses before the Select Committee exercised their Fifth Amendment privilege against self-incrimination and refused on that basis to provide testimony. They included individuals central to the investigation, such as John Eastman, Jeffrey Clark, Roger Stone, Michael Flynn, Kenneth Chesebro, and others.[683] The law allows a civil litigant to rely upon an "adverse inference" when a witness invokes the Fifth Amendment. "[T]he Fifth Amendment does not forbid adverse inferences against parties to civil actions . . .."[684] The Committee has not chosen to rely on any such inference in this Report or in its hearings.

We do note that certain witness assertions of the Fifth Amendment were particularly troubling, including this:

Vice Chair Cheney: General Flynn, do you believe the violence on January 6th was justified?

Counsel for the Witness: Can I get clarification, is that a moral question or are you asking a legal question?

Vice Chair Cheney: I'm asking both.

General Flynn: The Fifth.

Vice Chair Cheney: Do you believe the violence on January 6th was justified morally?

General Flynn: Take the Fifth.

Vice Chair Cheney: Do you believe the violence on January 6th was justified legally?

General Flynn: Fifth.

Vice Chair Cheney: General Flynn, do you believe in the peaceful transition of power in the United States of America?

General Flynn: The Fifth.[685]

President Trump refused to comply with the Committee's subpoena, and also filed suit to block the National Archives from supplying the Committee with White House records. The Committee litigated the National Archives case in Federal District Court, in the Federal Appellate Court for the District of Columbia, and before the Supreme Court. The Select Committee was successful in this litigation. The opinion of the D.C. Circuit explained:

> On January 6 2021, a mob professing support for then-President Trump violently attacked the United States Capitol in an effort to prevent a Joint Session of Congress from certifying the electoral college votes designating Joseph R. Biden the 46th President of the United States. The rampage left multiple people dead, injured more than 140 people, and inflicted millions of dollars in damage to the Capitol. Then-Vice President Pence, Senators, and Representatives were all forced to halt their constitutional duties and flee the House and Senate chambers for safety.[686]

> Benjamin Franklin said, at the founding, that we have "[a] Republic" – "if [we] can keep it." The events of January 6th exposed the fragility of those democratic institutions and traditions that we had perhaps come to take for granted. In response, the President of the United States and Congress have each made the judgment that access to this subset of presidential communication records is necessary to address a matter of great constitutional moment for the Republic. Former President Trump has given this court no legal reason to cast aside President Biden's assessment of the Executive Branch interests at stake, or to create a separation of powers conflict that the Political Branches have avoided.[687]

Several other witnesses have also avoided testifying in whole or in part by asserting Executive Privilege or Absolute Immunity from any obligation to appear before Congress. For example, the President's Chief of Staff Mark Meadows invoked both, and categorically refused to testify, even about text messages he provided to the Committee. The House of Representatives voted to hold him in criminal contempt.[688] Although the Justice Department has taken the position in litigation that a former high level White House staffer for a former President is not entitled to absolute immunity,[689] and that any interests in the confidentiality of his communications with President Trump and others are overcome in this case, the Justice Department declined to prosecute Meadows for criminal contempt. The reasons for Justice's refusal to do so are not apparent to the Committee.[690] Commentators have speculated that Meadows may be cooperating in the Justice Department's January 6th investigation.[691] The same may be true for Daniel Scavino, President Trump's White House Deputy Chief of Staff for Communications and Director of Social Media, whom the House also voted to hold in contempt.[692]

Steve Bannon also chose not to cooperate with the Committee, and the Justice Department prosecuted him for contempt of Congress.[693] Bannon has been sentenced and is currently appealing his conviction. Peter Navarro, another White House Staffer who refused to testify, is currently awaiting his criminal trial.[694]

Although the Committee issued letters and subpoenas to seven Republican members of Congress who have unique knowledge of certain developments on or in relation to January 6th, none agreed to participate in the investigation; none considered themselves obligated to comply with the subpoenas. A number of these same individuals were aware well in advance of January 6th of the plotting by Donald Trump, John Eastman, and others to overturn the election, and certain of them had an active role in that activity.[695] None seem to have alerted law enforcement of this activity, or of the known risk of violence. On January 5th, after promoting unfounded objections to election results, Rep. Debbie Lesko appears to have recognized the danger in a call with her colleagues:

> I also ask leadership to come up with a safety plan for Members [of Congress]. . . . We also have, quite honestly, Trump supporters who actually believe that we are going to overturn the election, and when that doesn't happen—most likely will not happen—they are going to go nuts.[696]

During our hearings, the Committee presented the testimony of numerous White House witnesses who testified about efforts by certain Republican Members of Congress to obtain Presidential pardons for their conduct in connection with January 6th.[697] Cassidy Hutchinson provided extensive detail in this regard:

> Vice Chair Cheney: And are you aware of any members of Congress seeking pardons?
>
> Hutchinson: I guess Mr. Gaetz and Mr. Brooks, I know, have both advocated for there'd be a blanket pardon for members involved in that meeting, and a — a handful of other members that weren't at the December 21st meeting as the presumptive pardons. Mr. Gaetz was personally pushing for a pardon, and he was doing so since early December.
>
> I'm not sure why Mr. Gaetz would reach out to me to ask if he could have a meeting with Mr. Meadows about receiving a presidential pardon.
>
> Vice Chair Cheney: Did they all contact you?

Hutchinson: Not all of them, but several of them did.

Vice Chair Cheney: So, you mentioned Mr. Gaetz, Mr. Brooks.

Hutchinson: Mr. Biggs did. Mr. Jordan talked about Congressional pardons, but he never asked me for one. It was more for an update on whether the White House was going to pardon members of Congress. Mr. Gohmert asked for one as well. Mr. Perry asked for a pardon, too. I'm sorry.

Vice Chair Cheney: Mr. Perry? Did he talk to you directly?

Hutchinson: Yes, he did.

Vice Chair Cheney: Did Marjorie Taylor Greene contact you?

Hutchinson: No, she didn't contact me about it. I heard that she had asked White House Counsel's Office for a pardon from Mr. Philbin, but I didn't frequently communicate with Ms. Greene.[698]

Many of these details were also corroborated by other sources. President Personnel Director Johnny McEntee confirmed that he was personally asked for a pardon by Representative Matt Gaetz (R-FL).[699] Eric Herschmann recalled that Rep. Gaetz "... asked for a very, very broad pardon.... And I said Nixon's pardon was never nearly that broad."[700] When asked about reporting that Reps. Mo Brooks and Andy Biggs also requested pardons, Herschmann did not reject either possibility out of hand, instead answering: "It's possible that Representative Brooks or Biggs, but I don't remember."[701] The National Archives produced to the Select Committee an email from Representative Mo Brooks to the President's executive assistant stating that "President Trump asked me to send you this letter" and "... pursuant to a request from Matt Gaetz" that recommended blanket Presidential pardons to every Member of Congress who objected to the electoral college votes on January 6th.[702]

These requests for pardons suggest that the members identified above were conscious of the potential legal jeopardy arising from their conduct. As noted *infra* [], the Committee has referred a number of these individuals to the House Ethics Committee for their failure to comply with subpoenas, and believes that they each owe the American people their direct and unvarnished testimony.

The Select Committee has also received a range of evidence suggesting specific efforts to obstruct the Committee's investigation. Much of this evidence is already known by the Department of Justice and by other prosecutorial authorities. For example:

1. The Committee received testimony from a witness about her decision to terminate a lawyer who was receiving payments for the representation from a group allied with President Trump. Among other concerns expressed by the witness:

- The lawyer had advised the witness that the witness could, in certain circumstances, tell the Committee that she did not recall facts when she actually did recall them;

- During a break in the Select Committee's interview, the witness expressed concerns to her lawyer that an aspect of her testimony was not truthful. The lawyer did not advise her to clarify the specific testimony that the witness believed was not complete and accurate, and instead conveyed that, "They don't know what you know, [witness]. They don't know that you can recall some of these things. So you saying 'I don't recall' is an entirely acceptable response to this.";

- The lawyer instructed the client about a particular issue that would cast a bad light on President Trump: "No, no, no, no, no. We don't want to go there. We don't want to talk about that.";

- The lawyer refused directions from the client not to share her testimony before the Committee with other lawyers representing other witnesses. The lawyer shared such information over the client's objection;

- The lawyer refused directions from the client not to share information regarding her testimony with at least one and possibly more than one member of the press. The lawyer shared the information with the press over her objection.

- The lawyer did not disclose who was paying for the lawyers' representation of the client, despite questions from the client seeking that information, and told her, "we're not telling people where funding is coming from right now";

- The client was offered potential employment that would make her "financially very comfortable" as the date of her testimony approached by entities apparently linked to Donald Trump and his associates. Such offers were withdrawn or did not materialize as reports of the content of her testimony circulated. The client believed this was an effort to impact her testimony.

Further details regarding these instances will be available to the public when transcripts are released.

2. Similarly, the witness testified that multiple persons affiliated with President Trump contacted her in advance of the witness's testimony and made the following statements:

- What they said to me is, as long as I continue to be a team player, they know that I am on the right team. I am doing the right thing. I am protecting who I need to protect. You know, I will continue to stay in good graces in Trump World. And they have reminded me a couple of times that Trump does read transcripts and just keep that in mind as I proceed through my interviews with the committee.

Here is another sample in a different context. This is a call received by one of our witnesses:

- [A person] let me know you have your deposition tomorrow. He wants me to let you know he's thinking about you. He knows you're a team player, you're loyal, and you're going do the right thing when you go in for your deposition.[703]

3. The Select Committee is aware of multiple efforts by President Trump to contact Select Committee witnesses. The Department of Justice is aware of at least one of those circumstances.

4. Rather than relying on representation by Secret Service lawyers at no cost, a small number of Secret Service agents engaged private counsel for their interviews before the Committee.[704] During one such witness's transcribed interview, a retained private counsel was observed writing notes to the witness regarding the content of the witness's testimony while the questioning was underway. The witness's counsel admitted on the record that he had done so.[705]

Recently, published accounts of the Justice Department's Mar-a-Lago investigation suggest that the Department is investigating the conduct of counsel for certain witnesses whose fees are being paid by President Trump's Save America Political Action Committee.[706] The public report implies the Department is concerned that such individuals are seeking to influence the testimony of the witnesses they represent.[707] This Committee also has these concerns, including that lawyers who are receiving such payments have specific incentives to defend President Trump rather than zealously represent their own clients. The Department of Justice and the Fulton County District Attorney have been provided with certain information related to this topic.

The Select Committee recognizes of course that most of the testimony we have gathered was given more than a year after January 6th. Recollections are not perfect, and the Committee expects that different accounts of the same events will naturally vary. Indeed, the lack of any inconsistencies in witness accounts would itself be suspicious. And many witnesses may simply recall different things than others.

Many of the witnesses before this Committee had nothing at all to gain from their testimony, gave straightforward responses to the questions posted, and made no effort to downplay, deflect, or rationalize. Trump Administration Justice Department officials such as Attorney General Bill Barr, Acting Attorney General Jeffrey Rosen, and Acting Deputy Attorney General Richard Donoghue are good examples. Multiple members of President Trump's White House staff were also suitably forthcoming, including Sarah Matthews, Matthew Pottinger, Greg Jacob, and Pat Philbin, as were multiple career White House and agency personnel whose names the Committee agreed not to disclose publicly; as were former Secretary of Labor Eugene Scalia, Bill Stepien, and certain other members of the Trump Campaign. The Committee very much appreciates the earnestness and bravery of Cassidy Hutchinson, Rusty Bowers, Shaye Moss, Ruby Freeman, Brad Raffensperger, Gabriel Sterling, Al Schmidt, and many others who provided important live testimony during the Committees hearings.[708]

The Committee, along with our nation, offers particular thanks to Officers Caroline Edwards, Michael Fanone, Harry Dunn, Aquilino Gonell, and Daniel Hodges, along with hundreds of other members of law enforcement who defended the Capitol on that fateful day, all of whom should be commended for their bravery and sacrifice. We especially thank the families of Officer Brian Sicknick, Howard Liebengood and Jeffrey Smith, whose loss can never be repaid.

The Committee very much appreciates the invaluable testimony of General Milley and other members of our military, Judge J. Michael Luttig, and the important contributions of Benjamin Ginsberg and Chris Stirewalt. This, of course is only a partial list, and the Committee is indebted to many others, as well.

The Committee believes that White House Counsel Pat Cipollone gave a particularly important account of the events of January 6th, as did White House lawyer, Eric Herschmann. For multiple months, Cipollone resisted giving any testimony at all, asserting concerns about executive privilege and other issues, until after the Committee's hearing with Hutchinson. When he did testify, Cipollone corroborated key elements of testimony given by several White House staff, including Hutchinson – most importantly, regarding what happened in the White House during the violence of January 6th – but also frankly recognized the limits on what he could say due to privilege: "Again, I'm not going to get into either my legal advice on matters, and the other thing I don't want to do is, again, other witnesses have their own recollections of things." Cipollone also told the Committee that, to the extent that other witnesses recall communications attributable to White House counsel that he does not, the communications might have been with his deputy Pat Philbin, or with Eric Herschmann, who had strong feelings and was particularly animated about certain issues.[709]

Of course, that is not to say that all witnesses were entirely frank or forthcoming. Other witnesses, including certain witnesses from the Trump White House, displayed a lack of full recollection of certain issues, or were not otherwise as frank or direct as Cipollone. We cite two examples here, both relating to testimony played during the hearings.

Kayleigh McEnany was President Trump's Press Secretary on January 6th. Her deposition was taken early in the investigation. McEnany seemed to acknowledge that President Trump: (1) should have instructed his violent supporters to leave the Capitol earlier than he ultimately did on January 6th;[710] (2) should have respected the rulings of the courts;[711] and (3) was wrong to publicly allege that Dominion voting machines stole the election.[712] But a segment of McEnany's testimony seemed evasive, as if she was testifying from pre-prepared talking points. In multiple instances, McEnany's testimony did not seem nearly as forthright as that of her press office staff, who testified about what McEnany said.

For example, McEnany disputed suggestions that President Trump was resistant to condemning the violence and urging the crowd at the Capitol to act peacefully when they crafted his tweet at 2:38 p.m. on January 6th.[713] Yet one of her deputies, Sarah Matthews, told the Select Committee that McEnany informed her otherwise: that McEnany and other advisors in the dining room with President Trump persuaded him to send the tweet, but that "... she said that he did not want to put that in and that they went through different phrasing of that, of the mention of peace, in order to get him to agree to include it, and that it was Ivanka Trump who came up with 'stay peaceful' and that he agreed to that phrasing to include in the tweet, but he was initially resistant to mentioning peace of any sort."[714] When the Select Committee asked "Did Ms. McEnany describe in any way how resistant the President was to including something about being peaceful," Matthews answered: "Just that he didn't want to include it, but they got him to agree on the phrasing 'stay peaceful.'"[715]

The Committee invites the public to compare McEnany's testimony with the testimony of Pat Cipollone, Sarah Matthews, Judd Deere, and others,

Ivanka Trump is another example. Among other things, Ivanka Trump acknowledged to the Committee that: (1) she agreed with Attorney General Barr's statements that there was no evidence of sufficient fraud to overturn the election; (2) the President and others are bound by the rulings of the courts and the rule of law; (3) President Trump pressured Vice President Pence on the morning of January 6th regarding his authorities at the joint session of Congress that day to count electoral votes; and (4) President Trump watched the violence on television as it was occurring.[716] But again, Ivanka Trump was not as forthcoming as Cipollone and others about President Trump's conduct.

Indeed, Ivanka Trump's Chief of Staff Julie Radford had a more specific recollection of Ivanka Trump's actions and statements. For example, Ivanka Trump had the following exchange with the Committee about her attendance at her father's speech on January 6th that was at odds with what the Committee learned from Radford:

Committee Staff: It's been reported that you ultimately decided to attend the rally because you hoped that you would calm the President and keep the event on an even keel. Is that accurate?

Ivanka Trump: No. I don't know who said that or where that came from.[717]

However, this is what Radford said about her boss's decision:

Committee Staff: What did she share with you about why it was concerning that her father was upset or agitated after that call with Vice President Pence in relation to the Ellipse rally? Why did that matter? Why did he have to be calmed down, I should say.

Radford: Well, she shared that he had called the Vice President a not – an expletive word. I think that bothered her. And I think she could tell based on the conversations and what was going on in the office that he was angry and upset and people were providing misinformation. And she felt like she might be able to help calm the situation down, at least before he went on stage.

Committee Staff: And the word that she relayed to you that the President called the Vice President – apologize for being impolite – but do you remember what she said her father called him?

Radford: The "P" word.[718]

When the Committee asked Ivanka Trump whether there were "[a]ny particular words that you recall your father using during the conversation" that morning with Vice President Pence, she answered simply: "No."⁷¹⁹

In several circumstances, the Committee has found that less senior White House aides had significantly better recollection of events than senior staff purported to have.

The Select Committee also has concerns regarding certain other witnesses, including those who still rely for their income or employment by organizations linked to President Trump, such as the America First Policy Institute. Certain witnesses and lawyers were unnecessarily combative, answered hundreds of questions with variants of "I do not recall" in circumstances where that answer seemed unbelievable, appeared to testify from lawyer-written talking points rather than their own recollections, provided highly questionable rationalizations or otherwise resisted telling the truth. The public can ultimately make its own assessment of these issues when it reviews the Committee transcripts and can compare the accounts of different witnesses and the conduct of counsel.

One particular concern arose from what the Committee realized early on were a number of intentional falsehoods in former White House Chief of Staff Mark Meadows's December 7, 2021 book, *The Chief's Chief*. ⁷²⁰ Here is one of several examples: Meadows wrote, "When he got offstage, President Trump let me know that he had been speaking metaphorically about going to the Capitol."⁷²¹ Meadows goes on in his book to claim that it "was clear the whole time" President Trump didn't intend to go to the Capitol.⁷²² This appeared to be an intentional effort to conceal the facts. Multiple witnesses directly contradicted Meadows's account about President Trump's desire to travel to the Capitol, including Kayleigh McEnany, Cassidy Hutchinson, multiple Secret Service agents, a White House employee with national security responsibilities and other staff in the White House, a member of the Metropolitan Police and others. This and several other statements in the Meadows book were false, and the Select Committee was concerned that multiple witnesses might attempt to repeat elements of these false accounts, as if they were the party line. Most witnesses did not, but a few did.

President Trump's desire to travel to the Capitol was particularly important for the Committee to evaluate because it bears on President Trump's intent on January 6th. One witness account suggests that President Trump even wished to participate in the electoral vote count from the House floor, standing with Republican Congressmen, perhaps in an effort to apply further pressure to Vice President Mike Pence and others.⁷²³

Mark Meadows's former Deputy Chief of Staff for Operations Anthony Ornato gave testimony consistent with the false account in Meadows's book. In particular, Ornato told the Committee that he was not aware of a genuine push by the President to go to the Capitol, suggesting instead that "it was one of those hypotheticals from the good idea fairy . . . [b]ecause it's ridiculous to think that a President of the United States can travel especially with, you know, people around just on the street up to the Capitol and peacefully protest outside the Capitol . . . ." ⁷²⁴ He told the Select Committee that the only conversation he had about the possibility of the President traveling to the Capitol was in a single meeting officials from the President's advance team,[725] and his understanding is that this idea "wasn't from the President."[726] Two witnesses before the Committee, including a White House employee with national security responsibilities and Hutchinson, testified that Ornato related an account of PresidentTrump's "irate" behavior when he was told in the Presidential SUV on January 6th that he would not be driven to the Capitol.[727] Both accounts recall Ornato doing so from his office in the White House, with another member of the Secret Service present.[728] Multiple other witness accounts indicate that the President genuinely was "irate," "heated," "angry," and "insistent" in the Presidential vehicle.[729] But Ornato professed that he did not recall either communication, and that he had no knowledge at all about the President's anger.[730]

Likewise, despite a significant and increasing volume of intelligence information in the days before January 6th showing that violence at the Capitol was indeed possible or likely, and despite other intelligence and law enforcement agencies similar conclusions,[731] Ornato claims never to have reviewed or had any knowledge of that specific information[732] He testified that he was only aware of warnings that opposing groups might "clash on the Washington Monument" and that is what he "would have brief to [Chief of Staff] Meadows."[733] The Committee has significant concerns about the credibility of this testimony, including because it was Ornato's responsibility to be aware of this information and convey it to decisionmakers.[734] The Committee will release Ornato's November Transcript so the public can review his testimony on these topics.

SUMMARY: CREATION OF THE SELECT COMMITTEE; PURPOSES.

In the week after January 6th, House Republican Leader Kevin McCarthy initially supported legislation to create a bipartisan commission to investigate the January 6th attack on the United States Capitol, stating that "the President bears responsibility for Wednesday's attack on Congress by mob rioters" and calling for creation of a "fact-finding commission."[735] Leader McCarthy repeated his support for a bipartisan commission during a press conference on January 21: "The only way you will be able to answer these questions is through a bipartisan commission."[736]

On February 15, House Speaker Nancy Pelosi announced in a letter to the House Democratic Caucus her intent to establish the type of independent commission McCarthy had supported, to "investigate and report on the facts and causes relating to the January 6, 2021 domestic terrorist attack upon the United States Capitol Complex."[737] A few days thereafter, Leader McCarthy provided the Speaker a wish list that mirrored "suggestions from the Co-Chairs of the 9/11 Commission" that he and House Republicans hoped would be included in the House's legislation to establish the Commission.[738]

In particular, Leader McCarthy requested an equal ratio of Democratic and Republican nominations, equal subpoena power for the Democratic Chair and Republican Vice Chair of the Commission, and the exclusion of predetermined findings or outcomes that the Commission itself would produce. Closing his letter, Leader McCarthy quoted the 9/11 Commission Co-Chairs, writing that a "bipartisan independent investigation will earn credibility with the American public."[739] He again repeated his confidence in achieving that goal.[740] In April 2021, Speaker Pelosi agreed to make the number of Republican and Democrat members of the Commission equal, and to provide both parties with an equal say in subpoenas, as McCarthy had requested.[741]

In May 2021, House Homeland Security Committee Chairman Bennie G. Thompson began to negotiate more of the details for the Commission with his Republican counterpart, Ranking Member John Katko.[742] On May 14, Chairman Thompson announced that he and Ranking Member Katko had reached an agreement on legislation to "form a bipartisan, independent Commission to investigate the January 6th domestic terrorism attack on the United States Capitol and recommend changes to further protect the Capitol, the citadel of our democracy."[743]

On May 18, the day before the House's consideration of the Thompson-Katko agreement, Leader McCarthy released a statement in opposition to the legislation.[744] Speaker Pelosi responded to that statement, saying: "Leader McCarthy won't take yes for an answer."[745] The Speaker referred to Leader McCarthy's February 22 letter where "he made three requests to be addressed in Democrats' discussion draft."[746] She noted that "every single one was granted by Democrats, yet he still says no."[747]

In the days that followed, Republican Ranking Member Katko defended the bipartisan nature of the bill to create the Commission:

> As I have called for since the days just after the attack, an independent, 9/11-style review is critical for removing the politics around January 6 and focusing solely on the facts and circumstances of the security breach at the Capitol, as well as other instances of violence relevant to such a review. Make no mistake about it, Mr. Thompson and I know this is about facts. It's not partisan politics. We would have never gotten to this point if it was about partisan politics.[748]

That evening, the House passed the legislation to establish a National Commission to Investigate the January 6th Attack on the United States Capitol Complex in a bipartisan fashion, with 35 Republicans joining 217 Democrats voting in favor and 175 Republicans voting against.[749] In the days thereafter, however, only six Senate Republicans joined Senate Democrats in supporting the legislation, killing the bill in the Senate.[750]

On June 24, Speaker Pelosi announced her intent to create a House select committee to investigate the attack.[751] On June 25, Leader McCarthy met with DC Metropolitan Police Officer Michael Fanone, who was seriously injured on January 6th.[752] Officer Fanone pressed Leader McCarthy "for a commitment not to put obstructionists and the wrong people in that position."[753]

On June 30, the House voted on H. Res. 503 to establish the 13-member Select Committee to Investigate the January 6th Attack on the United States Capitol by a vote of 222 Yeas and 190 Nays with just two Republicans supporting the measure: Representative Liz Cheney and Representative Adam Kinzinger.[754] On July 1, Speaker Pelosi named eight initial members to the Select Committee, including one Republican: Representative Cheney.[755]

On July 17th, Leader McCarthy proposed his selection of five members:

> *Rep. Jim Jordan, Ranking Member of the House Judiciary Committee;*
>
> *Rep. Kelly Armstrong of North Dakota; House Energy and Commerce Committee;*

Rep. Troy Nehls, House Transportation & Infrastructure and Veterans' Affairs Committees.

Rep. Jim Banks, Armed Services, Veterans' Affairs and Education and Labor Committees;

Rep. Rodney Davis, Ranking Member of the Committee on House Administration.[756]

Jordan was personally involved in the acts and circumstances of January 6th, and would be one of the targets of the investigation. By that point, Banks had made public statements indicating that he had already reached his own conclusions and had no intention of cooperating in any objective investigation of January 6th, proclaiming, for example, that the Select Committee was created "… solely to malign conservatives and to justify the Left's authoritarian agenda."[757]

On July 21, Speaker Nancy Pelosi exercised her power under H. Res. 503 not to approve the appointments of Rep. Jordan or Rep. Banks, expressing "concern about statements made and actions taken by these Members" and "the impact their appointments may have on the integrity of the investigation."[758] However, she also stated that she had informed Leader McCarthy "… that I was prepared to appoint Representatives Rodney Davis, Kelly Armstrong and Troy Nehls, and requested that he recommend two other Members."[759]

In response, Leader McCarthy *elected to remove all five* of his Republican appointments, refusing to allow Reps. Armstrong, Davis and Nehls to participate on the Select Committee.[760] On July 25, 2021, Speaker Pelosi then appointed Republican Rep. Adam Kinzinger.[761] In resisting the Committee's subpoenas, certain litigants attempted to argue that the Commission's composition violated House Rules or H. Res. 503, but those arguments failed in court.[762]

SELECT COMMITTEE WITNESSES WERE ALMOST ENTIRELY REPUBLICAN

In its ten hearings or business meetings, the Select Committee called live testimony or played video for several dozen witnesses, the vast majority of whom were Republicans. A full list is set forth below.

<u>Republicans</u>:

- **John McEntee** (served as Director of the White House Presidential Personnel Office in the Trump Administration)
- **Judd Deere** (served as deputy assistant to the President and White House deputy press secretary in the administration of Donald Trump)
- **Jared Kushner** (served as a senior advisor to President Donald Trump)
- **Pat Cipollone** (served as White House Counsel for President Donald Trump)
- **Eric Herschmann** (served as a senior advisor to former President Donald Trump)
- **Kayleigh McEnany** (served the administration of Donald Trump as the 33rd White House press secretary from April 2020 to January 2021)
- **Derek Lyons** (served as White House Staff Secretary and Counselor to the President in the administration of former U.S. President Donald Trump)
- **Cassidy Hutchinson** (assistant to former Chief of Staff Mark Meadows during the Trump administration)
- **Matt Pottinger** (served as the United States deputy national security advisor)

- **Ben Williamson** (senior advisor to chief of staff Mark Meadows)
- **Sarah Matthews** (served as the deputy press secretary for the Trump administration)
- **William Barr** (served as Attorney General for the Trump administration)
- **Mike Pompeo** (served as the director of the Central Intelligence Agency and as the 70th United States Secretary of State for the Trump administration)
- **Ivanka Trump** (served as a senior advisor and director of the Office of Economic Initiatives and Entrepreneurship for the Trump administration)
- **Donald Trump Jr.** (eldest child of Donald Trump)
- **Molly Michael** (served as Special Assistant to the President and Oval Office Operations Coordinator)
- **Tim Murtaugh** (served as director of communications for President Donald J. Trump's re-election campaign)
- **Richard Donoghue** (served as the acting United States deputy attorney general)
- **Jeffrey Rosen** (served as the acting United States attorney general from December 2020 to January 2021)
- **Steven Engel** (served as the United States Assistant Attorney General for the Office of Legal Counsel in the Trump administration)
- **Marc Short** (served as chief of staff to Vice President Mike Pence)
- **Greg Jacob** (served as White House lawyer to former Vice President Mike Pence)
- **Keith Kellogg** (served as National Security Advisor to the Vice President of the United States)
- **Chris Hodgson** (served as director of legislative affairs for Vice President Mike Pence)
- **Douglas Macgregor** (former advisor to the Secretary of Defense in the Trump administration)
- **Jason Miller** (served as spokesman for the Donald Trump 2016 Presidential Campaign and was a Senior Adviser to the Trump 2020 Re-election Campaign)
- **Alex Cannon** (an attorney for Donald Trump)
- **Bill Stepien** (served as the Campaign manager for Donald Trump's 2020 Presidential Campaign and was the White House Director of Political Affairs in the Trump administration from 2017 to 2018)
- **Rudolph Giuliani** (an attorney for Donald Trump)
- **John Eastman** (an attorney central to the Electoral College election theories to overturn the results of the election)
- **Michael Flynn** (served as former National Security Advisor for the Trump Administration)
- **Eugene Scalia** (served as the United States secretary of labor during the final 16 months of the Donald Trump administration)
- **Matthew Morgan** (Deputy Assistant to the Vice President and Deputy Counsel)
- **Sidney Powell** (served on President Trump's legal team to overturn the results of the 2020 election)
- **Jeffrey Clark** (former United States Assistant Attorney General for the Civil Division)
- **Cleta Mitchell** (served on President Trump's legal team to overturn the results of the 2020 election)
- **Ronna Romney McDaniel** (serving as the chair of the Republican National Committee)

- **Justin Clark** (served as Director of Public Liaison and Director of Intergovernmental Affairs at the White House under the Trump administration)
- **Robert Sinners** (a former campaign staffer for Donald Trump)
- **Andrew Hitt** (Former Wisconsin Republican Party Chair)
- **Laura Cox** (Former Michigan Republican Party Chair)
- **Mike Shirkey** (Majority Leader, Michigan State Senate - Republican)
- **Bryan Cutler** (Speaker, Pennsylvania House of Representatives - Republican)
- **Rusty Bowers** (Arizona House Speaker - Republican)
- **Brad Raffensperger** (Georgia Secretary of State - Republican)
- **Gabriel Sterling** (Georgia Secretary of State Chief Operating Officer - Republican)
- **BJay Pak** (Former United States Attorney for the Northern District of Georgia)
- **Al Schmidt** (Former City Commissioner of Philadelphia)
- **Chris Stirewalt** (Former Fox News Political Editor)
- **Benjamin Ginsberg** (Election Attorney)
- **J. Michael Luttig** (Retired judge for the U.S. Court of Appeals for the Fourth Circuit and informal advisor to Vice President Mike Pence)
- **Katrina Pierson** (served as a liaison for the White House and organizers at Donald Trump's "Save America" rally on January 6)
- **Nicholas Luna** (Former President Donald Trump's personal assistant in the White House)
- **Stephen Miller** (Senior Advisor to the President)
- **Vincent Haley** (Deputy Assistant to the President and Advisor for Policy, Strategy and Speechwriting)
- **Julie Radford** (Ivanka Trump's Former Chief of Staff)
- **Mick Mulvaney** (Former Chief of Staff and Special Envoy for Northern Ireland for the Trump administration)
- **Elaine Chao** (Former Transportation Secretary)
- **Roger Stone** (Trump associate)

Democrats:

- **Jocelyn Benson** (Michigan Secretary of State - Democrat)

Other:

- **U.S. Capitol Police Officer Harry Dunn**
- **DC Metropolitan Police Officer Michael Fanone**
- **U.S. Capitol Police Sgt. Aquilino Gonell**
- **DC Metropolitan Police Officer Daniel Hodges**
- **General Mark Milley** (chairman of the Joint Chiefs of Staff)
- **U.S. Capitol Police Officer Caroline Edwards**
- **Nick Quested** (award-winning British filmmaker)
- **Robert Schornack** (Sentenced to 36 months probation)
- **Eric Barber** (charged with theft and unlawful demonstration in the Capitol)
- **John Wright** (awaiting trial for felony civil disorder and other charges)

- **George Meza** (Proud Boy)
- **Daniel Herendeen** (sentenced to 36 months probation)
- **Matthew Walter** (Proud Boy)
- **Wandrea ArShaye "Shaye" Moss** (former Georgia election worker)
- **Ruby Freeman** (former Fulton County Election Worker)
- **Anika Collier Navaroli** (Former Twitter Employee)
- **White House Security Official**
- **Jim Watkins** (Founder and Owner, 8kun)
- **Jody Williams** (Former Owner of TheDonald.win)
- **Dr. Donell Harvin** (Former Chief of Homeland Security, DC)
- **Kellye SoRelle** (Oath Keepers General Counsel)
- **Shealah Craighead** (Former White House Photographer)
- **Jason Van Tatenhove** (Former Oath Keepers Spokesperson)
- **Stephen Ayres** (January 6th Defendant)
- **Sgt. Mark Robinson** (Ret.) (D.C. Metropolitan Police Department)
- **Janet Buhler** (Pleaded guilty to charges related to January 6th)

---

[1] A few weeks later, Rhodes and his associate Kelly Meggs were found guilty of seditious conspiracy, and other Oath Keepers were found guilty on numerous charges for obstructing the electoral count. Trial Transcript at 10502-508, *United States v. Rhodes et al.*, No. 1:22-cr-15 (D.D.C. Nov. 29, 2022); Alan Feuer and Zach Montague, "Oath Keepers Leader Convicted of Sedition in Landmark Jan. 6 Case," *New York Times*, (Nov. 29, 2022), available at https://www.nytimes.com/2022/11/29/us/politics/oath-keepers-trial-verdict-jan-6.html.
[2] Trial Transcript at 5698, 5759, *United States v. Rhodes et al.*, No. 1:22-cr-15 (D.D.C. Oct. 31, 2022).
[3] Trial Transcript at 5775, *United States v. Rhodes et al.*, No. 1:22-cr-15 (D.D.C. Oct. 31, 2022) ("for me at the time, it meant I felt it was like a Bastille type moment in history where in the French Revolution it was that big turning point moment where the population made their presence felt. I thought it was going to be a similar type of event for us").
[4] Trial Transcript at 5783, 5866, *United States v. Rhodes et al.*, No. 1:22-cr-15 (D.D.C. Oct. 31, 2022).
[5] Sentencing Transcript at 15-17, *United States v. Reimler*, No. 1:21-cr-239 (D.D.C. Jan. 11, 2022), ECF No. 37.
[6] Sentencing Transcript at 33, *United States v. Pert*, No. 1:21-cr-139 (D.D.C. Feb. 11, 2022), ECF No. 64.
[7] Sentencing Memorandum by Abram Markofski, Exhibit B, *United States v. Markofski*, No. 1:21-cr-344 (D.D.C. Dec. 2, 2021), ECF No. 44-2.
[8] Sentencing Transcript at 49, *United States v. Witcher*, No. 1:21-cr-235 (D.D.C. Feb. 24, 2022), ECF No. 53
[9] Sentencing Transcript at 19–20, *United States v. Edwards*, No. 1:21-cr-366 (D.D.C. Jan. 21, 2022), ECF No. 33. *See also*, Sentencing Memorandum by Brandon Nelson, Exhibit B, *United States v. Nelson*, No. 1:21-cr-344 (D.D.C. Dec. 6, 2021), ECF No. 51-2; Sentencing Transcript at 65–66, *United States v. Griffith*, No. 1:21-cr-204 (D.D.C. Oct. 30, 2021), ECF No. 137; Sentencing Transcript at 45, *United States v. Schornak*, 1:21-cr-278 (D.D.C. May 11, 2022), ECF No. 90; Sentencing Transcript at 35, *United States v. Wilkerson*, No. 1:21-cr-302 (D.D.C. Nov. 22, 2021), ECF No. 31; Select Committee to Investigate the January 6th Attack on the United States Capitol, Transcribed Interview of Eric Barber, (Mar. 16, 2022), pp. 50–51.
[10] Statement of Facts at 5, *United States v. Sandlin*, No. 1:21-cr-88 (D.D.C. Jan. 20, 2021), ECF No. 1-1; Ryan J. Reily (@ryanjreily), Twitter Oct. 1, 2022 3:33 p.m. ET, available at https://twitter.com/ryanjreily/status/1576295667412017157; Ryan J. Reily (@ryanjreily), Twitter, Oct. 1, 2022 3:40 p.m. ET, available at https://twitter.com/ryanjreily/status/1576296016512692225; Government's Sentencing Memorandum at 2, 16, *United States v. Sandlin*, No. 1:21-cr-88 (D.D.C. Dec. 2, 2022), ECF No. 92.
[11] Government's Opposition to Defendant's Motion to Revoke Magistrate Judge's Detention Order at 4, *United States v. Miller*, No. 1:21-cr-119 (D.D.C. Mar. 29, 2021), ECF No 16; Dan Mangan, "Capitol Rioter Garret Miller Says He Was Following Trump's Orders, Apologizes to AOC for Threat," CNBC, (Jan. 25, 2021), available at https://www.cnbc.com/2021/01/25/capitol-riots-garret-miller-says-he-was-following-trumps-orders-apologizes-to-aoc.html.

[12] Select Committee to Investigate the January 6th Attack on the United States Capitol, Transcribed Interview of John Douglas Wright, (Mar. 31, 2022), pp. 22, 63.

[13] Select Committee to Investigate the January 6th Attack on the United States Capitol, Transcribed Interview of Lewis Cantwell, (Apr. 26, 2022), p. 54.

[14] Select Committee to Investigate the January 6th Attack on the United States Capitol, Transcribed Interview of Stephen Ayres, (June 22, 2022), p. 8.

[15] Select Committee to Investigate the January 6th Attack on the United States Capitol, *Hearing on the January 6th Investigation*, 117th Cong., 2d sess., (July 12, 2022), available at https://www.govinfo.gov/committee/house-january6th.

[16] Affidavit at 8, *United States v. Ayres*, No. 1:21-cr-156 (D.D.C. Jan. 22, 2021), ECF No. 5-1.

[17] *See infra*, Chapter 6. *See also* Documents on file with the Select Committee to Investigate the January 6th Attack on the United States Capitol (Select Committee Chart Compiling Defendant Statements). The Select Committee Chart Compiling Defendant Statements identifies hundreds of examples of such testimony. Select Committee staff tracked cases filed by the Department of Justice against defendants who committed crimes related to the attack on the United States Capitol. Through Department of Justice criminal filings, through public reporting, through social media research, and through court hearings, staff collected a range of statements by these defendants about why they came to Washington, DC, on January 6th. Almost always, it was because President Trump had called upon them to support his big lie. Those defendants also discussed plans for violence at the Capitol, against law enforcement, against other American citizens, and against elected officials in the days leading up to January 6th. In the days immediately following the attack, defendants also bragged about their conduct. Some defendants later reflected on their actions at sentencing. The Select Committee Chart Compiling Defendant Statements is not meant to be comprehensive or polished; it is a small sampling of the tremendous work the Department of Justice has done tracking down and prosecuting criminal activity during the attempted insurrection.

Moreover, the trial of multiple members of the Proud Boys on seditious conspiracy and other charges is set to begin on December 19, 2022, and may provide additional information directly relevant to this topic. *See* Court Calendar: December 9, 2022 – December 31, 2022, United States District Court for the District of Columbia, available at https://media.dcd.uscourts.gov/datepicker/index.html (last accessed Dec. 9, 2022); Alan Feuer, "Outcome in Oath Keepers Trial Could Hold Lessons for Coming Jan. 6 Cases," *New York Times*, (Nov. 30, 2022), available at https://www.nytimes.com/2022/11/30/us/politics/oath-keepers-stewart-rhodes.html.

[18] Documents on file with the Select Committee to Investigate the January 6th Attack on the United States Capitol (National Archives Production), 076P-R000001890_00001 (December 28, 2020, email from Bernard Kerik to Mark Meadows explaining that "[w]e can do all the investigations we want later"); Documents on file with the Select Committee to Investigate the January 6th Attack on the United States Capitol (National Archives Production), 076P-R000005090_0001 (January. 6, 2021, email from John Eastman to Gregory Jacob acknowledging that President Trump had "been so advised" that Vice President Pence "DOES NOT have the power to decide things unilaterally"); Select Committee to Investigate the January 6th Attack on the United States Capitol, *Hearing on the January 6th Investigation*, 117th Cong., 2d sess., (June 21, 2022), available at https://www.govinfo.gov/committee/house-january6th (Russell "Rusty" Bowers testimony recalling Rudolph Giuliani stating that "[w]e've got lots of theories; we just don't have the evidence"); *see also* Select Committee to Investigate the January 6th Attack on the United States Capitol, Transcribed Interview of Eric Herschmann (Apr. 6, 2022), p. 128 ("Whether Rudy was at this stage of his life in the same abilities to manage things at this level or not, I mean, obviously, I think Bernie Kerik publicly said it, they never proved the allegations that they were making, and they were trying to develop.")

Note: Some documents cited in this report show timestamps based on a time zone other than Eastern Time – such as Greenwich Mean Time – because that is how they were produced to the Committee.

[19] The Committee notes that a number of these findings are similar to those Federal Judge David Carter reached after reviewing the evidence presented by the Committee. Order Re Privilege of Documents Dated January 4-7, 2021 at 31-40, *Eastman v. Thompson et al.*, 594 F. Supp. 3d 1156, (C.D. Cal. Mar. 28, 2022) (No. 8:22-cv-99-DOC-DFM); Order Re Privilege of 599 Documents Dated November 3, 2020 - January 20, 2021 at 23-24, *Eastman v. Thompson et al.*, No. 8:22-cv-99 (C.D. Cal. June 7, 2022), ECF No. 356; Order Re Privilege of Remaining Documents at 13-17, *Eastman v. Thompson et al.*, No. 8:22-cv-99 (C.D. Cal. Oct. 19, 2022), ECF No. 372.

[20] *See* Documents on file with the Select Committee to Investigate the January 6th Attack on the United States Capitol (Secret Service Production), CTRL0000091086 (United States Secret Service Protective Intelligence Division communication noting left-wing groups telling members to "stay at home" on January 6th).

[21] Committee on House Administration, *Oversight of the United States Capitol Police and Preparations for and Response to the Attack of January 6th: Part I*, 117th Cong., 1st sess., (Apr. 21, 2021), available at https://cha.house.gov/committee-activity/hearings/oversight-united-states-capitol-police-and-preparations-and-response; Committee on House Administration, *Oversight of the United States Capitol Police and Preparations for and Response to the Attack of January 6th: Part II*, 117th Cong., 1st sess.,, (May 10, 2021), available at https://cha.house.gov/committee-activity/hearings/oversight-january-6th-attack-united-states-capitol-police-threat; Committee on House Administration, *Oversight of the January 6th Attack: Review of the Architect of the Capitol's Emergency Preparedness*, 117th Cong., 1st sess., (May 12, 2021), available at https://cha.house.gov/committee-activity/hearings/oversight-january-6th-attack-review-architect-capitol-s-emergency; Committee on House Administration, *Reforming the Capitol Police and Improving Accountability for the Capitol Police Board*, 117th Cong., 1st sess., (May 19, 2021), available at https://cha.house.gov/committee-activity/hearings/reforming-capitol-police-and-improving-accountability-capitol-police; Committee on House Administration, *Oversight of the January 6th Attack: United States Capitol Police Containment Emergency Response Team and First Responders Unit*, 117th Cong., 1st sess., (June 15, 2021), available at https://cha.house.gov/committee-activity/hearings/oversight-january-6th-attack-united-states-capitol-police-containment; Committee on House Administration, *Oversight of the January 6th Capitol Attack: Ongoing Review of the United States Capitol Police Inspector General Flash Reports*, 117th Cong., 2d sess., (Feb. 17, 2022), available at https://cha.house.gov/committee-activity/hearings/oversight-january-6th-capitol-attack-ongoing-review-united-states.

[22] John Koblin, "At Least 20 Million Watched Jan. 6 Hearing," *New York Times*, (June 10, 2022), available at https://www.nytimes.com/2022/06/10/business/media/jan-6-hearing-ratings.html. Their findings were also widely noted by major media outlets, including conservative ones. "Editorial: What the Jan. 6 Hearings Accomplished," *Wall Street Journal*, (Oct. 14, 2022), available at https://www.wsj.com/articles/what-the-jan-6-inquiry-accomplished-donald-trump-liz-cheney-subpoena-congress-11665699321; "Editorial: The Jan. 6 Hearings are Over. Time to Vote.," *Washington Post*, (Oct. 13, 2022), available at https://www.washingtonpost.com/opinions/2022/10/13/jan-6-hearings-are-over-time-vote/; "Editorial: The President Who Stood Still on Jan. 6," *Wall Street Journal*, (July 22, 2022), available at https://www.wsj.com/articles/the-president-who-stood-still-donald-trump-jan-6-committee-mike-pence-capitol-riot-11658528548; "Editorial: 'We All have a Duty to Ensure that What Happened on Jan. 6 Never Happens Again'," *New York Times*, (June 10, 2022), available at https://www.nytimes.com/2022/06/10/opinion/january-6-hearing-trump.html; "Editorial: Trump's Silence on Jan. 6 is Damning," *New York Post*, (July 22, 2022), available at https://nypost.com/2022/07/22/trumps-jan-6-silence-renders-him-unworthy-for-2024-reelection/.

[23] Select Committee to Investigate the January 6th Attack on the United States Capitol, Transcribed Interview of William Stepien, (Feb. 10, 2022), p. 45 ("And I told him it was going to be a process. It was going to be, you know– you know, we're going to have to wait and see how this turned out. So I, just like I did in 2016, I did the same thing in 2020.").

[24] "When States Can Begin Processing and Counting Absentee/Mail-In Ballots, 2020," Ballotpedia (accessed on Dec. 5, 2022), available at https://ballotpedia.org/When_states_can_begin_processing_and_counting_absentee/mail-in_ballots,_2020.

[25] *See* Select Committee to Investigate the January 6th Attack on the United States Capitol, *Hearing on the January 6th Investigation*, 117th Cong., 2d sess., (June 13, 2022), available at https://www.govinfo.gov/committee/house-january6th.

[26] Select Committee to Investigate the January 6th Attack on the United States Capitol, Transcribed Interview of William Stepien, (Feb. 10, 2022), p. 45; Select Committee to Investigate the January 6th Attack on the United States Capitol, *Hearing on the January 6th Investigation*, 117th Cong., 2d sess., (June 13, 2022), available at https://www.govinfo.gov/committee/house-january6th.

[27] Select Committee to Investigate the January 6th Attack on the United States Capitol, *Hearing on the January 6th Investigation*, 117th Cong., 2d sess., (June 13, 2022), available at https://www.govinfo.gov/committee/house-january6th.

[28] Select Committee to Investigate the January 6th Attack on the United States Capitol, Transcribed Interview of William Stepien, (Feb. 10, 2022), p. 36.

[29] Select Committee to Investigate the January 6th Attack on the United States Capitol, Transcribed Interview of Jared Kushner, (Mar. 31, 2022), p. 21.
[30] John J. Martin, *Mail-in Ballots and Constraints on Federal Power under the Electors Clause*, 107 Va. L. Rev. Online 84, 86 (Apr. 2021) (noting that 45 States and DC permitted voters to request a mail-in ballot or automatically receive one in the 2020 election); Nathanial Rakich and Jasmine Mithani, "What Absentee Voting Looked Like In All 50 States," FiveThirtyEight, (Feb. 9, 2021), available at https://fivethirtyeight.com/features/what-absentee-voting-looked-like-in-all-50-states/; Lisa Danetz, "Mail Ballot Security Features: A Primer," Brennan Center for Justice, (Oct. 16, 2020), available at https://www.brennancenter.org/our-work/research-reports/mail-ballot-security-features-primer.
[31] Select Committee to Investigate the January 6th Attack on the United States Capitol, Transcribed Interview of Hope Hicks, (Oct. 25, 2022), p. 34.
[32] He also won in Utah, which mailed absentee ballots to all active voters, and won one or more electoral votes in both Maine and Nebraska, which allowed no-excuse absentee voting and assign their electoral votes proportionally. *See* "Table 1: States with No-Excuse Absentee Voting," National Conference of State Legislatures, (July 12, 2022), available at http://web.archive.org/web/20201004185006/https://www.ncsl.org/research/elections-and-campaigns/vopp-table-1-states-with-no-excuse-absentee-voting.aspx (archived); "Voting Outside the Polling Place: Absentee, All-Mail and Other Voting at Home Options," National Conference of State Legislatures, (Sep. 24, 2020), available at http://web.archive.org/web/20201103175057/https://www.ncsl.org/research/elections-and-campaigns/absentee-and-early-voting.aspx (archived); Federal Election Commission, "Federal Elections 2020 – Election Results for the U.S. President, the U.S. Senate and the U.S. House of Representatives," (Oct. 2022), p. 12, available at https://www.fec.gov/resources/cms-content/documents/federalelections2020.pdf.
[33] *See, e.g.*, Select Committee to Investigate the January 6th Attack on the United States Capitol, Transcribed Interview of William Stepien, (Feb. 10, 2022), p. 66; Select Committee to Investigate the January 6th Attack on the United States Capitol, Deposition of Jason Miller, (Feb. 3, 2022), pp. 75-76.
[34] Select Committee to Investigate the January 6th Attack on the United States Capitol, Transcribed Interview of William Stepien, (Feb. 10, 2022), pp. 54, 66.
[35] Select Committee to Investigate the January 6th Attack on the United States Capitol, Deposition of Jason Miller, (Feb. 3, 2022), pp. 74-77.
[36] Select Committee to Investigate the January 6th Attack on the United States Capitol, Transcribed Interview of William Stepien, (Feb. 10, 2022), pp. 60-61.
[37] "Donald Trump 2020 Election Night Speech Transcript," Rev, (Nov. 4, 2020), available at https://www.rev.com/blog/transcripts/donald-trump-2020-election-night-speech-transcript.
[38] Donald J. Trump (@realDonaldTrump), Twitter, Nov. 5, 2020 9:12 a.m. ET, available at http://web.archive.org/web/20201105170250/https://twitter.com/realdonaldtrump/status/1324353932022480896 (archived).

Note: Citations in this report that refer to an archived tweet may list a timestamp that is several hours earlier or later than the one shown on the suggested webpage because tweets are archived from various time zones.

[39] *See, e.g.*, 52 U.S.C. § 10307; Ariz. Rev. Stat. § 16-1010.
[40] Select Committee to Investigate the January 6th Attack on the United States Capitol, Deposition of Jason Miller, (Feb. 3, 2022), pp. 77-78.
[41] Select Committee to Investigate the January 6th Attack on the United States Capitol, Transcribed Interview of William Barr, (June 2, 2022), p. 8.
[42] Documents on file with the Select Committee to Investigate the January 6th Attack on the United States Capitol (National Archives Production), 076P-R000010020_0001 (November 3, 2020, email exchange between Tom Fitton and Molly Michael copying proposed election day victory statement).
[43] Dan Friedman, "Leaked Audio: Before Election Day, Bannon Said Trump Planned to Falsely Claim Victory," *Mother Jones*, (July 12, 2022), available at https://www.motherjones.com/politics/2022/07/leaked-audio-steve-bannon-trump-2020-election-declare-victory. We note that Mr. Bannon refused to testify and has been convicted of criminal contempt by a jury of his peers. "Stephen K. Bannon Sentenced to Four Months in Prison on Two counts of Contempt of Congress," Department of Justice, (Oct. 21, 2022), available at https://www.justice.gov/usao-dc/pr/stephen-k-bannon-sentenced-four-months-prison-two-counts-contempt-congress.

[44] At his interview, Stone invoked his Fifth Amendment Right not to incriminate himself in response to over 70 questions, including questions regarding his direct communications with Donald Trump and his role in January 6th. Select Committee to Investigate the January 6th Attack on the United States Capitol, Deposition of Roger Stone (Dec. 17, 2021). *See also* documents on file with the Select Committee to Investigate the January 6th Attack on the United States Capitol (Christoffer Guldbrandsen Production), Video file 201101_1 (November 1, 2020, footage of Roger Stone speaking to associates).

[45] Select Committee to Investigate the January 6th Attack on the United States Capitol, Deposition of Greg Jacob, (Feb. 1, 2022), pp. 12-13.

[46] Documents on file with the Select Committee to Investigate the January 6th Attack on the United States Capitol (National Archives Production), 79VP-R000011578_0001, 079VP-R000011579_0001, 079VP-R000011579_0002 (November 3, 2020, email and memorandum from Gregory Jacob to Marc Short regarding electoral vote count).

[47] Select Committee to Investigate the January 6th Attack on the United States Capitol, Transcribed Interview of William Stepien, (Feb. 10, 2022), pp. 117-18.

[48] Select Committee to Investigate the January 6th Attack on the United States Capitol, Deposition of Jason Miller, (Feb. 3, 2022), p. 91.

[49] Select Committee to Investigate the January 6th Attack on the United States Capitol, *Hearing on the January 6th Investigation*, 117th Cong., 2d sess., (June 13, 2022), available at https://www.govinfo.gov/committee/house-january6th.

[50] *See, e.g.*, Select Committee to Investigate the January 6th Attack on the United States Capitol, Transcribed Interview of General Mark A. Milley, (Nov. 17, 2021), p. 121; Select Committee to Investigate the January 6th Attack on the United States Capitol, Transcribed Interview of Alyssa Farah Griffin, (Apr. 15, 2022), p. 62; Select Committee to Investigate the January 6th Attack on the United States Capitol, Continued Interview of Cassidy Hutchinson, (Sep. 14, 2022), p. 113; Select Committee to Investigate the January 6th Attack on the United States Capitol, Transcribed Interview of Kellyanne Conway, (Nov. 28, 2022), pp. 79-84.

[51] *See* Select Committee to Investigate the January 6th Attack on the United States Capitol, Deposition of Keith Kellogg, Jr., (Dec. 14, 2021), pp. 212-21; Select Committee to Investigate the January 6th Attack on the United States Capitol, Transcribed Interview of General Mark A. Milley, (Nov. 17, 2021), pp. 108-10; Select Committee to Investigate the January 6th Attack on the United States Capitol, Deposition of John McEntee, (Mar. 28, 2022), pp. 44, 46, 48-51; Select Committee to Investigate the January 6th Attack on the United States Capitol, Transcribed Interview of Douglas Macgregor, (June 7, 2022), pp. 27-41.

[52] Select Committee to Investigate the January 6th Attack on the United States Capitol, Deposition of Keith Kellogg, Jr., (Dec. 14, 2021), p. 215.

[53] Select Committee to Investigate the January 6th Attack on the United States Capitol, Transcribed Interview of William Barr, (June 2, 2022), p. 6.

[54] Select Committee to Investigate the January 6th Attack on the United States Capitol, Transcribed Interview of Alex Cannon, (Apr. 13, 2022), pp. 22, 33-34.

[55] Select Committee to Investigate the January 6th Attack on the United States Capitol, Transcribed Interview of William Stepien, (Feb. 10, 2022), pp. 111-12.

[56] Select Committee to Investigate the January 6th Attack on the United States Capitol, Deposition of Jason Miller, (Feb. 3, 2022), p. 119.

[57] ABC News, "Pence Opens Up with David Muir on Jan. 6: Exclusive," YouTube, at 2:13, Nov. 14, 2022, available at https://youtu.be/-AAyKAoPFQs?t=133.

[58] "CNN Townhall: Former Vice President Mike Pence," CNN, (Nov. 16, 2022), available at https://transcripts.cnn.com/show/se/date/2022-11-16/segment/01.

[59] Select Committee to Investigate the January 6th Attack on the United States Capitol, Transcribed Interview of Matthew Morgan, (Apr. 25, 2022), p. 118.

[60] Select Committee to Investigate the January 6th Attack on the United States Capitol, Transcribed Interview of William Barr, (June 2, 2022), p. 18.

[61] Michael Balsamo, "Disputing Trump, Barr Says No Widespread Election Fraud," *Associated Press*, (Dec. 1, 2020, updated June 28, 2022), available at https://apnews.com/article/barr-no-widespread-election-fraud-b1f1488796c9a98c4b1a9061a6c7f49d.

[62] Select Committee to Investigate the January 6th Attack on the United States Capitol, Transcribed Interview of William Barr, (June 2, 2022), pp. 24-30; "Bill Barr Press Conference Transcript: No Special Counsels Needed to

Investigate Election or Hunter Biden," Rev, (Dec. 21, 2020), available at https://www.rev.com/blog/transcripts/bill-barr-press-conference-transcript-no-special-counsels-needed-to-investigate-election-or-hunter-biden

[63] "Joint Statement from Elections Infrastructure Government Coordinating Council & the Election Infrastructure Sector Coordinating Executive Committees," Cybersecurity and Infrastructure Security Agency, (Nov. 12, 2020), available at https://www.cisa.gov/news/2020/11/12/joint-statement-elections-infrastructure-government-coordinating-council-election (emphasis in original).

[64] Select Committee to Investigate the January 6th Attack on the United States Capitol, *Hearing on the January 6th Investigation*, 117th Cong., 2d sess., (June 23, 2022), available at https://www.govinfo.gov/committee/house-january6th.

[65] Select Committee to Investigate the January 6th Attack on the United States Capitol, Transcribed Interview of Richard Peter Donoghue, (Oct. 21, 2021), pp. 59-60.

[66] Select Committee to Investigate the January 6th Attack on the United States Capitol, Transcribed Interview of Richard Peter Donoghue, (Oct. 21, 2021), pp. 108-09.

[67] Senate Committee on the Judiciary, Transcribed Interview of Richard Donoghue, (Aug. 6, 2021), p. 156, available at https://www.judiciary.senate.gov/imo/media/doc/Donoghue%20Transcript.pdf.

[68] Select Committee to Investigate the January 6th Attack on the United States Capitol, Transcribed Interview of Jeffrey Rosen, (Oct. 13, 2021), pp. 18-19.

[69] Select Committee to Investigate the January 6th Attack on the United States Capitol, Transcribed Interview of Pasquale Anthony "Pat" Cipollone, (July 8, 2022), pp. 50, 123; Select Committee to Investigate the January 6th Attack on the United States Capitol, Transcribed Interview of Eric Herschmann, (Apr. 6, 2022), pp. 168-69, 184, 187.

[70] Select Committee to Investigate the January 6th Attack on the United States Capitol, Transcribed Interview of Pasquale Anthony "Pat" Cipollone, (July 8, 2022), p. 50.

[71] Select Committee to Investigate the January 6th Attack on the United States Capitol, Transcribed Interview of Eric Herschmann, (April 6, 2022), p. 128.

[72] Select Committee to Investigate the January 6th Attack on the United States Capitol, Transcribed Interview of William Stepien, (Feb. 10, 2022), pp. 172-73.

[73] Select Committee to Investigate the January 6th Attack on the United States Capitol, Transcribed Interview of William Stepien, (Feb. 10, 2022), p. 174.

[74] Select Committee to Investigate the January 6th Attack on the United States Capitol, Transcribed Interview of Justin Clark, (May 17, 2022), pp. 63-70; Select Committee to Investigate the January 6th Attack on the United States Capitol, Transcribed Interview of Matthew Morgan, (Apr. 25, 2022), pp. 57-62; Select Committee to Investigate the January 6th Attack on the United States Capitol, Transcribed Interview of Timothy Murtaugh, (May 19, 2022), pp, 66-68; Select Committee to Investigate the January 6th Attack on the United States Capitol, Transcribed Interview of Alex Cannon, (Apr. 19, 2022), pp. 37-38; Documents on file with the Select Committee to Investigate the January 6th Attack on the United States Capitol (Tim Murtaugh production), XXM-0021349 (text chain with Giuliani, Ellis, Epshteyn, Ryan, Bobb, and Herschmann).

[75] Select Committee to Investigate the January 6th Attack on the United States Capitol, Transcribed Interview of Matthew Morgan, (Apr. 25, 2022), p. 58.

[76] Select Committee to Investigate the January 6th Attack on the United States Capitol, Transcribed Interview of Matthew Morgan, (Apr. 25, 2022), p. 58.

[77] Select Committee to Investigate the January 6th Attack on the United States Capitol, Transcribed Interview of Matthew Morgan, (Apr. 25, 2022), p. 58.

[78] Select Committee to Investigate the January 6th Attack on the United States Capitol, Transcribed Interview of William Stepien, (Feb. 10, 2022), p. 173.

[79] *King v. Whitmer*, 505 F. Supp. 3d 720, 738 (E.D. Mich. 2020), also available at https://electioncases.osu.edu/wp-content/uploads/2020/11/King-v-Whitmer-Doc62.pdf; *Bowyer v. Ducey*, 506 F. Supp. 3d 699, 706 (D. Ariz. 2020), also available at https://storage.courtlistener.com/recap/gov.uscourts.azd.1255923/gov.uscourts.azd.1255923.84.0_2.pdf; *Donald J. Trump for President v. Boockvar*, 502 F. Supp. 3d 899, 906 (M.D. Pa. 2020), also available at https://storage.courtlistener.com/recap/gov.uscourts.pamd.127057/gov.uscourts.pamd.127057.202.0_1.pdf; *Law v. Whitmer*, No. 10 OC 00163 1B, 2020 Nev. Unpub. LEXIS 1160, at *1, 29-31, 33, 48-49, 52, 54 (Nev. Dec. 8, 2020), available at https://casetext.com/case/law-v-whitmer-1 (attaching and affirming lower court decision), also available at https://election.conservative.org/files/2020/12/20-OC-00163-Order-Granting-Motion-to-Dismiss-Statement-of-

Contest.pdf; *Wisconsin Voters Alliance v. Pence*, 514 F. Supp. 3d 117, 119 (D.D.C. 2021), also available at https://electioncases.osu.edu/wp-content/uploads/2020/12/WVA-v-Pence-Doc10.pdf.

[80] Documents on file with the Select Committee to Investigate the January 6th Attack on the United States Capitol (Zach Parkinson Production), Parkinson0620 (text message between Tim Murtaugh, Zach Parkinson, and "Matt").

[81] *In the Matter of Rudolph W. Giuliani*, No. 2021-00506, slip op at *2, 22 (N.Y. App. Div. May 3, 2021), available at https://int.nyt.com/data/documenttools/giuliani-law-license-suspension/1ae5ad6007c0ebfa/full.pdf.

[82] *In the Matter of Rudolph W. Giuliani*, No. 2021-00506, slip op at *2, 22 (N.Y. App. Div. May 3, 2021), available at https://int.nyt.com/data/documenttools/giuliani-law-license-suspension/1ae5ad6007c0ebfa/full.pdf.

[83] Opinion and Order at 1, *King v. Whitmer*, 505 F. Supp. 3d 720 (E.D. Mich. Aug. 25, 2020) (No. 20-13134), ECF No. 172.

[84] Senator John Danforth, Benjamin Ginsberg, The Honorable Thomas B. Griffith, et al., *Lost, Not Stolen: The Conservative Case that Trump Lost and Biden Won the 2020 Presidential Election*, (July 2022), p. 3, available at https://lostnotstolen.org/download/378/.

[85] Senator John Danforth, Benjamin Ginsberg, The Honorable Thomas B. Griffith, et al., *Lost, Not Stolen: The Conservative Case that Trump Lost and Biden Won the 2020 Presidential Election*, (July 2022), pp. 3-4, available at https://lostnotstolen.org/download/378/. We also note this: The authors of *Lost, Not Stolen* also conclude that one of the pieces of supposed evidence that President Trump and his allies have pointed to since January 6, 2021, to try to bolster their allegations that the 2020 election was stolen shows nothing of the sort. *Lost, Not Stolen* explains that Dinesh D'Souza's "2000 Mules" tries to establish widespread voter fraud in the 2020 election using phone-tracking data. "Yet the film, heartily endorsed by Trump at its Mar-a-Lago premiere, has subsequently been thoroughly debunked in analysis. What the film claims to portray is simply not supported by the evidence invoked by the film." *Id.*, at 6. Likewise, former Attorney General Bill Barr told the Select Committee: "… I haven't seen anything since the election that changes my mind…" to believe that fraud determined the outcome, "… including, the 2000 Mules movie." Select Committee to Investigate the January 6th Attack on the United States Capitol, Transcribed Interview of William Barr, (June 2, 2022), p. 37. He called its cell phone tracking data "singularly unimpressive" because "… in a big city like Atlanta or wherever, just by definition you're going to find many hundreds of them have passed by and spent time in the vicinity of these boxes" for submitting ballots, and to argue that those people must be "mules" delivering fraudulent ballots was "just indefensible." Select Committee to Investigate the January 6th Attack on the United States Capitol, Transcribed Interview of William Barr, (June 2, 2022), pp. 37-38.

[86] White House Senior Advisor Eric Herschmann told the Committee that when he disputed allegations of election fraud in a December 18th Oval Office meeting, Sidney Powell fired back that "the judges are corrupt. And I was like, every one? Every single case that you've done in the country you guys lost every one of them is corrupt, even the ones we appointed?" Select Committee to Investigate the January 6th Attack on the United States Capitol, Transcribed Interview of Eric Herschmann, (Apr. 6, 2022), p. 171.

[87] Select Committee to Investigate the January 6th Attack on the United States Capitol, *Hearing on the January 6th Investigation*, 117th Cong., 2d sess., (June 13, 2022), at 1:53:10-1:53:20, available at https://january6th.house.gov/legislation/hearings/06132022-select-committee-hearing.

[88] Verified Complaint for Declaratory and Injunctive Relief at 46-47, *Donald J. Trump for President, Inc. v. Boockvar*, No. 4:20-cv-02078 (M.D. Pa. Nov. 9, 2020), available at https://cdn.donaldjtrump.com/public-files/press_assets/2020-11-09-complaint-as-filed.pdf.

[89] Opinion at 2, 3, 16, *Donald J. Trump for President, Inc. v. Boockvar*, No. 20-3371 (3d Cir. Nov. 27, 2020), available at https://electioncases.osu.edu/wp-content/uploads/2020/11/Donald-J.-Trump-for-President-v-Boockvar-3rd-Cir-Doc91.pdf.

[90] Complaint for Expedited Declaratory and Injunctive Relief Pursuant to Article II of the United States Constitution, *Trump v. Wisconsin Elections Commission*, No. 2:20-cv-01785 (E.D. Wis. Dec. 2, 2020), available at https://electioncases.osu.edu/wp-content/uploads/2020/12/Trump-v-WEC-Doc1.pdf.

[91] *Trump v. Wisconsin Elections Commission*, 506 F. Supp. 3d 620, 21, 22 (E.D. Wis. 2020), available at https://electioncases.osu.edu/wp-content/uploads/2020/12/Trump-v-WEC-Doc134.pdf.

[92] Select Committee to Investigate the January 6th Attack on the United States Capitol, *Hearing on the January 6th Investigation*, 117th Cong., 2d sess., (June 13, 2022), at 1:52:45 to 1:53:20, available at https://january6th.house.gov/legislation/hearings/06132022-select-committee-hearing.

[93] The authors determined that thirty cases were dismissed by a judge after an evidentiary hearing had been held, compared to twenty cases that were dismissed by a judge beforehand, while the remaining fourteen were withdrawn

voluntarily by plaintiffs. *See* Senator John Danforth, Benjamin Ginsberg, The Honorable Thomas B. Griffith, et al, *Lost, Not Stolen: The Conservative Case that Trump Lost and Biden Won the 2020 Presidential Election*, (July 2022), p. 3, available at https://lostnotstolen.org/download/378/.

[94] Select Committee to Investigate the January 6th Attack on the United States Capitol, Deposition of Rudolph Giuliani, (May 20, 2022), p. 111.

[95] Letter from Timothy C. Parlatore to Chairman Bennie G. Thompson on "Re: Subpoena to Bernard B. Kerik," (Dec. 31, 2021).

[96] Documents on file with the Select Committee to Investigate the January 6th Attack on the United States Capitol (National Archives Production), 076P-R000004125_0001 (December 28, 2020, email from Kerik to Meadows).

[97] When our courts weigh evidence to determine facts, they often infer that disputed facts do not favor a witness who refuses to testify by invoking his Fifth Amendment right against incriminating himself. *See Baxter v. Palmigiano*, 425 U.S. 308, 318 (1976) (the Fifth Amendment allows for "adverse inferences against parties to civil actions when they refuse to testify to probative evidence offered against them").

[98] Nor was there such evidence of widespread fraud in any of the documents produced in response to Select Committee subpoenas issued to the proponents of the claims, including Rudy Giuliani and his team members and investigators Bernard Kerik and Christina Bobb, or other proponents of election fraud claims such as Pennsylvania Senator Doug Mastriano, Arizona legislator Mark Finchem, disbarred attorney Phill Kline, and attorneys Sidney Powell, Cleta Mitchell, and John Eastman. Not one of them provided evidence raising genuine questions about the election outcome. In short, it was a big scam.

[99] Select Committee to Investigate the January 6th Attack on the United States Capitol, *Business Meeting on the January 6th Investigation*, 117th Cong., 2d sess., (Oct. 19, 2022), at 56:30 to 58:10, available at https://january6th.house.gov/legislation/hearings/101322-select-committee-hearing

[100] Select Committee to Investigate the January 6th Attack on the United States Capitol, Transcribed Interview of Eugene Scalia (June 30, 2022), pp. 11-13. Then-Secretary Scalia also sent a memorandum to President Trump on January 8, 2021. In that memorandum, he requested that the President "convene an immediate meeting of the Cabinet." He told the President that he was "concerned by certain statements you made since the election . . . of further actions you may be considering," and he "concluded that [his] responsibilities as a Cabinet Secretary obligate[d] [him] to take further steps to address those concerns." The Select Committee will make this memorandum available to the public. Documents on file with the Select Committee to Investigate the January 6th Attack on the United States Capitol (Department of Labor Production), CTRL0000087637, (January 8, 2021, Memorandum for The President of the United States from Secretary of Labor Eugene Scalia, regarding Request for Cabinet Meeting).

[101] Select Committee to Investigate the January 6th Attack on the United States Capitol, Deposition of Judson Deere, (Mar. 3, 2022), pp. 23-25.

[102] Select Committee to Investigate the January 6th Attack on the United States Capitol, Transcribed Interview of Pasquale Anthony "Pat" Cipollone (July 8, 2022), p. 12.

[103] Select Committee to Investigate the January 6th Attack on the United States Capitol, Transcribed Interview of William Barr, (June 3, 2022), p. 62.

[104] Select Committee to Investigate the January 6th Attack on the United States Capitol, Transcribed Interview of William Barr, (June 3, 2022), pp. 19-20.

[105] Senate Committee on the Judiciary, Transcribed Interview of Jeffrey Rosen, (Aug. 7, 2021), pp. 30-31, available at https://www.judiciary.senate.gov/imo/media/doc/Rosen%20Transcript.pdf; Select Committee to Investigate the January 6th Attack on the United States Capitol, Transcribed Interview of Jeffrey Rosen, (Oct. 13, 2021), pp. 14-15 (in which Rosen confirms the general accuracy of the transcription of his Senate testimony and then is asked and agrees to the following question: [Committee staff]: "And we are going to – the select committee is going to essentially incorporate those transcripts as part of our record and rely upon your testimony there for our purposes going forward, as long as you're comfortable with that?" [Rosen]: "Yes.")

[106] "Donald Trump Vlog: Contesting Election Results – December 22, 2020," Factba.se, at 9:11-9:25 (Dec. 22, 2020), available at https://factba.se/transcript/donald-trump-vlog-contesting-election-results-december-22-2020.

[107] Select Committee to Investigate the January 6th Attack on the United States Capitol, Transcribed Interview of Richard Peter Donoghue, (Oct. 1, 2021), p. 43.

[108] Brad Raffensperger, *Integrity Counts* (New York: Simon & Schuster, 2021), p. 191 (reproducing the call transcript); Amy Gardner and Paulina Firozi, "Here's the Full Transcript and Audio of the Call Between Trump and

Raffensperger," *Washington Post*, (Jan. 5, 2021), available at https://www.washingtonpost.com/politics/trump-raffensperger-call-transcript-georgia-vote/2021/01/03/2768e0cc-4ddd-11eb-83e3-322644d82356_story.html

[109] Brad Raffensperger, *Integrity Counts* (New York: Simon & Schuster, 2021), p. 191 (reproducing the call transcript); Amy Gardner and Paulina Firozi, "Here's the Full Transcript and Audio of the Call Between Trump and Raffensperger," *Washington Post*, (Jan. 5, 2021), available at https://www.washingtonpost.com/politics/trump-raffensperger-call-transcript-georgia-vote/2021/01/03/2768e0cc-4ddd-11eb-83e3-322644d82356_story.html

[110] Donald J. Trump (@realDonaldTrump), Twitter, Jan. 3, 2021 8:57 a.m. ET, available at http://web.archive.org/web/20210103135742/https://twitter.com/realdonaldtrump/status/1345731043861659650 (archived).

[111] Select Committee to Investigate the January 6th Attack on the United States Capitol, Transcribed Interview of William Barr, (June 2, 2022), pp. 25-26.

[112] "Donald Trump Speech on Election Fraud Claims Transcript December 2," Rev, at 15:12-15:44, (Dec. 2, 2020), available at https://www.rev.com/blog/transcripts/donald-trump-speech-on-election-fraud-claims-transcript-december-2.

[113] Select Committee to Investigate the January 6th Attack on the United States Capitol, Transcribed Interview of Richard Peter Donoghue, (Oct. 1, 2021), p. 64.

[114] PBS NewsHour, "WATCH LIVE: Trump Speaks as Congress Prepares to Count Electoral College Votes in Biden Win," YouTube, at 1:42:58-1:43:02, Jan. 6, 2021, available at https://youtu.be/pa9sT4efsqY?t=6178.

[115] Senate Committee on the Judiciary, Interview of Richard Donoghue, (Aug. 6, 2021), p. 156, available at https://www.judiciary.senate.gov/imo/media/doc/Donoghue%20Transcript.pdf.

[116] PBS NewsHour, "WATCH LIVE: Trump Speaks as Congress Prepares to Count Electoral College Votes in Biden Win," YouTube, at 1:15:19-1:15:39, Jan. 6, 2021, available at https://youtu.be/pa9sT4efsqY?t=4519.

[117] Brad Raffensperger, Integrity Counts (New York: Simon & Schuster, 2021), p. 191 (reproducing the call transcript); Amy Gardner and Paulina Firozi, "Here's the Full Transcript and Audio of the Call Between Trump and Raffensperger," *Washington Post*, (Jan. 5, 2021), available at https://www.washingtonpost.com/politics/trump-raffensperger-call-transcript-georgia-vote/2021/01/03/2768e0cc-4ddd-11eb-83e3-322644d82356_story.html

[118] "Donald Trump Rally Speech Transcript Dalton, Georgia: Senate Runoff Election," Rev, at 51:38-52:01, (Jan. 4, 2021), available at https://www.rev.com/blog/transcripts/donald-trump-rally-speech-transcript-dalton-georgia-senate-runoff-election.

[119] Brad Raffensperger, *Integrity Counts* (New York: Simon & Schuster, 2021), p. 191 (reproducing the call transcript); Amy Gardner and Paulina Firozi, "Here's the Full Transcript and Audio of the Call Between Trump and Raffensperger," *Washington Post*, (Jan. 5, 2021), available at https://www.washingtonpost.com/politics/trump-raffensperger-call-transcript-georgia-vote/2021/01/03/2768e0cc-4ddd-11eb-83e3-322644d82356_story.html

[120] PBS NewsHour, "WATCH LIVE: Trump Speaks as Congress Prepares to Count Electoral College Votes in Biden Win," YouTube, at 1:32:25-1:32:43, Jan. 6, 2021, available at https://youtu.be/pa9sT4efsqY?t=5545.

[121] Brad Raffensperger, *Integrity Counts* (New York: Simon & Schuster, 2021), p. 191 (reproducing the call transcript); Amy Gardner and Paulina Firozi, "Here's the Full Transcript and Audio of the Call Between Trump and Raffensperger," *Washington Post*, (Jan. 5, 2021), available at https://www.washingtonpost.com/politics/trump-raffensperger-call-transcript-georgia-vote/2021/01/03/2768e0cc-4ddd-11eb-83e3-322644d82356_story.html

[122] PBS NewsHour, "WATCH LIVE: Trump Speaks as Congress Prepares to Count Electoral College Votes in Biden Win," YouTube, at 1:33:35-1:33:44, Jan. 6, 2021, available at https://youtu.be/pa9sT4efsqY?t=5615.

[123] Select Committee to Investigate the January 6th Attack on the United States Capitol, Deposition of Kayleigh McEnany, (Jan. 12, 2022), pp. 143, 290-91.

[124] Search results for "dominion", Trump Twitter Archive v2, (accessed Sep. 20, 2022), https://www.thetrumparchive.com/?searchbox=%22dominion%22&results=1.

[125] Select Committee to Investigate the January 6th Attack on the United States Capitol, Deposition of Jason Miller (Feb. 3, 2022), pp. 117, 133.

[126] "Donald Trump Thanksgiving Call to Troops Transcript 2020: Addresses Possibility of Conceding Election," Rev, at 23:35-23:46, (Nov. 26, 2020), available at https://www.rev.com/blog/transcripts/donald-trump-thanksgiving-call-to-troops-transcript-2020-addresses-possibility-of-conceding-election.

[127] Select Committee to Investigate the January 6th Attack on the United States Capitol, Transcribed Interview of William Barr, (Jun. 2, 2022), p. 19.

[128] "Donald Trump Thanksgiving Call to Troops Transcript 2020: Addresses Possibility of Conceding Election," Rev, at 24:16-24:35 (Nov. 26, 2020), available at https://www.rev.com/blog/transcripts/donald-trump-thanksgiving-call-to-troops-transcript-2020-addresses-possibility-of-conceding-election.

[129] Select Committee to Investigate the January 6th Attack on the United States Capitol, Transcribed Interview of William Barr, (Jun. 2, 2022), p. 27.

[130] "Donald Trump Speech on Election Fraud Claims Transcript December 2," Rev, at 10:46-11:06, (Dec. 2, 2020), available at https://www.rev.com/blog/transcripts/donald-trump-speech-on-election-fraud-claims-transcript-december-2.

[131] William P. Barr, *One Damn Thing After Another: Memoirs of an Attorney General*, (New York: HarperCollins, 2022), at p. 554.

[132] Donald J. Trump (@realDonaldTrump), Twitter, Nov. 15, 2020 12:21 a.m. ET, available at https://media-cdn.factba.se/realdonaldtrump-twitter/1338715842931023873.jpg (archived).

[133] Senate Committee on the Judiciary, Transcribed Interview of Jeffrey Rosen, (Aug. 7, 2021), pp. 25, 31, available at https://www.judiciary.senate.gov/imo/media/doc/Rosen%20Transcript.pdf.

[134] Donald J. Trump (@realDonaldTrump), Twitter, Dec. 16, 2020 1:09 a.m. ET, available at https://media-cdn.factba.se/realdonaldtrump-twitter/1339090279429775363.jpg (archived).

[135] Select Committee to Investigate the January 6th Attack on the United States Capitol, Transcribed Interview of Robert O'Brien, (Aug. 23, 2022), pp. 164-65.

[136] Donald J. Trump (@realDonaldTrump), Twitter, Dec. 19, 2020 11:30 a.m. ET, available at https://media-cdn.factba.se/realdonaldtrump-twitter/1340333619299147781.jpg (archived).

[137] Select Committee to Investigate the January 6th Attack on the United States Capitol, Transcribed Interview of Richard Peter Donoghue, (Oct. 1, 2021), p. 109.

[138] Brad Raffensperger, *Integrity Counts* (New York: Simon & Schuster, 2021), p. 191 (reproducing the call transcript); Amy Gardner and Paulina Firozi, "Here's the Full Transcript and Audio of the Call Between Trump and Raffensperger," *Washington Post*, (Jan. 5, 2021), available at https://www.washingtonpost.com/politics/trump-raffensperger-call-transcript-georgia-vote/2021/01/03/2768e0cc-4ddd-11eb-83e3-322644d82356_story.html

[139] Brad Raffensperger, Integrity Counts (New York: Simon & Schuster, 2021), p. 191 (reproducing the call transcript); Amy Gardner and Paulina Firozi, "Here's the Full Transcript and Audio of the Call Between Trump and Raffensperger," *Washington Post*, (Jan. 5, 2021), available at https://www.washingtonpost.com/politics/trump-raffensperger-call-transcript-georgia-vote/2021/01/03/2768e0cc-4ddd-11eb-83e3-322644d82356_story.html

[140] PBS NewsHour, "WATCH LIVE: Trump Speaks as Congress Prepares to Count Electoral College Votes in Biden Win," YouTube, at 1:39:09 to 1:39:27 and 1:40:51 to 1:41:01, Jan. 6, 2021, available at https://youtu.be/pa9sT4efsqY?t=5949.

[141] Select Committee to Investigate the January 6th Attack on the United States Capitol, *Hearing on the January 6th Investigation*, 117th Cong., 2d sess., (June 13, 2022), available at https://www.govinfo.gov/committee/house-january6th

[142] Select Committee to Investigate the January 6th Attack on the United States Capitol, Transcribed Interview of William Barr, (June 2, 2022), p. 15.

[143] The framers specifically considered and rejected two constitutional plans that would have given Congress the power to select the Executive. Under both the Virginia and New Jersey Plans, the national executive would have been chosen by the national legislature. *See* Curtis A. Bradley & Martin S. Flaherty, *Executive Power Essentialism and Foreign Affairs*, 102 Mich. L. Rev. 545, 592, 595 (2004); *see also* 1 The Records of the Federal Convention of 1787, at 21, 244 (Max Farrand ed., 1911) (introducing Virginia and New Jersey Plans), available at https://oll.libertyfund.org/title/farrand-the-records-of-the-federal-convention-of-1787-vol-1; James Madison, *Notes of the Constitutional Convention* (Sep. 4, 1787) (Gov. Morris warning of "the danger of intrigue & faction" if Congress selected the President), available at https://www.consource.org/document/james-madisons-notes-of-the-constitutional-convention-1787-9-4/.

[144] The Federalist No. 68, at 458 (Alexander Hamilton) (Jacob E. Cooke ed., 1961).

[145] The Federalist No. 68, at 459 (Alexander Hamilton) (Jacob E. Cooke ed., 1961).

[146] The Federalist No. 68, at 459 (Alexander Hamilton) (Jacob E. Cooke ed., 1961).

[147] The Federalist No. 68, at 459 (Alexander Hamilton) (Jacob E. Cooke ed., 1961). *See also* U.S. Const. art. II, § 1, cl. 2 ("but no Senator or Representative, or Person holding an Office of Trust or Profit under the United States, shall be appointed an Elector").

[148] Documents on file with the Select Committee to Investigate the January 6th Attack on the United States Capitol (Chapman University Production), Chapman052976 (Eastman Jan 6 scenario dual slates of electors memo); Documents on file with the Select Committee to Investigate the January 6th Attack on the United States Capitol (Chapman University Production), CTRL0000923171 (Eastman Jan. 6 scenario conduct by elected officials memo).

[149] Documents on file with the Select Committee to Investigate the January 6th Attack on the United States Capitol (Chapman University Production), Chapman003228 (Eastman memo to President Trump).

[150] *See Eastman v. Thompson et al.* at 6-8, 594 F. Supp. 3d 1156, (C.D. Cal. Mar. 28, 2022) (No. 8:22-cv-99-DOC-DFM)

[151] Documents on file with the Select Committee to Investigate the January 6th Attack on the United States Capitol (Chapman University Production), Chapman003228 (Eastman memo to President Trump).

[152] Select Committee to Investigate the January 6th Attack on the United States Capitol, Deposition of Greg Jacob (Feb. 1, 2022), p. 118.

[153] Select Committee to Investigate the January 6th Attack on the United States Capitol, Deposition of Greg Jacob (Feb. 1, 2022), p. 110, 117.

[154] Select Committee to Investigate the January 6th Attack on the United States Capitol, Deposition of Greg Jacob (Feb. 1, 2022), pp. 109-10; Select Committee to Investigate the January 6th Attack on the United States Capitol, *Hearing on the January 6th Investigation*, 117th Cong., 2d sess., (June 16, 2022), available at https://www.govinfo.gov/committee/house-january6th.

[155] Select Committee to Investigate the January 6th Attack on the United States Capitol, *Hearing on the January 6th Investigation*, 117th Cong., 2d sess., (June 16), available at https://www.govinfo.gov/committee/house-january6th.

[156] "Former Vice President Pence Remarks at Federalist Society Conference," C-SPAN (Feb. 4, 2022), available at https://www.c-span.org/video/?517647-2/vice-president-pence-remarks-federalist-society-conference.

[157] Select Committee to Investigate the January 6th Attack on the United States Capitol, Deposition of Greg Jacob, (Feb. 1, 2022), p. 122.

[158] Document on file with the Select Committee (National Archives Production), VP-R0000107 (January 5, 2021, Greg Jacob memo to Vice President); *see also* Select Committee to Investigate the January 6th Attack on the United States Capitol, Deposition of Greg Jacob, (Feb. 1, 2022), pp. 127-28 (discussing memorandum).

[159] Select Committee to Investigate the January 6th Attack on the United States Capitol, Deposition of Greg Jacob, (Feb. 1, 2022), pp. 122-23.

[160] Select Committee to Investigate the January 6th Attack on the United States Capitol, Deposition of Marc Short, (Jan. 26, 2022), pp. 26-27.

[161] Judge Luttig (@judgeluttig), Twitter, Jan. 5, 2021 9:53 a.m. ET available at https://twitter.com/judgeluttig/status/1346469787329646592.

[162] Select Committee to Investigate the January 6th Attack on the United States Capitol, *Hearing on the January 6th Investigation*, 117th Cong., 2d sess., (June 16, 2022), available at https://www.govinfo.gov/committee/house-january6th.

[163] Select Committee to Investigate the January 6th Attack on the United States Capitol, *Hearing on the January 6th Investigation*, 117th Cong., 2d sess., (June 16, 2022), available at https://www.govinfo.gov/committee/house-january6th.

[164] Documents on file with the Select Committee, (Chapman University Production), Chapman005442 (Eastman emails with Greg Jacob).

[165] Select Committee to Investigate the January 6th Attack on the United States Capitol, Transcribed Interview of Pasquale Anthony "Pat" Cipollone, (July 8, 2022), p. 88.

[166] Select Committee to Investigate the January 6th Attack on the United States Capitol, Transcribed Interview of Pasquale Anthony "Pat" Cipollone, (July 8, 2022), p. 85.

[167] Select Committee to Investigate the January 6th Attack on the United States Capitol, Transcribed Interview of Pasquale Anthony "Pat" Cipollone, (July 8, 2022), pp. 85-86.

[168] Select Committee to Investigate the January 6th Attack on the United States Capitol, Deposition of Jason Miller, (Feb. 3, 2022), p. 157.

[169] Select Committee to Investigate the January 6th Attack on the United States Capitol, Transcribed Interview of Pasquale Anthony "Pat" Cipollone, (July 8, 2022), pp. 86-87.

[170] Select Committee to Investigate the January 6th Attack on the United States Capitol, Transcribed Interview of Eric Herschmann, (Apr. 6, 2022), p. 34.

[171] Select Committee to Investigate the January 6th Attack on the United States Capitol, Transcribed Interview of Eric Herschmann, (Apr. 6, 2022), p. 26.
[172] Select Committee to Investigate the January 6th Attack on the United States Capitol, Transcribed Interview of Pasquale Anthony "Pat" Cipollone, (July 8, 2022), p. 85.
[173] Select Committee to Investigate the January 6th Attack on the United States Capitol, Transcribed Interview of Eric Herschmann, (Apr. 6, 2022), p. 40.
[174] Maggie Haberman and Annie Karni, "Pence Said to Have Told Trump He Lacks Power to Change Election Result," *New York Times*, (Jan. 5, 2021), available at https://www.nytimes.com/2021/01/05/us/politics/pence-trump-election-results.html.
[175] Meredith Lee (@meredithllee), Twitter, Jan. 5, 2021 9:58 p.m. ET, available at https://twitter.com/meredithllee/status/1346652403605647367; Select Committee to Investigate the January 6th Attack on the United States Capitol, Deposition of Jason Miller, (Feb. 3, 2022), p. 174-76; Greg Jacob testified that the President's statement was "categorically untrue." Select Committee to Investigate the January 6th Attack on the United States Capitol, *Hearing on the January 6th Investigation*, 117th Cong., 2d sess., (June 16, 2022), available at https://www.govinfo.gov/committee/house-january6th; Marc Short testified that the statement was "incorrect" and "false." Select Committee to Investigate the January 6th Attack on the United States Capitol, Deposition of Marc Short, (Jan. 26, 2022), p. 224; Chris Hodgson testified that it was not an accurate statement. Select Committee to Investigate the January 6th Attack on the United States Capitol, Deposition of Chris Hodgson, (Mar. 30, 2022), pp. 184-85.
[176] Select Committee to Investigate the January 6th Attack on the United States Capitol, Deposition of Jason Miller, (Feb. 3, 2022), pp. 175-77 (acknowledging that Miller normally would have called the Vice President's office before issuing a public statement describing the Vice President's views but stating "I don't think that ultimately -- don't know if it ultimately would have changed anything as the President was very adamant that this is where they both were" and acknowledging that "the way this [statement] came out was the way that [Trump] wanted [it] to.").
[177] Donald J. Trump (@realDonaldTrump), Twitter, Jan. 6, 2021 1:00 a.m. ET, available at http://web.archive.org/web/20210106072109/https://twitter.com/realDonaldTrump/status/1346698217304584192 (archived).
[178] Donald J. Trump (@realDonaldTrump), Twitter, Jan. 6, 2021 8:17 a.m. ET, available at http://web.archive.org/web/20210106175200/https://twitter.com/realDonaldTrump/status/1346808075626426371 (archived).
[179] Select Committee to Investigate the January 6th Attack on the United States Capitol, Transcribed Interview of Eric Herschmann, (Apr. 6, 2022), p. 47; Select Committee to Investigate the January 6th Attack on the United States Capitol, Deposition of Nicholas Luna, (Mar. 21, 2022), p. 126.
[180] Select Committee to Investigate the January 6th Attack on the United States Capitol, Deposition of General Keith Kellogg, Jr., (Dec. 14, 2021), p. 90; *See also,* Select Committee to Investigate the January 6th Attack on the United States Capitol, Transcribed Interview of Donald John Trump Jr., (May 3, 2022), p. 84; Select Committee to Investigate the January 6th Attack on the United States Capitol, Transcribed Interview of Eric Herschmann, (Apr. 6, 2022), p. 49; Select Committee to Investigate the January 6th Attack on the United States Capitol, Transcribed Interview of White House Employee, (June 10, 2022), pp. 21-22. The Select Committee is not revealing the identity of this witness to guard against the risk of retaliation.
[181] Select Committee to Investigate the January 6th Attack on the United States Capitol, Deposition of Nicholas Luna, (Mar. 21, 2022), p. 127.
[182] Select Committee to Investigate the January 6th Attack on the United States Capitol, Transcribed Interview of White House Employee (June 10, 2022), p. 20. The Select Committee is not revealing the identity of this witness to guard against the risk of retaliation.
[183] Select Committee to Investigate the January 6th Attack on the United States Capitol, Deposition of General Keith Kellogg, Jr., (Dec. 14, 2021), p. 92.
[184] Select Committee to Investigate the January 6th Attack on the United States Capitol, Transcribed Interview of Julie Radford, (May 24, 2022), p. 19. *See also* Peter Baker, Maggie Haberman, and Annie Karni, "Pence Reached His Limit with Trump. It Wasn't Pretty," *New York Times*, (Jan. 12, 2021), available at https://www.nytimes.com/2021/01/12/us/politics/mike-pence-trump.html; Jonathan Karl, *Betrayal: The Final Act of the Trump Show*, (New York: Dutton, 2021), at pp. 273-74.

185 At 11:33 a.m., Stephen Miller's assistant, Robert Gabriel, emailed the speechwriting team with the line: "REINSERT THE MIKE PENCE LINES." Documents on file with the Select Committee to Investigate the January 6th Attack on the United States Capitol (National Archives Production), 076P-R000007531_0001 (January 6, 2021, Robert Gabriel email to Trump speechwriting team at 11:33 a.m.).

186 Select Committee to Investigate the January 6th Attack on the United States Capitol, Deposition of Stephen Miller (Apr. 14, 2022), p. 153.

187 Document on file with the Select Committee (Ross Worthington Production), RW_0002341-2351 (S. Miller Jan. 6 Speech Edits Native File), pp. 2-3.

188 "Transcript of Trump's Speech at Rally Before US Capitol Riot," *Associated Press*, (Jan. 13, 2021), available at https://apnews.com/article/election-2020-joe-biden-donald-trump-capitol-siege-media-e79eb5164613d6718e9f4502eb471f27; Documents on file with the Select Committee to Investigate the January 6th Attack on the United States Capitol (Ross Worthington Production), CTRL0000924249, (changes in speech between draft and as delivered), pp. 2, 5, 12, 16, 22.

189 "Transcript of Trump's Speech at Rally Before US Capitol Riot," *Associated Press*, (Jan. 13, 2021), available at https://apnews.com/article/election-2020-joe-biden-donald-trump-capitol-siege-media-e79eb5164613d6718e9f4502eb471f27.

190 "Transcript of Trump's Speech at Rally Before US Capitol Riot," *Associated Press*, (Jan. 13, 2021), available at https://apnews.com/article/election-2020-joe-biden-donald-trump-capitol-siege-media-e79eb5164613d6718e9f4502eb471f27.

191 "Transcript of Trump's Speech at Rally Before US Capitol Riot," *Associated Press*, (Jan. 13, 2021), available at https://apnews.com/article/election-2020-joe-biden-donald-trump-capitol-siege-media-e79eb5164613d6718e9f4502eb471f27.

192 Select Committee to Investigate the January 6th Attack on the United States Capitol, *Hearing on the January 6th Investigation*, 117th Cong., 2d sess., (June 16, 2022), at 0:14:11-0:14:29, available at https://youtu.be/vBjUWVKuDj0?t=851.

193 Select Committee to Investigate the January 6th Attack on the United States Capitol, *Hearing on the January 6th Investigation*, 117th Cong., 2d sess., (June 16, 2022), at 2:07:02-2:07:07, available at https://youtu.be/vBjUWVKuDj0?t=7609.

194 Select Committee to Investigate the January 6th Attack on the United States Capitol, *Hearing on the January 6th Investigation*, 117th Cong., 2d sess., (June 16, 2022), at 2:07:02-2:07:07, available at https://youtu.be/vBjUWVKuDj0?t=7609.

195 Select Committee to Investigate the January 6th Attack on the United States Capitol, *Hearing on the January 6th Investigation*, 117th Cong., 2d sess., (July 21, 2022), at 1:00:46-1:01:12, available at https://youtu.be/pbRVqWbHGuo?t=3645.

196 Select Committee to Investigate the January 6th Attack on the United States Capitol, *Hearing on the January 6th Investigation*, 117th Cong., 2d sess., (July 21, 2022), at 1:01:13-1:01:26, available at https://youtu.be/pbRVqWbHGuo?t=3645.

197 Select Committee to Investigate the January 6th Attack on the United States Capitol, *Hearing on the January 6th Investigation*, 117th Cong., 2d sess., (June 16, 2022), at 0:14:37-0:14:46, available at https://youtu.be/vBjUWVKuDj0?t=851.

198 Select Committee to Investigate the January 6th Attack on the United States Capitol, *Hearing on the January 6th Investigation*, 117th Cong., 2d sess., (June 16, 2022), at 0:14:47-0:14:55, available at https://youtu.be/vBjUWVKuDj0?t=851.

199 Select Committee to Investigate the January 6th Attack on the United States Capitol, Transcribed Interview of White House Employee, (June 10, 2022), pp. 26-27 (establishing time as 1:21 p.m. based on time stamp of a photograph recognized and described).

200 Donald J. Trump (@realDonaldTrump), Twitter, Jan. 6, 2021 2:24 p.m. ET, available at https://web.archive.org/web/20210106192450/https://twitter.com/realdonaldtrump/status/1346900434540240897 (archived).

201 Government's Sentencing Memorandum at 32-33, *United States v. Cusanelli*, No. 1:21-cr-37 (D.D.C. Sept. 15, 2022), ECF No. 110.

202 *See* Affidavit in Support of Criminal Complaint and Arrest Warrant at 5, *United States v. Black*, No. 1:21-cr-127 (D.D.C. Jan. 13, 2021), ECF No. 1-1, available at https://www.justice.gov/opa/page/file/1354806/download.

203 Indictment at 9, *United States v. Neefe*, No. 1:21-cr-567 (D.D.C. Sept. 8, 2021), ECF No. 1, available at https://www.justice.gov/usao-dc/case-multi-defendant/file/1432686/download.

204 Affidavit in Support of Criminal Complaint and Arrest Warrant at 8, *United States v. Evans*, No. 1:21-cr-337 (D.D.C. Jan. 8, 2021), ECF No. 1-1, available at https://www.justice.gov/usao-dc/press-release/file/1351946/download.

205 Select Committee to Investigate the January 6th Attack on the United States Capitol, *Business Meeting on the January 6th Investigation*, 117th Cong., 2d sess., (Oct. 13, 2022), at 2:26:06-2:26:26, available at https://youtu.be/IQvuBoLBuC0?t=8766; Sentencing Transcript at 19, United States v. Yo*ung, No. 1:21-cr-291 (*D.D.C. Sept. 27, 2022), ECF No. 170 (testifying for a victim impact statement, Officer Michael Fanone said: "At approximately 1435 hours, with rapidly mounting injuries and most of the MPD less than lethal munitions expended, the defending officers were forced to conduct a fighting withdrawal back towards the United States Capitol Building entrance. This is the first fighting withdrawal in the history of the Metropolitan Police Department").

206 *See* Transcript of Trump's Speech at Rally Before US Capitol Riot," *Associated Press*, (Jan. 13, 2021), available at https://apnews.com/article/election-2020-joe-biden-donald-trump-capitol-siege-media-e79eb5164613d6718e9f4502eb471f27.

207 United States Secret Service Radio Tango Frequency at 14:16.

208 United States Secret Service Radio Tango Frequency at 14:25; *see also* Spencer S. Hsu, "Pence Spent Jan. 6 at Underground Senate Loading Dock, Secret Service Confirms," *Washington Post*, (Mar. 21, 2022), available at https://www.washingtonpost.com/dc-md-va/2022/03/21/couy-griffin-cowboys-trump-jan6/.

209 Select Committee to Investigate the January 6th Attack on the United States Capitol, *Hearing on the January 6th Investigation*, 117th Cong., 2d sess., (June 16, 2022), at 2:11:22-2:13:55, available at https://youtu.be/vBjUWVKuDj0?t=7882.

210 Select Committee to Investigate the January 6th Attack on the United States Capitol, Transcribed Interview of Eric Herschmann, (Apr. 6, 2022), pp. 43-44.

211 Select Committee to Investigate the January 6th Attack on the United States Capitol, Transcribed Interview of Eric Herschmann, (Apr. 6, 2022), p. 44.

212 Complaint, Exhibit 2 (Select Committee to Investigate the January 6th Attack on the United States Capitol subpoena to Chapman University, dated Jan. 21, 2022), *Eastman v. Thompson et al. et al.*, No. 8:22-cv-99, (C.D. Cal. Jan. 20, 2022) ECF No. 1-2.

213 Order Re Privilege of Documents Dated January 4-7, 2021 at 51-52, *Eastman v. Thompson et al.*, 594 F. Supp. 3d 1156, (C.D. Cal. Mar. 28, 2022) (No. 8:22-cv-99-DOC-DFM).

214 Order Re Privilege of Documents Dated January 4-7, 2021 at 56-57, *Eastman v. Thompson et al.*, 594 F. Supp. 3d 1156, (C.D. Cal. Mar. 28, 2022) (No. 8:22-cv-99-DOC-DFM).

215 Order Re Privilege of Documents Dated January 4-7, 2021 at 63-64, *Eastman v. Thompson et al.*, 594 F. Supp. 3d 1156, (C.D. Cal. Mar. 28, 2022) (No. 8:22-cv-99-DOC-DFM).

216 Select Committee to Investigate the January 6th Attack on the United States Capitol, *Hearing on the January 6th Investigation*, 117th Cong., 2d sess., (June 16, 2022), available at https://www.govinfo.gov/committee/house-january6th.

217 Select Committee to Investigate the January 6th Attack on the United States Capitol, Deposition of Greg Jacob, (Feb. 1, 2022), p. 223.

218 Select Committee to Investigate the January 6th Attack on the U.S. Capitol, Transcribed Interview of Ronna Romney McDaniel, (June 1, 2022), pp. 7-8.

219 Select Committee to Investigate the January 6th Attack on the U.S. Capitol, Transcribed Interview of Ronna Romney McDaniel, (June 1, 2022), pp. 9-11.

220 On December 13th, Chesebro memorialized the strategy in an email he sent Rudy Giuliani with the subject line: "PRIVILEGED AND CONFIDENTIAL – Brief notes on 'President of the Senate strategy." Documents on file with the Select Committee to Investigate the January 6th Attack on the United States Capitol (Chapman University Production), Chapman004708 (Dec. 13, 2020, Kenneth Chesebro email to Rudy Giuliani). Chesebro argued that the Trump team could use the fake slates of electors to complicate the joint session on January 6th if the President of the Senate "firmly t[ook] the position that he, and he alone, is charged with the constitutional responsibility not just to open the votes, but to count them—including making judgments about what to do if there are conflicting votes." *Id.* In the weeks that followed, Chesebro and John Eastman would build upon that framework and write two memos asserting that Joe Biden's certification could be derailed on January 6th if Vice President Pence

acted as the "ultimate arbiter" when opening the real and fake Electoral College votes during the joint session of Congress. Documents on file with the Select Committee to Investigate the January 6th Attack on the United States Capitol (Chapman University Production), Chapman053476 (December 23, 2020, Eastman memo titled "PRIVILEGED AND CONFIDENTIAL – Dec 23 memo on Jan 6 scenario.docx"); *see also* Documents on file with the Select Committee to Investigate the January 6th Attack on the United States Capitol (Chapman University Production), Chapman061863 (January 1, 2021, Chesebro email to Eastman).

[221] Select Committee to Investigate the January 6th Attack on the U.S. Capitol, Transcribed Interview of Justin Clark, (May 17, 2022), pp. 114, 116.

[222] Select Committee to Investigate the January 6th Attack on the U.S. Capitol, Transcribed Interview of Justin Clark, (May 17, 2022), pp. 116.

[223] The "certificate of ascertainment" is a State executive's official documentation announcing the official electors appointed pursuant to State law. *See* 3 U.S.C. § 6.

[224] Select Committee to Investigate the January 6th Attack on the U.S. Capitol, Transcribed Interview of Matthew Morgan, (Apr. 25, 2022), p. 70.

[225] Select Committee to Investigate the January 6th Attack on the U.S. Capitol, Transcribed Interview of Pasquale Anthony "Pat" Cipollone (July 8, 2022), pp. 70-72.

[226] Select Committee to Investigate the January 6th Attack on the U.S. Capitol, Informal Interview of Patrick Philbin (Apr. 13, 2022).

[227] Select Committee to Investigate the January 6th Attack on the U.S. Capitol, Transcribed Interview of Pasquale Anthony "Pat" Cipollone (July 8, 2022), p. 75.

[228] Select Committee to Investigate the January 6th Attack on the United States Capitol, Continued Interview of Cassidy Hutchinson, (Mar. 7, 2022), p. 64.

[229] Select Committee to Investigate the January 6th Attack on the United States Capitol, Deposition of Shawn Still, (Feb. 25, 2022), p. 24.

[230] Select Committee to Investigate the January 6th Attack on the United States Capitol, Deposition of Andrew Hitt, (Feb. 28, 2022), pp. 50–51.

[231] The National Archives produced copies of the seven slates of electoral votes they received from Trump electors in States that Trump lost. *See* Documents on file with the Select Committee to Investigate the January 6th Attack on the United States Capitol (National Archives Production), CTRL0000037568, CTRL0000037944, CTRL0000037945, CTRL0000037946, CTRL0000037947, CTRL0000037948, CTRL0000037949 (December 14, 2020, memoranda from slates of purported electors in Arizona, Georgia, Michigan, New Mexico, Nevada, Pennsylvania, and Wisconsin); Documents on file with the Select Committee to Investigate the January 6th Attack on the United States Capitol (National Archives Production), VP-R0000323_0001 (Senate Parliamentarian office tracking receipt and attaching copies of the seven slates); *See also* Documents on file with the Select Committee to Investigate the January 6th Attack on the United States Capitol (Robert Sinners Production), CTRL0000083893 (Trump campaign staffers emailing regarding submission); Documents on file with the Select Committee to Investigate the January 6th Attack on the United States Capitol (Bill Stepein Production), WS 00096 – WS 00097 (Trump campaign staffers emailing regarding submission).

[232] Documents on file with the Select Committee to Investigate the January 6th Attack on the United States Capitol (David Shafer Production), 108751.0001 000004 (December 10, 2020, Kenneth Chesebro email to David Shafer).

[233] Documents on file with the Select Committee to Investigate the January 6th Attack on the United States Capitol (National Archives Production), CTRL0000037944 (December 14, 2020, certificate and mailing envelope from Georgia); Documents on file with the Select Committee to Investigate the January 6th Attack on the United States Capitol (National Archives Production), CTRL0000037941 (December 14, 2020, certificate and mailing envelope from Arizona), Documents on file with the Select Committee to Investigate the January 6th Attack on the United States Capitol (National Archives Production), CTRL0000037945 (December 14, 2020, certificate and mailing envelope from Michigan).

[234] Documents on file with the Select Committee to Investigate the January 6th Attack on the United States Capitol (Andrew Hitt Production), Hitt000080 (January 4, 2021, Hitt text message with Mark Jefferson); Documents on file with the Select Committee to Investigate the January 6th Attack on the United States Capitol (Angela McCallum Production), McCallum_01_001576 - McCallum_01_001577 (January 5, 2021, McCallum text messages with G. Michael Brown); Documents on file with the Select Committee to Investigate the January 6th Attack on the United States Capitol (Chris Hodgson Production) CTRL0000056548_00007 (January 6, 2021, Hodgson text messages with

Matt Stroia); Documents on file with the Select Committee to Investigate the January 6th Attack on the United States Capitol (Chris Hodgson Production), CTRL0000056548_00035 (January 6, 2021, text messages from Senator Johnson's Chief of Staff, Sean Riley, to Chris Hodgson around 12:37 p.m.).

[235] Select Committee to Investigate the January 6th Attack on the United States Capitol, Deposition of Chris Hodgson (Mar. 30, 2022), pp. 206–07; Documents on file with the Select Committee to Investigate the January 6th Attack on the United States Capitol (Chris Hodgson Production) CTRL0000056548_00007 (January 6, 2021, text message from Rep. Kelly's Chief of Staff, Matt Stroia, to Chris Hodgson at 8:41 a.m.), CTRL0000056548_00035 (January 6, 2021, text messages from Senator Johnson's Chief of Staff, Sean Riley, to Chris Hodgson around 12:37 p.m.); Jason Lennon, "Johnson Says Involvement with 1/6 Fake Electors Plan Only 'Lasted Seconds'," *Newsweek*, (Aug. 21, 2022), available at https://www.newsweek.com/johnson-says-involvement-1-6-fake-electors-plan-only-lasted-seconds-1735486.

[236] Select Committee to Investigate the January 6th Attack on the United States Capitol, Deposition of Greg Jacob, (Feb. 1, 2022), pp. 52–54.

[237] Order Re Privilege of 599 Documents Dated November 3, 2020 - January 20, 2021 at 6, *Eastman v. Thompson et al.*, No. 8:22-cv-99 (C.D. Cal June 7, 2022), ECF No. 356.

[238] Order Re Privilege of 599 Documents Dated November 3, 2020 - January 20, 2021 at 20, *Eastman v. Thompson et al.*, No. 8:22-cv-99 (C.D. Cal June 7, 2022), ECF No. 356.

[239] Brad Raffensperger, *Integrity Counts* (New York: Simon & Schuster, 2021), p. 191 (reproducing the call transcript); Amy Gardner and Paulina Firozi, "Here's the Full Transcript and Audio of the Call Between Trump and Raffensperger," *Washington Post*, (Jan. 5, 2021), available at https://www.washingtonpost.com/politics/trump-raffensperger-call-transcript-georgia-vote/2021/01/03/2768e0cc-4ddd-11eb-83e3-322644d82356_story.html.

[240] Order Re Privilege of Documents Dated January 4-7, 2021 at 5, E*astman v. Thompson et al.*, 594 F. Supp. 3d 1156, (C.D. Cal. Mar. 28, 2022) (No. 8:22-cv-99-DOC-DFM), also available at https://www.cacd.uscourts.gov/sites/default/files/documents/Dkt%20260%2C%20Order%20RE%20Privilege%20of%20Jan.%204-7%2C%202021%20Documents_0.pdf. .

[241] Order Re Privilege of Documents Dated January 4-7, 2021 at 35, *Eastman v. Thompson et al.*, 594 F. Supp. 3d 1156, (C.D. Cal. Mar. 28, 2022) (No. 8:22-cv-99-DOC-DFM), also available at https://www.cacd.uscourts.gov/sites/default/files/documents/Dkt%20260%2C%20Order%20RE%20Privilege%20of%20Jan.%204-7%2C%202021%20Documents_0.pdf.

[242] After a journalist tweeted a video clip of key remarks from Gabriel Sterling's warning addressed to President Trump, President Trump responded by quote-tweeting that post, along with a comment that doubled down on demonizing Georgia election workers in spite of Sterling's stark and detailed warning. *See* Donald J. Trump (@realDonaldTrump), Twitter, Dec. 1, 2020 10:27 p.m. ET, available at http://web.archive.org/web/20201203173245/https://mobile.twitter.com/realDonaldTrump/status/1333975991518187521 (archived) ("Rigged Election. Show signatures and envelopes. Expose the massive voter fraud in Georgia. What is Secretary of State and @BrianKempGA afraid of. They know what we'll find!!! [linking to] twitter.com/BrendanKeefe/status/1333884246277189633"); Brendan Keefe (@BrendanKeefe), Twitter, Dec. 1, 2020 4:22 p.m. ET, available at https://twitter.com/BrendanKeefe/status/1333884246277189633 (""It. Has. All. Gone. Too. Far," says @GabrielSterling with Georgia Sec of State after a Dominion tech's life was threatened with a noose. "Mr. President, you have not condemned these actions or this language....all of you who have not said a damn word are complicit in this."" with embedded video of Gabriel Sterling's remarks); Select Committee to Investigate the January 6th Attack on the United States Capitol, *Hearing on the January 6th Investigation*, 117th Cong., 2d sess., (June 21, 2022), available at https://www.govinfo.gov/committee/house-january6th.

[243] Stephen Fowler, "'Someone's Going to Get Killed': Election Official Blasts GOP Silence on Threats," GPB News, (Dec. 1, 2020, updated Dec. 2, 2020), available at https://www.gpb.org/news/2020/12/01/someones-going-get-killed-election-official-blasts-gop-silence-on-threats.

[244] House Governmental Affairs Committee, Georgia House of Representatives, Public Hearing (Dec. 10, 2020), YouTube, at 1:55:10-1:59:10, available at https://youtu.be/9EfgETUKfsI?t=6910.

[245] Select Committee to Investigate the January 6th Attack on the United States Capitol, *Hearing on the January 6th Investigation*, 117th Cong., 2d sess., (June 21, 2022), at 2:25:45 to 2:26:00, available at https://youtu.be/xa43_z_82Og?t=8745.

[246] Jason Szep and Linda So, "A Reuters Special Report: Trump Campaign Demonized Two Georgia Election Workers – and Death Threats Followed," *Reuters* (Dec. 1, 2021), available at https://www.reuters.com/investigates/special-report/usa-election-threats-georgia/.

247 Amended Complaint at 52, *Freeman v. Giuliani*, No. 21-cv-03354-BAH (D.D.C. filed May 10, 2022), ECF No. 22, available at https://www.courtlistener.com/docket/61642105/22/freeman-v-herring-networks-inc.

248 Select Committee to Investigate the January 6th Attack on the United States Capitol, Transcribed Interview of Ruby Freeman, (May 31, 2022), pp. 7-8.

249 Select Committee to Investigate the January 6th Attack on the United States Capitol, *Hearing on the January 6th Investigation*, 117th Cong., 2d sess., (June 21, 2022), at 41:30-46:35, available at https://www.youtube.com/watch?v=xa43_z_82Og; Yvonne Wingett Sanchez and Ronald J. Hansen, "White House Phone Calls, Baseless Fraud Charges: The Origins of the Arizona Election Review," *Arizona Republic*, (Nov. 17, 2021), available at https://www.azcentral.com/in-depth/news/politics/elections/2021/11/17/arizona-audit-trump-allies-pushed-to-undermine-2020-election/6045151001/; Yvonne Wingett Sanchez and Ronald J. Hansen, "'Asked to do Something Huge': An Audacious Pitch to Reserve Arizona's Election Results," *Arizona Republic*, (Nov. 18, 2021, updated Dec. 2, 2021), available at https://www.azcentral.com/in-depth/news/politics/elections/2021/11/18/arizona-audit-rudy-giuliani-failed-effort-replace-electors/6349795001/.

250 Select Committee to Investigate the January 6th Attack on the United States Capitol, *Hearing on the January 6th Investigation*, 117th Cong., 2d sess., (June 21, 2022), at 53:00-53:40, available at https://www.youtube.com/watch?v=xa43_z_82Og.

251 Select Committee to Investigate the January 6th Attack on the United States Capitol, *Hearing on the January 6th Investigation*, 117th Cong., 2d sess., (June 21, 2022), at 41:30-46:35, available at https://www.youtube.com/watch?v=xa43_z_82Og.

252 Dennis Welch (@dennis_welch), Twitter, Dec. 8, 2020 11:23 p.m. ET, available at https://twitter.com/dennis_welch/status/1336526978640302080 (retweeting people who were posting Bowers's personal information); Dennis Welch (@dennis_welch), Twitter, Dec. 8, 2020 11:28 p.m. ET, available at https://twitter.com/dennis_welch/status/1336528029791604737.

253 Select Committee to Investigate the January 6th Attack on the U.S. Capitol, Transcribed Interview of Russel "Rusty" Bowers, (June 19, 2022), pp. 50-52; Kelly Weill, "Arizona GOP Civil War Somehow Keeps Getting Weirder," *Daily Beast*, (Dec. 11, 2020), available at https://www.thedailybeast.com/arizona-republican-party-civil-war-somehow-keeps-getting-weirder; Yvonne Wingett Sanchez and Ronald J. Hansen, "'Asked to do Something Huge': An Audacious Pitch to Reserve Arizona's Election Results," *Arizona Republic*, (Nov. 18, 2021, updated Dec. 2, 2021), available at https://www.azcentral.com/in-depth/news/politics/elections/2021/11/18/arizona-audit-rudy-giuliani-failed-effort-replace-electors/6349795001/.

254 Select Committee to Investigate the January 6th Attack on the United States Capitol, *Hearing on the January 6th Investigation*, 117th Cong., 2d sess., (June 21, 2022), available at https://www.govinfo.gov/committee/house-january6th.

255 Select Committee to Investigate the January 6th Attack on the United States Capitol, Transcribed Interview of Michael Shirkey, (June 8, 2022), pp. 16-22.

256 Select Committee to Investigate the January 6th Attack on the United States Capitol, Informal Interview of Lee Chatfield, (Oct. 15, 2021).

257 Select Committee to Investigate the January 6th Attack on the United States Capitol, Transcribed Interview of Michael Shirkey, (June 8, 2022), p. 57.

258 "Legislative Leaders Meet with President Trump," State Senator Mike Shirkey, (Nov. 20, 2020), available at https://www.senatormikeshirkey.com/legislative-leaders-meet-with-president-trump/.

259 Team Trump (Text TRUMP to 88022) (@TeamTrump), Twitter, Jan. 3, 2021 9:00 a.m. ET, available at http://web.archive.org/web/20210103170109/https://twitter.com/TeamTrump/status/1345776940196659201 (archived); Beth LeBlanc, "Trump Campaign Lists Lawmakers' Cells, Misdirects Calls for Chatfield to Former Petoskey Resident," *Detroit News*, (Jan. 4, 2021), available at https://www.detroitnews.com/story/news/politics/2021/01/04/trump-campaign-lists-michigan-lawmakers-cell-numbers-misdirects-private-citizen/4130279001/; Jaclyn Peiser, "Trump Shared the Wrong Number for a Michigan Lawmaker: A 28-Year-Old Has Gotten Thousands of Angry Calls," *Washington Post*, (Jan. 5, 2021), available at https://www.washingtonpost.com/nation/2021/01/05/michigan-trump-wrong-number-chatfield/.

260 Select Committee to Investigate the January 6th Attack on the United States Capitol, Transcribed Interview of Michael Shirkey, (June 8, 2022), p. 52; Aaron Parseghian, "Former Michigan Resident Slammed with Calls After Trump Campaign Mistakenly Posts Number on Social Media," Fox 17 West Michigan, (Jan. 4, 2021), available at

https://www.fox17online.com/news/politics/former-michigan-resident-slammed-with-calls-after-trump-campaign-mistakenly-posts-number-on-social-media.

[261] Nor would any State legislature have had such authority.

[262] Order Re Privilege of Remaining Documents at 16-17, *Eastman v. Thompson et al..*, No. 8:22-cv-99 (C.D. Cal Oct. 19, 2022), ECF No. 372, available at https://www.cacd.uscourts.gov/sites/default/files/documents/Dkt.%20372%2C%20Order%20Re%20Privilege%20of%20Remaining%20Documents.pdf.

[263] Documents on file with the Select Committee to Investigate the January 6th Attack on the United States Capitol (Chapman University Production), Chapman060742, (December 31, 2020, from John Eastman to Alex Kaufman and Kurt Hilbert)

[264] Documents on file with the Select Committee to Investigate the January 6th Attack on the United States Capitol (Chapman University Production), Chapman060742, (December 31, 2020, from John Eastman to Alex Kaufman and Kurt Hilbert).

[265] Order Re Privilege of Remaining Documents at 17, *Eastman v. Thompson et al.*, No. 8:22-cv-99 (C.D. Cal Oct. 19, 2022), ECF No. 372, available at https://www.cacd.uscourts.gov/sites/default/files/documents/Dkt.%20372%2C%20Order%20Re%20Privilege%20of%20Remaining%20Documents.pdf..

[266] Order Re Privilege of Remaining Documents at 17, *Eastman v. Thompson et al.*, No. 8:22-cv-099 (C.D. Cal Oct. 19, 2022), ECF No. 372, available at https://www.cacd.uscourts.gov/sites/default/files/documents/Dkt.%20372%2C%20Order%20Re%20Privilege%20of%20Remaining%20Documents.pdf.

[267] Select Committee to Investigate the January 6th Attack on the United States Capitol, *Hearing on the January 6th Investigation*, 117th Cong., 2d sess., (June 23, 2022), available at https://www.govinfo.gov/committee/house-january6th.

[268] Select Committee to Investigate the January 6th Attack on the United States Capitol, Transcribed Interview of Richard Peter Donoghue, (Oct. 1, 2021), p. 53.

[269] Select Committee to Investigate the January 6th Attack on the United States Capitol, Transcribed Interview of Richard Peter Donoghue, (Oct. 1, 2021), pp. 47-48, 53; Select Committee to Investigate the January 6th Attack on the United States Capitol, *Hearing on the January 6th Investigation*, 117th Cong., 2d sess., (June 23, 2022), available at https://www.govinfo.gov/committee/house-january6th.

[270] Select Committee to Investigate the January 6th Attack on the United States Capitol, *Hearing on the January 6th Investigation*, 117th Cong., 2d sess., (June 23, 2022), available at https://www.govinfo.gov/committee/house-january6th.

[271] Select Committee to Investigate the January 6th Attack on the United States Capitol, *Hearing on the January 6th Investigation*, 117th Cong., 2d sess., (June 23, 2022), available at https://www.govinfo.gov/committee/house-january6th.

[272] Select Committee to Investigate the January 6th Attack on the United States Capitol, *Hearing on the January 6th Investigation*, 117th Cong., 2d sess., (June 23, 2022), available at https://www.govinfo.gov/committee/house-january6th.

[273] Select Committee to Investigate the January 6th Attack on the United States Capitol, *Hearing on the January 6th Investigation*, 117th Cong., 2d sess., (June 23, 2022), available at https://www.govinfo.gov/committee/house-january6th.

[274] Select Committee to Investigate the January 6th Attack on the United States Capitol, Transcribed Interview of Richard Peter Donoghue, (Oct. 1, 2021), p. 58; Documents on file with the Select Committee to Investigate the January 6th Attack on the United States Capitol (Department of Justice Production), HCOR-Pre-Certification-Events-07282021-000738, HCOR-Pre-Certification-Events-07282021-000739 (December 27, 2020, handwritten notes from Richard Donoghue about call with President Trump).

[275] Select Committee to Investigate the January 6th Attack on the United States Capitol, Transcribed Interview of Richard Peter Donoghue, (Oct. 1, 2021), p. 59.

[276] Select Committee to Investigate the January 6th Attack on the United States Capitol, Transcribed Interview of Richard Peter Donoghue, (Oct. 1, 2021), p. 59.

[277] The Select Committee has reviewed evidence including a series of text messages between Rep. Scott Perry and Mark Meadows—sometimes referring to separate messages conducted over the Signal app—after the 2020 election,

some, if not all of which, relate to the appointment of Jeffrey Clark. *See, e.g.*, Documents on file with the Select Committee to Investigate the January 6th Attack on the United States Capitol (Mark Meadows Production), MM014099 (December 26, 2020, message from Representative Perry to Meadows stating: "Mark, just checking in as time continues to count down. 11 days to 1/6 and 25 days to inauguration. We gotta get going!"); Documents on file with the Select Committee to Investigate the January 6th Attack on the United States Capitol (Mark Meadows Production), MM014100 (December 26, 2020, message from Representative Perry to Meadows stating: "Mark, you should call Jeff. I just got off the phone with him and he explained to me why the principal deputy won't work especially with the FBI. They will view it as as [sic] not having the authority to enforce what needs to be done."); Documents on file with the Select Committee to Investigate the January 6th Attack on the United States Capitol (Mark Meadows Production), MM014101 (Dec. 26, 2020 Message from Meadows to Rep. Perry stating: "I got it. I think I understand. Let me work on the deputy position"); Documents on file with the Select Committee to Investigate the January 6th Attack on the United States Capitol (Mark Meadows Production), MM014102 (Dec. 26, 2020 Message from Rep. Perry to Meadows stating: "Roger. Just sent you something on Signal"); Documents on file with the Select Committee to Investigate the January 6th Attack on the United States Capitol (Mark Meadows Production), MM014162 (December 27, 2020, message from Rep. Perry to Meadows stating: "Can you call me when you get a chance? I just want to talk to you for a few moments before I return the presidents [sic] call as requested."); Documents on file with the Select Committee to Investigate the January 6th Attack on the United States Capitol (Mark Meadows Production), MM014178 (December 28, 2020, message from Rep. Perry to Meadows stating: "Did you call Jeff Clark?"); Documents on file with the Select Committee to Investigate the January 6th Attack on the United States Capitol (Mark Meadows Production), MM014208 (December 29, 2020, message from Representative Perry to Meadows stating: "Mark, I sent you a note on signal"); Documents on file with the Select Committee to Investigate the January 6th Attack on the United States Capitol (Mark Meadows Production), MM014586 (January 2, 2021, message from Representative Perry to Meadows stating: "Please call me the instant you get off the phone with Jeff."). President Trump, Mark Meadows, and Representative Perry refused to testify before the Select Committee, and Jeffrey Clark asserted his Fifth Amendment rights in refusing to answer questions from the Select Committee. "Thompson & Cheney Statement on Donald Trump's Defiance of Select Committee Subpoena," Select Committee to Investigate the January 6th Attack on the United States Capitol, (Nov. 14, 2022), available at https://january6th.house.gov/news/press-releases/thompson-cheney-statement-donald-trump-s-defiance-select-committee-subpoena; Luke Broadwater, "Trump Sues to Block Subpoena from Jan. 6 Committee," *New York Times*, (Nov. 11, 2022), available at https://www.nytimes.com/2022/11/11/us/politics/trump-subpoena-jan-6-committee.html; H. Rept. 117-216, Resolution Recommending that the House of Representatives Find Mark Randall Meadows in Contempt of Congress for Refusal to Comply with a Subpoena Duly Issued by the Select Committee to Investigate the January 6th Attack on the United States Capitol, 117th Cong., 1st Sess. (2021), available at https://www.congress.gov/117/crpt/hrpt216/CRPT-117hrpt216.pdf; Letter from John P. Rowley III to the Honorable Bennie G. Thompson, re: Subpoena to Representative Scott Perry, May 24, 2022, available at https://keystonenewsroom.com/wp-content/uploads/sites/6/2022/05/575876667-Rep-perry-Ltr-SelectComm.pdf; Select Committee to Investigate the January 6th Attack on the United States Capitol, Deposition of Jeffrey Clark, (Nov. 5, 2021); Select Committee to Investigate the January 6th Attack on the United States Capitol, Continued Deposition of Jeffrey Clark, (Feb. 2, 2022). *See also* Jonathan Tamari and Chris Brennan, "Pa. Congressman Scott Perry Acknowledges Introducing Trump to Lawyer at the Center of Election Plot," *Philadelphia Inquirer*, (Jan. 25, 2021), available at https://www.inquirer.com/politics/pennsylvania/scott-perry-trump-georgia-election-results-20210125.html.

[278] Documents on file with the Select Committee to Investigate the January 6th Attack on the United States Capitol (Mark Meadows Production), MM014099-014103, MM014178.

[279] Select Committee to Investigate the January 6th Attack on the United States Capitol, Transcribed Interview of Jeffrey Rosen, (Oct. 13, 2021), pp. 54-55.

[280] Select Committee to Investigate the January 6th Attack at the United States Capitol, Transcribed Interview of Jeffrey Rosen, (Oct. 13, 2021), p. 55.

[281] Select Committee to Investigate the January 6th Attack at the United States Capitol, Transcribed Interview of Jeffrey Rosen, (Oct. 13, 2021), p. 56.

[282] Select Committee to Investigate the January 6th Attack on the United States Capitol, Transcribed Interview of Richard Peter Donoghue, (Oct. 1, 2021), p. 114; Documents on file with the Select Committee to Investigate the January 6th Attack on the United States Capitol (Department of Justice Production), HCOR-Pre-CertificationEvents-

07262021-000681-84 (Department of Justice policy), HCOR-Pre-CertificationEvents-07262021-000685-86 (White House policy).

[283] Select Committee to Investigate the January 6th Attack at the United States Capitol, Transcribed Interview of Jeffrey Rosen, (Oct. 13, 2021), p. 56.

[284] Select Committee to Investigate the January 6th Attack on the United States Capitol, Transcribed Interview of Richard Peter Donoghue, (Oct. 1, 2021), p. 82.

[285] Select Committee to Investigate the January 6th Attack on the United States Capitol, Transcribed Interview of Richard Peter Donoghue, (Oct. 1, 2021), pp. 72-73; Documents on file with the Select Committee to Investigate the January 6th Attack on the United States Capitol (Department of Justice Production), HCOR-Pre-CertificationEvents-07262021-000698, (December 27, 2020, handwritten notes from Richard Donoghue about call with Congressman Perry).

[286] Select Committee to Investigate the January 6th Attack on the United States Capitol, Deposition of Kenneth Klukowski, (Dec. 15, 2021), pp. 15-17, 64-80, 179-191; Documents on file with the Select Committee to Investigate the January 6th Attack on the United States Capitol (Department of Justice Production), HCOR-Pre-CertificationEvents-07262021-000697, HCOR-Pre-CertificationEvents-07262021-000698 (email with draft letter attached to December 28, 2020, email from Jeffrey Clark to Jeffrey Rosen and Richard Donoghue).

[287] Select Committee to Investigate the January 6th Attack on the United States Capitol, Deposition of Kenneth Klukowski, (Dec. 15, 2021), pp. 184-88; Documents on file with the Select Committee to Investigate the January 6th Attack on the United States Capitol (Department of Justice Production), HCOR-Pre-CertificationEvents-07262021-000697, HCOR-Pre-CertificationEvents-07262021-000698 (email with draft letter attached to Dec. 28 email from Jeffrey Clark to Jeffrey Rosen and Richard Donoghue). As further discussed in Chapter 4 of this report, Klukowski, a lawyer, joined DOJ's Civil Division with just weeks remaining in President Trump's term and helped Clark on issues related to the 2020 election, despite the fact that "election-related matters are not part of the Civil portfolio." Select Committee to Investigate the January 6th Attack on the United States Capitol, Deposition of Kenneth Klukowski (Dec. 15, 2021), p. 66-67. Although Klukowski told the Select Committee that the Trump Campaign was his client before joining DOJ, *id.* at p. 190, and despite the fact that he had sent John Eastman draft talking points titled "TRUMP RE-ELECTION" that encouraged Republican State legislatures to "summon" new Electoral College electors for the 2020 election less than a week before starting at DOJ, Klukowski nevertheless helped Clark draft the December 28th letter described in this Report that, if sent, would have encouraged one or more State legislatures to take actions that they believed could have changed the outcome of the 2020 election, *see* Documents on file with the Select Committee to Investigate the January 6th Attack on the United States Capitol (Chapman University Production), Chapman028219, Chapman028220 (December 9, 2020, email from Klukowski to Eastman with attached memo). The Select Committee has concerns about whether his actions at DOJ, and his continued contacts with those working for, or to benefit, the Trump Campaign, may have presented a conflict of interest to the detriment of DOJ's mission. In addition, the Select Committee has concerns about many of the "privilege" claims Klukowski used to withhold information responsive to his subpoena, as well as concerns about some of his testimony, including his testimony about contacts with, among others, John Eastman. The Committee has learned that their communications included at least four known calls between December 22, 2020, and January 2, 2021. Documents on file with the Select Committee to Investigate the January 6th Attack on the United States Capitol (Verizon Production, July 1, 2022) (showing that Klukowski called Eastman on 12/22 at 7:38 a.m. EST for 22.8 min, that Klukowski called Eastman on 12/22 at 7:09 p.m. EST for 6.4 min, that Eastman called Klukowski on 12/30 at 9:11 p.m. EST for 31.9 min, and that Klukowski called Eastman on 1/02 at 6:59 p.m. EST for 6.4 min.

[288] Documents on file with the Select Committee to Investigate the January 6th Attack on the United States Capitol (Chapman University Production), Chapman061893 (Jan. 1, 2021, emails between Jeffrey Clark and John Eastman); *see* Documents on file with the Select Committee to Investigate the January 6th Attack on the United States Capitol (Verizon Production, July 1, 2022) (showing five calls between John Eastman and Jeffrey Clark from January 1, 2021, through January 8, 2021).

[289] Documents on file with the Select Committee to Investigate the January 6th Attack on the United States Capitol (Department of Justice Production), HCOR-Pre-CertificationEvents-07262021-000697 (Dec. 28 email from Jeffrey Clark to Jeffrey Rosen and Richard Donoghue titled "Two Urgent Action Items") ("The concept is to send it to the Governor, Speaker, and President pro temp of each relevant state…"); Select Committee to Investigate the January 6th Attack on the United States Capitol, Deposition of Kenneth Klukowski, (Dec. 15, 2021), pp. 68-69, 79.

[290] Documents on file with the Select Committee to Investigate the January 6th Attack on the United States Capitol (Department of Justice Production), HCOR-Pre-CertificationEvents-07262021-00069 (draft letter attached to December 28, 2020, email from Jeffrey Clark to Jeffrey Rosen and Richard Donoghue).

[291] Documents on file with the Select Committee to Investigate the January 6th Attack on the United States Capitol (Department of Justice Production), HCOR-Pre-CertificationEvents-07262021-00069 (draft letter attached to December 28, 2020, email from Jeffrey Clark to Jeffrey Rosen and Richard Donoghue).

[292] Documents on file with the Select Committee to Investigate the January 6th Attack on the United States Capitol (Department of Justice Production), HCOR-Pre-CertificationEvents-07262021-000703.

[293] Documents on file with the Select Committee to Investigate the January 6th Attack on the United States Capitol (Department of Justice Production), HCOR-Pre-CertificationEvents-07262021-00069 (draft letter attached to December 28, 2020, email from Jeffrey Clark to Jeffrey Rosen and Richard Donoghue).

[294] Documents on file with the Select Committee to Investigate the January 6th Attack on the United States Capitol (Department of Justice Production), HCOR-Pre-CertificationEvents-07262021-00069 (draft letter attached to December 28, 2020, email from Jeffrey Clark to Jeffrey Rosen and Richard Donoghue).

[295] Documents on file with the Select Committee to Investigate the January 6th Attack on the United States Capitol (Department of Justice Production), HCOR-Pre-CertificationEvents-07262021-00069 (draft letter attached to December 28, 2020, email from Jeffrey Clark to Jeffrey Rosen and Richard Donoghue).

[296] Documents on file with the Select Committee to Investigate the January 6th Attack on the United States Capitol (Department of Justice Production), HCOR-Pre-CertificationEvents-06032021-000200 (January 2, 2021, email from Jeffrey Rosen to Richard Donoghue titled "RE: Two Urgent Action Items").

[297] Documents on file with the Select Committee to Investigate the January 6th Attack on the United States Capitol (Department of Justice Production), HCOR-Pre-CertificationEvents-06032021-000200 (January 2, 2021, email from Jeffrey Rosen to Richard Donoghue titled "RE: Two Urgent Action Items").

[298] Documents on file with the Select Committee to Investigate the January 6th Attack on the United States Capitol (Department of Justice Production), HCOR-Pre-CertificationEvents-06032021-000200 (January 2, 2021, email from Jeffrey Rosen to Richard Donoghue titled "RE: Two Urgent Action Items").

[299] Select Committee to Investigate the January 6th Attack on the United States Capitol, *Hearing on the January 6th Investigation*, 117th Cong., 2d sess., (June 23, 2022), available at https://www.govinfo.gov/committee/house-january6th.

[300] Select Committee to Investigate the January 6th Attack on the United States Capitol, Transcribed Interview of Richard Peter Donoghue, (Oct. 1, 2021), p. 82.

[301] Select Committee to Investigate the January 6th Attack on the United States Capitol, Transcribed Interview of Richard Peter Donoghue, (Oct. 1, 2021), p. 82.

[302] Select Committee to Investigate the January 6th Attack on the United States Capitol, *Hearing on the January 6th Investigation*, 117th Cong., 2d sess., (June 23, 2022), available at https://www.govinfo.gov/committee/house-january6th; Select Committee to Investigate the January 6th Attack on the United States Capitol, Transcribed Interview of Richard Peter Donoghue, (Oct. 1, 2021), pp. 79-82; Documents on file with the Select Committee to Investigate the January 6th Attack on the United States Capitol (Department of Justice Production), HCOR-Pre-CertificationEvents-07262021-000703 (December 28, 2020, email from Richard Donoghue to Jeffrey Clark, cc'ing Jeffrey Rosen re: Two Urgent Action Items in which Donoghue writes: "there is no chance that I would sign this letter or anything remotely like this.").

[303] Select Committee to Investigate the January 6th Attack at the United States Capitol, Transcribed Interview of Jeffrey Rosen, (Oct. 13, 2021), p. 73; Documents on file with the Select Committee to Investigate the January 6th Attack on the United States Capitol (Department of Justice Production), HCOR-Pre-CertificationEvents-07262021-000703 (December 28, 2020, email from Richard Donoghue to Jeffrey Clark, cc'ing Jeffrey Rosen re: Two Urgent Action Items in which Donoghue writes: "there is no chance that I would sign this letter or anything remotely like this."); Senate Committee on the Judiciary, Interview of Richard Donoghue, (August 6, 2021), at p. 99, available at https://www.judiciary.senate.gov/imo/media/doc/Donoghue%20Transcript.pdf.

[304] Select Committee to Investigate the January 6th Attack on the United States Capitol, Transcribed Interview of Richard Peter Donoghue, (Oct. 1, 2021), p. 113.

[305] Select Committee to Investigate the January 6th Attack on the United States Capitol, *Hearing on the January 6th Investigation*, 117th Cong., 2d sess., (June 23, 2022), available at https://www.govinfo.gov/committee/house-january6th.

[306] Select Committee to Investigate the January 6th Attack on the United States Capitol, *Hearing on the January 6th Investigation*, 117th Cong., 2d sess., (June 23, 2022), available at https://www.govinfo.gov/committee/house-january6th.

[307] Documents on file with the Select Committee to Investigate the January 6th Attack on the United States Capitol (National Archives Production), CTRL0000083040 (January 3, 2021, White House Presidential Call Log).

[308] Select Committee to Investigate the January 6th Attack on the United States Capitol, Transcribed Interview of Richard Peter Donoghue, (Oct. 1, 2021), p. 119.

[309] Select Committee to Investigate the January 6th Attack on the United States Capitol, Transcribed Interview of Richard Peter Donoghue, (Oct. 1, 2021), p. 119-20. ("And so it was unanimous; everyone was going to resign if Jeff Rosen was removed from the seat." The only exception was John Demers, the Assistant Attorney General for the National Security Division. Donohue encouraged Demers to stay on because he didn't want to further jeopardize national security.)

[310] Select Committee to Investigate the January 6th Attack on the United States Capitol, Transcribed Interview of Richard Peter Donoghue, (Oct. 1, 2021), p. 124.

[311] Select Committee to Investigate the January 6th Attack on the United States Capitol, Transcribed Interview of Richard Peter Donoghue, (Oct. 1, 2021), pp. 126-28; Select Committee to Investigate the January 6th Attack on the United States Capitol, Transcribed Interview of Pasquale Anthony "Pat" Cipollone, (July 8, 2022), p. 120.

[312] Select Committee to Investigate the January 6th Attack on the United States Capitol, Transcribed Interview of Richard Peter Donoghue, (Oct. 1, 2021), p. 126.

[313] Select Committee to Investigate the January 6th Attack on the United States Capitol, Transcribed Interview of Richard Peter Donoghue, (Oct. 1, 2021), p. 125.

[314] Select Committee to Investigate the January 6th Attack on the United States Capitol, Transcribed Interview of Steven A. Engel, (Jan. 13, 2022), p. 64.

[315] Select Committee to Investigate the January 6th Attack on the United States Capitol, Transcribed Interview of Richard Peter Donoghue, (Oct. 1, 2021), p. 125.

[316] Select Committee to Investigate the January 6th Attack on the United States Capitol, Transcribed Interview of Richard Peter Donoghue, (Oct. 1, 2021), pp. 131-132.

[317] Select Committee to Investigate the January 6th Attack on the United States Capitol, Transcribed Interview of Richard Peter Donoghue, (Oct. 1, 2021), pp. 131-32.

[318] Select Committee to Investigate the January 6th Attack on the United States Capitol, Deposition of Sidney Powell, (May 7, 2022), pp. 75, 84.

[319] Donald J. Trump (@realDonaldTrump), Twitter, Dec. 19, 2020 1:42 a.m. ET, available at http://web.archive.org/web/20201219064257/https://twitter.com/realDonaldTrump/status/1340185773220515840 (archived).

[320] Donald J. Trump (@realDonaldTrump), Twitter, Dec. 26, 2020 8:14 a.m. ET, available at https://twitter.com/realDonaldTrump/status/1342821189077622792; Donald J. Trump (@realDonaldTrump), Twitter, Dec. 27, 2020 5:51 p.m. ET, available at https://twitter.com/realDonaldTrump/status/1343328708963299338; Donald J. Trump (@realDonaldTrump), Twitter, Dec. 30, 2020 2:06 p.m. ET, available at https://twitter.com/realDonaldTrump/status/1344359312878149634; Donald J. Trump (@realDonaldTrump), Twitter, Jan. 1, 2021 12:52 p.m. ET, available at https://www.thetrumparchive.com/?searchbox=%22RT+%40KylieJaneKremer%22 (archived) (retweeting @KylieJaneKremer, Dec. 19, 2020 3:50 p.m. ET, available at https://twitter.com/KylieJaneKremer/status/1340399063875895296)); Donald J. Trump (@realDonaldTrump), Twitter, Jan. 1, 2021 2:53 p.m. ET, available at https://twitter.com/realDonaldTrump/status/1345095714687377418; Donald J. Trump (@realDonaldTrump), Twitter, Jan. 1, 2021 3:34 p.m. ET, available at https://twitter.com/realDonaldTrump/status/1345106078141394944; Donald J. Trump (@realDonaldTrump), Twitter, Jan. 1, 2021 6:38 p.m. ET, available at https://twitter.com/realDonaldTrump/status/1345152408591204352; Donald J. Trump (@realDonaldTrump), Twitter, Jan. 2, 2021 9:04 p.m. ET, available at https://twitter.com/realDonaldTrump/status/1345551634907209730; Donald J. Trump (@realDonaldTrump), Twitter, Jan. 3, 2021 1:29 a.m. ET, available at https://www.thetrumparchive.com/?searchbox=%22RT+%40realDonaldTrump%3A+https%3A%2F%2Ft.co%2FnslWcFwkCj%22 (archived) (retweeting Donald J. Trump (@realDonaldTrump), Jan. 2, 2021 9:04 p.m. ET, available at https://twitter.com/realDonaldTrump/status/1345551634907209730)); Donald J. Trump (@realDonaldTrump),

Twitter, Jan. 3, 2021 10:15 a.m. ET, available at https://www.thetrumparchive.com/?searchbox=%22RT+%40JenLawrence21%22 (archived) (retweeting Jennifer Lynn Lawrence (@JenLawrence21)), Jan. 3, 2021 12:17 a.m. ET, available at https://twitter.com/JenLawrence21/status/1345600194826686464); Donald J. Trump (@realDonaldTrump), Twitter, Jan. 3, 2021 10:17 a.m. ET, available at https://www.thetrumparchive.com/?searchbox=%22RT+%40CodeMonkeyZ+if%22 (archived) (retweeting Ron Watkins (@CodeMonkeyZ) Jan. 2, 2021 9:14 p.m. ET, available at http://web.archive.org/web/20210103151826/https://twitter.com/CodeMonkeyZ/status/1345599512560078849 (archived)); Donald J. Trump, (@realDonaldTrump), Twitter, Jan. 3, 2021 10:24 a.m. ET, available at https://www.thetrumparchive.com/?searchbox=%22RT+%40realMikeLindell%22 (archived) (retweeting Mike Lindell (@realMikeLindell), Jan. 2, 2021 5:47 p.m. ET, available at http://web.archive.org/web/20210103152421/https://twitter.com/realMikeLindell/status/1345547185836978176 (archived)); Donald J. Trump (@realDonaldTrump), Twitter, Jan. 3, 2021 10:27 a.m. ET, available at https://twitter.com/realDonaldTrump/status/1345753534168506370; Donald J. Trump (@realDonaldTrump), Twitter, Jan. 3, 2021 10:28 a.m. ET, available at https://www.thetrumparchive.com/?searchbox=%22RT+%40AmyKremer+we%22 (archived) (retweeting Amy Kremer (@AmyKremer), Jan. 2, 2021 2:58 p.m. ET, available at https://twitter.com/AmyKremer/status/1345459488107749386); Donald J. Trump (@realDonaldTrump), Twitter, Jan. 4, 2021 9:46 a.m. ET, available at https://www.thetrumparchive.com/?searchbox=%22RT+%40realDonaldTrump+I+will+be+there.+Historic+day%21%22 (retweeting Donald J. Trump (@realDonaldTrump), Jan. 3, 2021 10:27 a.m. ET, available at https://twitter.com/realDonaldTrump/status/1345753534168506370); Donald J. Trump (@realDonaldTrump), Twitter, Jan. 5, 2021 10:27 a.m. ET, available at https://twitter.com/realDonaldTrump/status/1346478482105069568; Donald J. Trump (@realDonaldTrump), Twitter, Jan. 5, 2021 5:43 p.m. ET, available at https://twitter.com/realDonaldTrump/status/1346588064026685443.

[321] *See, e.g.*, Sentencing Memorandum of Daniel Johnson at 5, *United States v. Johnson*, No. 1:21-cr-407 (D.D.C. May 25, 2022), ECF No. 56 ("Mr. Johnson believed what he read on the internet and heard from the President himself - that the election had been stolen."); Select Committee to Investigate the January 6th Attack on the United States Capitol, Transcribed Interview of Zac Martin, (Mar. 9, 2022), p. 20 (answering that he believed President Trump wanted "patriots to show up in Washington, DC on January 6th" because "we felt like our rights were being taken away from us" given the election results).

[322] *See, e.g.*, Trial Transcript at 4106-08, *United States v. Rhodes et al.*, No. 1:22-cr-15 (D.D.C. Oct. 18, 2022) (Oath Keeper Jason Dolan testified that the Oath Keepers came to Washington, DC "to stop the certification of the election. … [b]y any means necessary. That's why we brought our firearms."); Motion to Suppress, Exhibit A at 34, 85-86, *United States v. Rodriguez*, No. 1:21-cr-246 (D.D.C. Oct. 15, 2021), ECF No. 38-1 ("Trump called us. Trump called us to D.C. ... and he's calling for help -- I thought he was calling for help. I thought he was -- I thought we were doing the right thing."); Statement of Facts at 2, *United States v. Martin*, No. 1:21-cr-394 (D.D.C. Apr. 20, 2021) ("MARTIN reported that he decided to travel to Washington, DC after reading then-President Donald Trump's tweets regarding the election being stolen and a protest on January 6, 2021, flying to DC on January 5, 2021, and attending the rallies on January 6, 2021, and then heading to the U.S. Capitol where he entered along with a crowd of other individuals."); Statement of Facts at 9-10, *United States v. Denney*, No. 1:22-cr-70 (D.D.C. Dec. 7, 2021) ("So Trump has called this himself. For everyone to come. It's the day the electoral college is suppose [sic] to be certified by congress to officially elect Biden."); Select Committee to Investigate the January 6th Attack on the United States Capitol, Transcribed Interview of Dustin Thompson (Nov. 16, 2022), pp. 34, 44, 70-71 (noting that he went to the Capitol at President Trump's direction and that he "figured [stopping the certification of the vote] was [President Trump's] plan"; *see also*, Documents on file with the Select Committee to Investigate the January 6th Attack on the United States Capitol (Select Committee Chart Compiling Defendant Statements).

[323] Indictment at 6, *United States v. Smith*, No. 1:21-cr-567 (D.D.C. Sept. 9, 2021), ECF No. 1.

[324] Statement of Facts at 3, *United States v. Sulenta*, No. 1:22-mj-00129-ZMF (D.D.C. June 6, 2022), ECF No. 1-1.

[325] Stipulated Statement of Facts at 7, *United States v. Morss*, No. 1:21-cr-40 (D.D.C. August 23, 2022), ECF No. 430.

[326] Statement of Facts at 9, *United States v. Grayson*, No. 1:21-cr-224 (D.D.C. Jan. 25, 2021), ECF No. 1-1.

[327] Statement of Facts at 11, *United States v. Denney*, No. 1:21-mj-00686-RMM-ZMF (D.D.C. Dec. 7, 2021), ECF No. 1-1.

[328] Gieswein denies that he was a Three Percenter as of January 6, 2021, even though he affiliated with an apparent Three Percenter group at previous times. *See* Gieswein's Motion for Hearing & Revocation of Detention Order at 2-3, 18-19, 25, *United States v. Gieswein*, No. 1:21-cr-24 (D.D.C. June 8, 2021), ECF No. 18. When the FBI arrested Gieswein, the criminal complaint noted that he "appears to be affiliated with the radical militia group known as the Three Percenters." Criminal Complaint at 5, *United States v. Gieswein*, No. 1:21-cr-24 (D.D.C. Jan. 16, 2021), available at https://www.justice.gov/opa/page/file/1360831/download. *See also* Adam Rawnsley (@arawnsley), Twitter, Jan. 17, 2021 9:13 p.m. ET, available at https://twitter.com/arawnsley/status/1350989535954530315 (highlighting photos of Gieswein flashing a Three Percenter symbol).

[329] Second Superseding Indictment at 9-10, *United States v. Nordean et al.*, No. 1:21-cr-175 (D.D.C. March 7, 2022), ECF No. 305.

[330] Statement of Offense at 5, *United States v. Bertino*, No. 1:22-cr-329 (D.D.C. Oct. 6, 2022), ECF No. 5; Third Superseding Indictment at 6, *United States v. Nordean, et al.*, No. 1:21-cr-175 (D.D.C. June 6, 2022), ECF No. 380; Statement of Offense at 3, *United States v. Donohoe*, No. 1:21-cr-175 (D.D.C. Apr. 8, 2022), ECF No. 336.

[331] Third Superseding Indictment at 13, *United States v. Nordean, et al.*, No. 1:21-cr-175 (D.D.C. June 6, 2022), ECF No. 380; Georgia Wells, Rebecca Ballhaus, and Keach Hagey, "Proud Boys, Seizing Trump's Call to Washington, Helped Lead Capitol Attack," *Wall Street Journal*, (Jan.17, 2021), available at https://www.wsj.com/articles/proud-boys-seizing-trumps-call-to-washington-helped-lead-capitol-attack-11610911596.

[332] Documents on file with the Select Committee to Investigate the January 6th Attack on the United States Capitol (Jay Thaxton Production), CTRL0000070865, (December 29, 2020, Telegram chat at 11:09 a.m. from Enrique Tarrio under the name "HEIKA NOBLELEAD.").

[333] "Former Leader of Proud Boys Pleads Guilty to Seditious Conspiracy for Efforts to Stop Transfer of Power Following 2020 Presidential Election," Department of Justice, (Oct. 6, 2022), available at https://www.justice.gov/opa/pr/former-leader-proud-boys-pleads-guilty-seditious-conspiracy-efforts-stop-transfer-power; "Leader of North Carolina Chapter of Proud Boys Pleads Guilty to Conspiracy and Assault Charges in Jan. 6 Capitol Breach," Department of Justice, (Apr. 8, 2022), available at https://www.justice.gov/opa/pr/leader-north-carolina-chapter-proud-boys-pleads-guilty-conspiracy-and-assault-charges-jan-6.

[334] Statement of Offense at 2, *United States v. Bertino*, No. 1:22-cr-329 (D.D.C. Oct. 6, 2022), ECF No. 5.

[335] Statement of Offense at 4, *United States v. Bertino*, No. 1:22-cr-329 (D.D.C. Oct. 6, 2022), ECF No. 5.

[336] Statement of Offense at 4-5, *United States v. Bertino*, No. 1:22-cr-329 (D.D.C. Oct. 6, 2022), ECF No. 5.

[337] Statement of Offense at 4, *United States v. Donohoe*, No. 1:21-cr-175 (D.D.C. Apr. 8, 2022), ECF No. 336. Indeed, Proud Boys leaders Biggs and Nordean told MOSD on January 5th about a plan they had discussed with Tarrio for January 6th. Although Biggs and Nordean did not share the plan's precise details, Proud Boys like Bertino and Donohoe nonetheless understood the "objective in Washington, D.C., on January 6, 2021, was to obstruct, impede, or interfere with the certification of the Electoral College vote, including by force if necessary," and that the Proud Boys "would accomplish this through the use of force and violence, which could include storming the Capitol through police lines and barricades if necessary." Statement of Offense at 8, *United States v. Bertino*, No. 1:22-cr-329 (D.D.C. Oct. 6, 2022), ECF No. 5; Statement of Offense at 6, *United States v. Donohoe*, No. 1:21-cr-175 (D.D.C. Apr. 8, 2022), ECF No. 336.

[338] Superseding Indictment at 2-3, *United States v. Rhodes et al*, No. 1:22-cr-15 (D.D.C. June 22, 2022), ECF No. 167.

[339] Caldwell testified that he was not an Oath Keeper. *See* Trial Transcript at 8778-79, *United States v. Rhodes et al.*, No. 1:22-cr-15 (D.D.C. Nov. 15, 2022); Hannah Rabinowitz and Holmes Lybrand, "Capitol Riot Defendant Calls Himself a 'Little Bit of a Goof' Regarding Pelosi and Pence Comments," CNN, (Nov. 15, 2022), available at https://www.cnn.com/2022/11/15/politics/thomas-caldwell-testifies-oath-keeper-trial. Because the government tried Caldwell in a conspiracy case with known Oath Keepers, the Select Committee has referred to him as an Oath Keeper.

[340] *See* Trial Transcript at 10502-08, *United States v. Rhodes et al.*, No. 1:22-cr-15 (D.D.C. Nov. 29, 2022).

[341] Trial Exhibit 6860 (1.S.656.9328 - 9396), *United States v. Rhodes*, No. 1:22-cr-15 (D.D.C. Oct. 13, 2022).

[342] Superseding Indictment at 13, *United States v. Rhodes, III, et al.*, No. 22-cr-15 (D.D.C. June 22, 2022), ECF No 167.

[343] Superseding Indictment at 13-14, *United States v. Rhodes, et al.*, No. 1:22-cr-15 (D.D.C. June 22, 2022), ECF No. 167.

[344] Superseding Indictment at 15-17, *United States v. Rhodes, et al.*, No. 22-cr-15 (D.D.C. June 22, 2022), ECF No 167.

[345] Statement of Offense at 5, *United States v. Ulrich*, No. 1:22-cr-15 (D.D.C. Apr. 29, 2022), ECF No. 117.

[346] Statement of Offense at 5, *United States v. James*, No. 1:22-cr-15 (D.D.C. Mar. 2, 2022), ECF No. 60.
[347] "TTPO Stance on Election Fraud," The Three Percenters - Original, available at https://archive.ph/YemCC#selection-289.0-289.29 (archived).
[348] Statement of Facts at 7-8, *United States v. Buxton*, No. 1:21-cr-739 (D.D.C. Dec. 8, 2021), ECF No. 1-1; Post: "Oath Keepers claim to stand for the constitution yet will not call up its 30k membership to attend the 6th. I thought you guys stood for the constitution? It's your only job as an organization...now or never boys," Patriots.win, Dec. 29, 2020, available at https://patriots.win/p/11RO2hdyR2/x/c/4DrwV8RcV1s.
[349] Indictment at 1, 7, *United States v. Hostetter et al.*, No. 1:21-cr-392 (D.D.C. June 9, 2021), ECF No. 1.
[350] Indictment at 7, *United States v. Hostetter et al.*, No. 1:21-cr-392 (D.D.C. June 9, 2021), ECF No. 1.
[351] Indictment at 8-13, *United States v. Hostetter et al.*, No. 1:21-cr-392 (D.D.C. June 9, 2021), ECF No. 1.
[352] Indictment at 9, *United States v. Hostetter et al.*, No. 1:21-cr-392 (D.D.C. June 9, 2021), ECF No. 1.
[353] Statement of Facts at 4, *United States v. Cole et al.*, No. 1:22-mj-184, (D.D.C. Aug. 29, 2022), ECF No. 5-1.
[354] Statement of Facts at 5, *United States v. Cole et al.*, No. 1:22-mj-184, (D.D.C. Aug. 29, 2022), ECF No. 5-1. When the Select Committee asked about this post to the leader of the Florida Guardians of Freedom, Liggett downplayed any significance or any knowledge about other Three Percenter groups that might "show in record numbers." Select Committee to Investigate the January 6th Attack on the United States Capitol, Deposition of Jeremy Liggett, (May 17, 2022), pp. 51-52.
[355] Statement of Facts at 5-6, *United States v. Cole et al.*, No. 1:22-mj-184, (D.D.C. Aug. 29, 2022), ECF No. 5-1; #SeditionHunters (@SeditionHunters), Twitter, June 7, 2021 2:11 p.m. ET, available at https://twitter.com/SeditionHunters/status/1401965056980627458.
[356] Statement of Facts at 15-17, *United States v. Cole et al.*, No. 1:22-mj-184, (D.D.C. Aug. 29, 2022), ECF No. 5-1. The "tunnel" is actually a flight of stairs leading to a doorway from which the President emerges on Inauguration Day to take the oath of office. When the inauguration stage is present, the stairs leading to the doorway are converted into a "10-foot-wide, slightly sloped, short tunnel that was approximately 15 feet long." Government's Sentencing Memorandum at 5-6, *United States v. Young*, No. 1:21-cr-291-3 (D.D.C. Sept. 13, 2022), ECF No. 140. For other examples of how extremist groups responded to President Trump's call to action, *see* Chapter 6.
[357] Indictment at 11, *United States v. Rodriguez et al.*, No. 1:21-cr-246 (D.D.C. Nov. 19, 2021), ECF No. 65; Motion to Suppress, Exhibit A at 70, *United States v. Rodriguez*, No. 1:21-cr-246 (D.D.C. Oct. 15, 2021), ECF No. 38-1.
[358] Motion to Suppress, Exhibit A at 34, 85-86, *United States v. Rodriguez*, No. 1:21-cr-246 (D.D.C. Oct. 15, 2021), ECF No. 38-1.
[359] Government's Opposition to Defendant's Renewed Request for Pretrial Release at 7, *United States v. Meggs*, No. 1:21-cr-28 (D.D.C Mar. 23, 2021), ECF No. 98.
[360] Documents on file with the Select Committee to Investigate the January 6th Attack on the United States Capitol (Documents on file with the Select Committee to Investigate the January 6th Attack on the United States Capitol (Google Voice Production, Feb. 25, 2022).
[361] Trial Exhibit 6868 (2000.T.420), *United States v. Rhodes et al.*, No. 1:22-cr-15 (D.D.C. Oct. 13, 2022).
[362] Trial Exhibit 6868 (2000.T.420), *United States v. Rhodes et al.*, No. 1:22-cr-15 (D.D.C. Oct. 13, 2022).
[363] Trial Exhibit 9221, *United States v. Rhodes et al.*, No.1:22-cr-15 (D.D.C. Nov. 9, 2022).
[364] Motion for Bond, Exhibit 1 at 125-26, *United States v. Vallejo*, No. 1:22-cr-15 (D.D.C. Apr. 18, 2022), ECF No. 102-1 (Collection of redacted text messages, labeled as Exhibit 8, showing Rhodes adding "a CA Oath Keeper who is in with a four man team, followed by that person announcing his identifiable radio frequency) Ryan J. Reilly, "New Evidence Reveals Coordination Between Oath Keepers, Three Percenters on Jan. 6," NBC News, (May 28, 2022), available at https://www.nbcnews.com/politics/justice-department/new-evidence-reveals-coordination-oath-keepers-three-percenters-jan-6-rcna30355 (noting how public source investigators linked the identifiable radio frequency to Derek Kinnison, who is one of the California Three Percenters indicted on conspiracy charges for their conduct on January 6th. *See* Indictment, *United States v. Hostetter et al.*, No. 1:21-cr-392 (D.D.C. June 9, 2021), ECF No. 1).
[365] Documents on file with the Select Committee to Investigate the January 6th Attack on the United States Capitol (Department of Justice Production), CTRL 0000010471, at 7:01 (January 6, 2021, video footage recorded by Samuel Montoya at the U.S. Capitol).
[366] Documents on file with the Select Committee to Investigate the January 6th Attack on the United States Capitol, (District of Columbia Production), Axon Body 3 X6039BKH5 13.53.47 20210106-FELONYRIOT-FIRSTSTSE, at 15:28:13 (MPD body camera footage); Statement of Facts at 3, *United States v. Cale*, No. 1:22-cr-139 (D.D.C. Mar. 28, 2022), ECF No. 1-1.

367 Documents on file with the Select Committee to Investigate the January 6th Attack on the United States Capitol (Department of Justice Production), HCOR-Jan6-07222021-000603.
368 Select Committee to Investigate the January 6th Attack on the United States Capitol, Transcribed Interview of Richard Peter Donoghue, (Oct. 1, 2021), p. 143.
369 Select Committee to Investigate the January 6th Attack on the United States Capitol, Transcribed Interview of General Mark A. Milley, (Nov. 17, 2021), p. 199.
370 Documents on file with the Select Committee to Investigate the January 6th Attack on the United States Capitol (Mary McCord Production), CTRL0000930476 (December 22, 2020, email to the FBI noting troubling Oath Keepers chats),
371 Documents on file with the Select Committee to Investigate the January 6th Attack on the United States Capitol (Mary McCord Production), CTRL0000930476 (December 22, 2020, email to the FBI noting troubling Oath Keepers chats).
372 Documents on file with the Select Committee to Investigate the January 6th Attack on the United States Capitol (Secret Service Production), USSS0000038637, (December 25, 2020, email chain from PIOC on January 6th intelligence).
373 Documents on file with the Select Committee to Investigate the January 6th Attack on the United States Capitol (Secret Service Production), USSS0000038637, (December 25, 2020, email chain from PIOC on January 6th intelligence).
374 Documents on file with the Select Committee to Investigate the January 6th Attack on the United States Capitol (Secret Service Production), USSS0000038637, (December 25, 2020, email chain from PIOC on January 6th intelligence).
375 Documents on file with the Select Committee to Investigate the January 6th Attack on the United States Capitol (Secret Service Production), USSS0000038637, (December 25, 2020, email chain from PIOC on January 6th intelligence).
376 Documents on file with the Select Committee to Investigate the January 6th Attack on the United States Capitol (Secret Service Production), USSS0000038637, (December 25, 2020, email chain from PIOC on January 6th intelligence).
377 Documents on file with the Select Committee to Investigate the January 6th Attack on the United States Capitol (Secret Service Production), USSS0000038637, (December 25, 2020, email chain from PIOC on January 6th intelligence).
378 Documents on file with the Select Committee to Investigate the January 6th Attack on the United States Capitol (Secret Service Production), USSS0000038637, (December 25, 2020, email chain from PIOC on January 6th intelligence).
379 Documents on file with the Select Committee to Investigate the January 6th Attack on the United States Capitol (Capitol Police Production), CTRL0000000080 (December 28, 2020, email to John Donohue re: (LES) Armed and Ready SITE.pdf.); Select Committee to Investigate the January 6th Attack on the United States Capitol, Transcribed Interview of Jack Donohue, (Jan. 31, 2022), p. 8; Select Committee to Investigate the January 6th Attack on the United States Capitol, Informal Interview of Jack Donohue, (Jan. 7, 2022).
380 Documents on file with the Select Committee to Investigate the January 6th Attack on the United States Capitol (Secret Service Production), USSS0000067420 (December 26, 2020, email to PIOC regarding possible Proud Boys plan for January 6, 2021).
381 Documents on file with the Select Committee to Investigate the January 6th Attack on the United States Capitol (Secret Service Production), USSS0000067420 (December 26, 2020, email to PIOC regarding possible Proud Boys plan for January 6, 2021).
382 Documents on file with the Select Committee to Investigate the January 6th Attack on the United States Capitol (Capitol Police Production), CTRL0000001473 (December 29, 2020, email from PIOC-ONDUTY to THREAT ASSESSMENT re: FW: [EXTERNAL EMAIL] - Neo-Nazi Calls on D.C. Pro-Trump Protesters to Occupy Federal Building.).
383 Documents on file with the Select Committee to Investigate the January 6th Attack on the United States Capitol (Capitol Police Production), CTRL0000000087 (December 28, 2020, email re: 1/6 warning.).
384 Documents on file with the Select Committee to Investigate the January 6th Attack on the United States Capitol (Capitol Police Production), CTRL0000001473 (December 29, 2020, email from PIOC-

ONDUTY@USSS.DHS.GOV to THREATS@uscp.gov titled "FW: [EXTERNAL EMAIL] - Neo-Nazi Calls on D.C. Pro-Trump Protesters to Occupy Federal Building.").

[385] Documents on file with the Select Committee to Investigate the January 6th Attack on the United States Capitol (Secret Service Production), CTRL0000101135.0001, pp. 1, 3 (December 30, 2020, Protective Intelligence Brief titled "Wild Protest").

[386] *See* Documents on file with the Select Committee to Investigate the January 6th Attack on the United States Capitol (Capitol Police Production), CTRL0000001527 (Email titled "Fwd: MPD MMS Text Tip.").

[387] *See* Documents on file with the Select Committee to Investigate the January 6th Attack on the United States Capitol (Capitol Police Production), CTRL0000001527 (Email titled "Fwd: MPD MMS Text Tip.").

[388] Documents on file with the Select Committee to Investigate the January 6th Attack on the United States Capitol, (Parler Production) PARLER_00000013 (January 2, 2021, email from Parler to the FBI re: Another to check out, attaching Parler posts).

[389] Documents on file with the Select Committee to Investigate the January 6th Attack on the United States Capitol (Capitol Police Production), CTRL0000001487 (January 2, 2021, email to Capitol Police and Department of Justice with screenshots of Parler posts); Documents on file with the Select Committee to Investigate the January 6th Attack on the United States Capitol (Capitol Police Production), CTRL0000000116, CTRL0000000116.0001 (January 4, 2021, email from U.S. Capitol Police re: Comments of concern for Jan 6 rally, collecting Parler posts).

[390] Documents on file with the Select Committee to Investigate the January 6th Attack on the United States Capitol (Capitol Police Production), CTRL0000001532.0001, p.2 (January 5, 2021, FBI Situational Information Report).

[391] Documents on file with the Select Committee to Investigate the January 6th Attack on the United States Capitol (Capitol Police Production), CTRL0000001532.0001, p.2 (January 5, 2021, FBI Situational Information Report).

[392] Documents on file with the Select Committee to Investigate the January 6th Attack on the United States Capitol (Secret Service Production), CTRL0000293417 (December 30, 2020, email to OSU-ALL titled "Discovery of Event Website- MAGA Drag the Interstate & Occupy the Capitol").

[393] Documents on file with the Select Committee to Investigate the January 6th Attack on the United States Capitol (Capitol Police Production), CTRL0000000083, CTRL0000000083.0001 (January 5, 2021, email re: (U//FOUO//LES) OSINT Post of Concern.).

[394] Documents on file with the Select Committee to Investigate the January 6th Attack on the United States Capitol (Capitol Police Production), CTRL0000000083, CTRL0000000083.0001 (January 5, 2021, email re: (U//FOUO//LES) OSINT Post of Concern.).

[395] Documents on file with the Select Committee to Investigate the January 6th Attack on the United States Capitol (Capitol Police Production), CTRL0000000083, CTRL0000000083.0001 (January 5, 2021, email re: (U//FOUO//LES) OSINT Post of Concern.).

[396] Documents on file with the Select Committee to Investigate the January 6th Attack on the United States Capitol (Secret Service Production), USSS0000066986, USSS0000066986.0001 (January 5, 2021, Secret Service email noting social media user threatening to bring a firearm to Washington, D.C. on January 6th).

[397] Documents on file with the Select Committee to Investigate the January 6th Attack on the United States Capitol (Department of Interior Production), DOI_46000114_00000238, DOI_46000114_00000239 (January 5, 2021, Situational Information Report Federal Bureau of Investigation. "Potential for Violence in Washington, D.C. Area in Connection with Planned 'StopTheSteal' Protest on 6 January 2021.").

[398] *See* Documents on file with the Select Committee to Investigate the January 6th Attack on the United States Capitol (Department of Interior Production), DOI_46000114_00000238, DOI_46000114_00000239 (January 5, 2021, Situational Information Report Federal Bureau of Investigation. "Potential for Violence in Washington, D.C. Area in Connection with Planned 'StopTheSteal' Protest on 6 January 2021.").

[399] Trial Exhibit 6923 (1.S.159.817, 955), *United States v. Rhodes et al.*, No. 22-cr-15 (D.D.C. Oct. 14, 2022) (Rhodes sent an encrypted message to Oath Keeper leadership on January 5, 2021, stating: "We will have several well equipped QRFs outside DC. And there are many, many others, from other groups, who will be watching and waiting on the outside in case of worst case scenarios.").

[400] Documents on file with the Select Committee to Investigate the January 6th Attack on the United States Capitol (Mark Meadows Production), MM014441-42 (December 30, 2020, 6:05 p.m. ET text from Jason Miller to Mark Meadows).

[401] Select Committee to Investigate the January 6th Attack on the United States Capitol, Deposition of Jason Miller, (Feb. 3, 2022), Exhibit 45, pp. 4, 13. Miller claimed he had no idea about the comments and would have "flag[ged]"

them for "Secret Service" had he seen them. Select Committee to Investigate the January 6th Attack on the United States Capitol, Deposition of Jason Miller, (Feb. 3, 2022), pp. 210-12.

402 On his way to the Capitol, Proud Boy David Nicholas Dempsey stopped on the National Mall in front of an erected gallows, fitted with a noose, to tell the world what he hoped would happen: "Them worthless shitholes like Jerry Nadler, fuckin Pelosi ... They don't need a jail cell. They need to hang from these motherfuckers [pointing to gallows]. They need to get the point across that the time for peace is over. ... For four, or five years really, they've been fucking demonizing us, belittling us, ... doing everything they can to stop what this is, and people are sick of that shit .... Hopefully one day soon we really have someone hanging from one of these motherfuckers ... ." Statement of Facts at 2-3, *United States v. Dempsey*, No. 1:21-cr-566 (D.D.C. Aug. 25, 2021); #SeditionHunters (@SeditionHunters), Twitter, Mar. 11, 2021 8:12 p.m. ET, available at https://twitter.com/SeditionHunters/status/1370180789770588163.

403 Select Committee to Investigate the January 6th Attack on the United States Capitol, Continued Interview of Cassidy Hutchinson, (June 20, 2022), p. 49.

404 Select Committee to Investigate the January 6th Attack on the United States Capitol, Continued Interview of Cassidy Hutchinson, (May 17, 2022), p. 92.

405 Documents on file with the Select Committee to Investigate the January 6th Attack on the United States Capitol (Hope Hicks Production), SC_HH_035, SC_HH_036 (January 6, 2021, text messages with Hogan Gidley).

406 Select Committee to Investigate the January 6th Attack on the United States Capitol, Transcribed Interview of Hope Hicks, (Oct. 25, 2022), pp. 109-10.

407 Documents on file with the Select Committee to Investigate the January 6th Attack on the United States Capitol (Homeland Security and Emergency Management Agency, DC Production), CTRL0000926794 (Talking points put together by Dr. Christopher Rodriguez, Director of HSEMA, for a briefing with Mayor Muriel Bowers on December 30, 2020).

408 Select Committee to Investigate the January 6th Attack on the United States Capitol, *Hearing on the January 6th Investigation*, 117th Cong., 2d sess., (July 12, 2022), available at https://www.govinfo.gov/committee/house-january6th; Select Committee to Investigate the January 6th Attack on the United States Capitol, Transcribed Interview of Donnell Harvin, (Jan. 24, 2022), pp. 22-23.

409 Given the timing of receipt of much of this intelligence immediately in advance of January 6th, it is unclear that any comprehensive intelligence community analytical product could have been reasonably expected. But it is clear that the information itself was communicated.

410 Documents on file with the Select Committee to Investigate the January 6th Attack on the United States Capitol (Caroline Wren Production), REVU_000181 (January 2, 2021, email from Katrina Pierson to Caroline Wren and Taylor Budowich re: 1/6 Speaker Schedule).

411 Documents on file with the Select Committee to Investigate the January 6th Attack on the United States Capitol (Kylie Kremer Production), KKremer5449; Select Committee to Investigate the January 6th Attack on the United States Capitol, *Hearing on the January 6th Investigation*, 117th Cong., 2d sess., (July 12, 2022), available at https://www.govinfo.gov/committee/house-january6th.

412 Select Committee to Investigate the January 6th Attack on the United States Capitol, Deposition of Judson P. Deere, (Mar. 3, 2022), pp. 83, 86.

413 Select Committee to Investigate the January 6th Attack on the United States Capitol, *Hearing on the January 6th Investigation*, 117th Cong., 2d sess., (June 28, 2022), available at https://www.govinfo.gov/committee/house-january6th.

414 Select Committee to Investigate the January 6th Attack on the United States Capitol, Transcribed Interview of Robert "Bobby" Engel, (Nov. 17, 2022), p. 64.

415 Select Committee to Investigate the January 6th Attack on the United States Capitol, Continued Interview of Robert Engel, (Nov. 17, 2022), p. 21.

416 Select Committee to Investigate the January 6th Attack on the United States Capitol, Continued Interview of Anthony Ornato, (Nov. 29, 2022), p. 152.

417 Select Committee to Investigate the January 6th Attack on the United States Capitol, Continued Interview of Anthony Ornato, (Nov. 29, 2022), p. 152.

418 Select Committee to Investigate the January 6th Attack on the United States Capitol, Continued Interview of Anthony Ornato, (Nov. 29, 2022), p. 152.

419 Select Committee to Investigate the January 6th Attack on the United States Capitol, Continued Interview of Anthony Ornato, (Mar. 29, 2022), p. 16.

420 Documents on file with the Select Committee to Investigate the January 6th Attack on the United States Capitol (Capitol Police Production), CTRL0000086772, p. 4 (November 18, 2021, document titled: United States Secret Service - Coordinated Response to a Request for Information from the Select Committee to Investigate the January 6th Attack on the United States Capitol).

421 Documents on file with the Select Committee to Investigate the January 6th Attack on the United States Capitol (Nick Quested Production), Video file ML_DC_20210106_Sony_FS7-GC_1935.mov; Documents on file with the Select Committee to Investigate the January 6th Attack on the United States Capitol (Secret Service Production), CTRL0000882478 (Summary of updates from January 6, 2021); Select Committee to Investigate the January 6th Attack on the United States Capitol, Transcribed Interview of Dustin Thompson, (Nov. 16, 2022), pp. 30-31 ("I was seeing these, like, piles of backpacks and flagpoles [outside the magnetometers]. And some people were watching that for other people. And I just -- there were lots of piles all over the place of stuff like that.").

422 Tom Jackman, Rachel Weiner, and Spencer S. Hsu, "Evidence of Firearms in Jan. 6 Crowd Grows as Arrests and Trials Mount," *Washington Post*, (July 8, 2022), https://www.washingtonpost.com/dc-md-va/2022/07/08/jan6-defendants-guns/.

423 Documents on file with the Select Committee to Investigate the January 6th Attack on the United States Capitol (Secret Service Production), CTRL0000882478 (summary of radio traffic on January 6, 2021).

424 Documents on file with the Select Committee to Investigate the January 6th Attack on the United States Capitol (District of Columbia Production), MPD 73-78 (District of Columbia, Metropolitan Police Department, Transcript of Radio Calls, January 6, 2021); Documents on file with the Select Committee to Investigate the January 6th Attack on the United States Capitol (District of Columbia Production), CTRL0000070375, at 3:40 (District of Columbia, Metropolitan Police Department, audio file of radio traffic from January 6, 2021, from 12:00 - 13:00).

425 Documents on file with the Select Committee to Investigate the January 6th Attack on the United States Capitol (Cassidy Hutchinson Production), CH-CTRL0000000069.

426 Select Committee to Investigate the January 6th Attack on the United States Capitol, *Hearing on the January 6th Investigation*, 117th Cong., 2d sess., (June 28, 2022), available at https://www.govinfo.gov/committee/house-january6th.

427 Select Committee to Investigate the January 6th Attack on the United States Capitol, Transcribed Interview of United States Secret Service Employee, (Nov. 7, 2022), p. 77 ("The most--the thing that sticks out most was he kept asking why we couldn't go, why we couldn't go, and that he wasn't concerned about the people that were there or referenced them being Trump people or Trump supporters.").

428 "Transcript of Trump's Speech at Rally before US Capitol Riot," *Associated Press*, (Jan. 13, 2021), available at https://apnews.com/article/election-2020-joe-biden-donald-trump-capitol-siege-media-e79eb5164613d6718e9f4502eb471f27.

429 "Transcript of Trump's Speech at Rally before US Capitol Riot," *Associated Press*, (Jan. 13, 2021), available at https://apnews.com/article/election-2020-joe-biden-donald-trump-capitol-siege-media-e79eb5164613d6718e9f4502eb471f27.

430 Select Committee to Investigate the January 6th Attack on the United States Capitol, Transcribed Interview of Eric Herschmann, (Apr. 6, 2022), pp. 20-21.

431 Select Committee to Investigate the January 6th Attack on the United States Capitol, Transcribed Interview of Eric Herschmann, (Apr. 6, 2022), pp. 24, 26.

432 Select Committee to Investigate the January 6th Attack on the United States Capitol, Transcribed Interview of Eric Herschmann, (Apr. 6, 2022), p. 26.

433 Select Committee to Investigate the January 6th Attack on the United States Capitol, Transcribed Interview of Eric Herschmann, (Apr. 6, 2022), p. 23.

434 *See* "Donald Trump Speech 'Save America' Rally Transcript January 6," Rev, (Jan. 6, 2021), at 1:00:00 – 1:02:31, available at https://www.rev.com/blog/transcripts/donald-trump-speech-save-america-rally-transcript-january-6 (timestamping the speech).

435 "Transcript of Trump's Speech at Rally before US Capitol Riot," *Associated Press*, (Jan. 13, 2021), available at https://apnews.com/article/election-2020-joe-biden-donald-trump-capitol-siege-media-e79eb5164613d6718e9f4502eb471f27.

436 Select Committee to Investigate the January 6th Attack on the United States Capitol, *Hearing on the January 6th Investigation*, 117th Cong., 2d sess., (July 21, 2022), at 1:00:45-1:01:12, available at

https://youtu.be/pbRVqWbHGuo?t=3645; Select Committee to Investigate the January 6th Attack on the United States Capitol, Transcribed Interview of Janet West Buhler, (Feb. 28, 2022), p. 40.

[437] "Transcript of Trump's Speech at Rally before US Capitol Riot," *Associated Press*, (Jan. 13, 2021), available at https://apnews.com/article/election-2020-joe-biden-donald-trump-capitol-siege-media-e79eb5164613d6718e9f4502eb471f27.

[438] "Transcript of Trump's Speech at Rally before US Capitol Riot," *Associated Press*, (Jan. 13, 2021), available at https://apnews.com/article/election-2020-joe-biden-donald-trump-capitol-siege-media-e79eb5164613d6718e9f4502eb471f27.

[439] "Transcript of Trump's Speech at Rally before US Capitol Riot," *Associated Press*, (Jan. 13, 2021), available at https://apnews.com/article/election-2020-joe-biden-donald-trump-capitol-siege-media-e79eb5164613d6718e9f4502eb471f27.

[440] Select Committee to Investigate the January 6th Attack on the United States Capitol, *Hearing on the January 6th Investigation*, 117th Cong., 2d sess., (June 16, 2022), at 0:14:11-0:15:00, available at https://youtu.be/vBjUWVKuDj0?t=851; Hearing on Motion to Modify Conditions of Release, Exhibit 07 at 7:43 - 8:00, *United States v. Nichols*, No. 1:21-cr-117 (D.D.C. Dec. 20, 2021).

[441] Unframe of Mind, "Unframe of Mind in DC #stopthesteal Rally," YouTube, at 9:40 – 9:47, Jan. 6, 2021, available at https://www.youtube.com/watch?v=OFbvpBu_7ws&t=579s; Select Committee to Investigate the January 6th Attack on the United States Capitol, *Hearing on the January 6th Investigation*, 117th Cong., 2d sess., (June 16, 2022), at, at 0:14:11-0:15:00, available at https://youtu.be/vBjUWVKuDj0?t=851.

[442] Walter Masterson, "Live from the Trump Rally in Washington, D.C.," YouTube, at 17:32 – 17:50, Jan. 11, 2021, available at https://www.youtube.com/watch?v=OFbvpBu_7ws&t=579s; Select Committee to Investigate the January 6th Attack on the United States Capitol, *Hearing on the January 6th Investigation*, 117th Cong., 2d sess., (June 16, 2022), at, at 2:07:02-2:07:07, available at https://youtu.be/vBjUWVKuDj0?t=7609.

[443] Select Committee to Investigate the January 6th Attack on the United States Capitol, *Hearing on the January 6th Investigation*, 117th Cong., 2d sess., (June 16, 2022) at, at 2:07:13-2:07:47, available at https://youtu.be/vBjUWVKuDj0?t=7609.

[444] Select Committee to Investigate the January 6th Attack on the United States Capitol, *Hearing on the January 6th Investigation*, 117th Cong., 2d sess., (July 21, 2022), at 1:00:45-1:01:12, available at https://youtu.be/pbRVqWbHGuo?t=3645; On the Media, "Jessica Watkins on 'Stop the Steal J6' Zello Channel (Unedited)," Soundcloud, at 4:00-4:18, available at https://soundcloud.com/user-403747081/jessica-watkins-on-stop-the-steal-j6-zello-channel-unedited .

[445] For a video of the interview, *see* "Crown Point, Indiana Man Charged in Jan. 6 Capitol Riot Says He Has 'No Regrets'," CBS Chicago, Nov. 29, 2022, available at https://www.cbsnews.com/chicago/video/crown-point-indiana-man-charged-in-jan-6-capitol-riot-says-he-has-no-regrets/#x.

[446] "Transcript of Trump's Speech at Rally before US Capitol Riot," *Associated Press*, (Jan. 13, 2021), available at https://apnews.com/article/election-2020-joe-biden-donald-trump-capitol-siege-media-e79eb5164613d6718e9f4502eb471f27 (emphasis added).

[447] Select Committee to Investigate the January 6th Attack on the United States Capitol, *Hearing on the January 6th Investigation*, 117th Cong., 2d sess., (June 28, 2022), available at https://www.govinfo.gov/committee/house-january6th; Select Committee to Investigate the January 6th Attack on the United States Capitol, Continued Interview of Cassidy Hutchinson, (June 20, 2022), p. 49.

[448] Select Committee to Investigate the January 6th Attack on the United States Capitol, Transcribed Interview of Pasquale Anthony "Pat" Cipollone, (July 8, 2022), p. 131 ("I just didn't think it would be, you know, a good idea for the President to go up to the Capitol."). While Cipollone did not specifically recall talking with Cassidy Hutchinson about this topic, he informed the Select Committee that he was sure that he did express his view to some people. *Id*. Hutchinson believes it was Pat Cipollone, but also testified that it may have been a different lawyer. *See* Select Committee to Investigate the January 6th Attack on the United States Capitol, Transcribed Interview of Cassidy Hutchinson, (Feb. 23, 2022), pp. 113-16.

[449] For security reasons, the Select Committee is not releasing the name of this employee. Select Committee to Investigate the January 6th Attack on the United States Capitol, Transcribed Interview of White House employee with national security responsibilities, (July 19, 2022) at p. 73. *See also* Chapter 7, which discusses this topic in greater detail.

[450] Select Committee to Investigate the January 6th Attack on the United States Capitol, Transcribed Interview of United States Secret Service Agent, (Nov. 21, 2022), pp. 22-23. The Select Committee has agreed to keep confidential the identity of this witness due to their sensitive national security responsibilities.

[451] A book written by Chief of Staff Mark Meadows in December 2021 made the categorical claim that the President never intended to travel to the Capitol that day. *See* Mark Meadows, *The Chief's Chief* (St. Petersburg, FL: All Seasons Press, 2021), p. 250. The Committee's evidence demonstrates that Meadows's claim is categorically false. Because the Meadows book conflicted sharply with information that was being received by the Select Committee, the Committee became increasingly wary that other witnesses might intentionally conceal what happened. That appeared to be the case with Ornato. Ornato does not recall that he conveyed the information to Cassidy Hutchinson regarding the SUV, and also does not recall that he conveyed similar information to a White House employee with national security responsibilities who testified that Ornato recalled a similar account to him. The Committee is skeptical of Ornato's account.

[452] Select Committee to Investigate the January 6th Attack on the United States Capitol, Transcribed Interview of White House Security Official, (July 11, 2022), p. 45. The Select Committee has agreed to keep confidential the identity of this witness due to their sensitive national security responsibilities.

[453] Select Committee to Investigate the January 6th Attack on the United States Capitol, Deposition of Kayleigh McEnany, (Jan. 12, 2022), p. 159.

[454] Select Committee to Investigate the January 6th Attack on the United States Capitol, Continued Interview of Cassidy Hutchinson, (June 20, 2022), p. 8.

[455] Government's Sentencing Memorandum at 2-9, *United States v. Young*, No. 1:21-cr-291 (D.D.C. Sept. 13, 2022), ECF No. 140; 167 Cong. Rec. S619 (daily ed. Feb. 10, 2021), available at https://www.congress.gov/117/crec/2021/02/10/CREC-2021-02-10-pt1-PgS615-4.pdf; Michael S. Schmidt and Luke Broadwater, "Officers' Injuries, Including Concussions, Show Scope of Violence at Capitol Riot," *New York Times*, (Feb. 11, 2021), available at https://www.nytimes.com/2021/02/11/us/politics/capitol-riot-police-officer-injuries.html.

[456] *See* Sentencing Transcript at 35, *United States v. Griffith*, No. 1:21-cr-204 (D.D.C. Oct. 30, 2021), ECF No. 137; Kyle Cheney and Josh Gerstein, "Where Jan. 6 Prosecutions Stand, 18 Months after the Attack," *Politico*, (July 7, 2022), available at https://www.politico.com/news/2022/07/07/jan-6-prosecutions-months-later-00044354.

[457] Select Committee to Investigate the January 6th Attack on the United States Capitol, *Hearing on the January 6th Investigation*, 117th Cong., 2d sess., (July 12, 2022), at 2:36:58-2:37:30, 2:44:00-2:45:05, available at https://www.youtube.com/watch?v=rrUa0hfG6Lo ("[W]hen President Trump put his tweet out, we literally left right after that come out . . . As soon as that come out, everybody started talking about it . . . it definitely dispersed a lot of the crowd. . . . We left."); Select Committee to Investigate the January 6th Attack on the United States Capitol, *Hearing on the January 6th Investigation*, 117th Cong., 2d sess., (July 21, 2022), at 1:58:00, available at https://www.youtube.com/watch?v=pbRVqWbHGuo ("I'm here delivering the President's message. Donald Trump has asked everybody to go home. ... That's our order.").

[458] Select Committee to Investigate the January 6th Attack on the United States Capitol, *Hearing on the January 6th Investigation*, 117th Cong., 2d sess., (July 21, 2022), at 1:50:59-1:52:19, available at https://youtu.be/pbRVqWbHGuo?t=6659; Select Committee to Investigate the January 6th Attack on the United States Capitol, *Business Meeting on the January 6th Investigation*, 117th Cong., 2d sess., (Oct. 13, 2022), at 2:15:45-2:17:12, available at https://youtu.be/IQvuBoLBuC0?t=8145; CBS News, "Former Vice President Mike Pence on 'Face the Nation with Margaret Brennan' | Full Interview," YouTube, at 16:23-19:01, Nov. 21, 2022, available at https://youtu.be/U9GbkPhG1Lo?t=983; Select Committee to Investigate the January 6th Attack on the United States Capitol, Transcribed Interview of Steven Andrew Sund, (Apr. 20, 2022), p. 173.

[459] Select Committee to Investigate the January 6th Attack on the United States Capitol, Transcribed Interview of White House Employee, (June 10, 2022), p. 27. The Select Committee is not revealing the identity of this witness to guard against the risk of retaliation; *See* "Donald Trump Speech 'Save America' Rally Transcript January 6," Rev, (Jan. 6, 2021), available at https://www.rev.com/blog/transcripts/donald-trump-speech-save-america-rally-transcript-january-6 (timestamping the speech).

[460] Documents on file with the Select Committee to Investigate the January 6th Attack on the United States Capitol (National Archives Production), 40a8_hi_j0087_0bea; Select Committee to Investigate the January 6th Attack on the United States Capitol, *Hearing on the January 6th Investigation*, 117th Cong., 2d sess., (July 21, 2022), at 34:18, available at https://youtu.be/pbRVqWbHGuo?t=2058.

461 Washington Post, "D.C. Police requested backup at least 17 times in 78 minutes during Capitol riot | Visual Forensics," YouTube, at 7:58 to 8:45, Apr. 15, 2021, available at https://youtu.be/rsQTY9083r8?t=478; Senate Committee on Homeland Security and Governmental Affairs and Senate Committee on Rules and Administration, Public Hearing, (Mar. 3, 2021), Written Testimony of William J. Walker, Commanding General District of Columbia National Guard, p. 3, available at https://www.hsgac.senate.gov/imo/media/doc/Testimony-Walker-2021-03-03.pdf.

462 Select Committee to Investigate the January 6th Attack on the United States Capitol, Transcribed Interview of Shealah Craighead, (June 8, 2022), pp. 42, 46.

463 Documents on file with the Select Committee to Investigate the January 6th Attack on the United States Capitol (National Archives Production), P-R000261; Select Committee to Investigate the January 6th Attack on the United States Capitol, *Hearing on the January 6th Investigation*, 117th Cong., 2d sess., (July 21, 2022), available at https://www.govinfo.gov/committee/house-january6th

464 Documents on file with the Select Committee to Investigate the January 6th Attack on the United States Capitol (National Archives Production), P-R000257; Select Committee to Investigate the January 6th Attack on the United States Capitol, *Hearing on the January 6th Investigation*, 117th Cong., 2d sess., (July 21, 2022), available at https://www.govinfo.gov/committee/house-january6th

465 Select Committee to Investigate the January 6th Attack on the United States Capitol, Deposition of Molly Michael, (Mar. 24, 2022), p. 138.

466 Select Committee to Investigate the January 6th Attack on the United States Capitol, Transcribed Interview of Pasquale Anthony "Pat" Cipollone, (Jul. 8, 2022), p. 174; Select Committee to Investigate the January 6th Attack on the United States Capitol, Deposition of Keith Kellogg Jr., (Dec. 14, 2021), pp. 126–27; Select Committee to Investigate the January 6th Attack on the United States Capitol, Deposition of Nicholas Luna, (Mar. 21, 2022), pp. 151-52; Select Committee to Investigate the January 6th Attack on the United States Capitol, Transcribed Interview of Christopher Charles Miller, (Jan. 14, 2022), pp. 124-26; Select Committee to Investigate the January 6th Attack on the United States Capitol, Transcribed Interview of General Mark A. Milley, (Nov. 17, 2021), pp. 80-82; Select Committee to Investigate the January 6th Attack on the United States Capitol, *Hearing on the January 6th Investigation*, 117th Cong., 2d sess., (June 23, 2022), available at https://www.govinfo.gov/committee/house-january6th; Select Committee to Investigate the January 6th Attack on the United States Capitol, Transcribed Interview of Richard Peter Donoghue, (Oct. 1, 2021), pp. 186-90.

467 Select Committee to Investigate the January 6th Attack on the United States Capitol, Deposition of Molly Michael, (Mar. 24, 2022), pp. 127, 129, 131-32, 137, 141, 143-44, 148-49, 159.

468 Documents on file with the Select Committee to Investigate the January 6th Attack on the United States Capitol (AT&T Production, Feb. 9, 2022).

469 Select Committee to Investigate the January 6th Attack on the United States Capitol, Deposition of Kayleigh McEnany, (Jan. 12, 2022), pp. 163-64; Select Committee to Investigate the January 6th Attack on the United States Capitol, *Hearing on the January 6th Investigation*, 117th Cong., 2d sess., (July 21, 2022), available at https://www.govinfo.gov/committee/house-january6th.

470 Senator Lee wrote to a reporter that he received a call from the President moments after the Senate halted its proceedings and that the President claimed he had dialed Sen. Tommy Tuberville (R-AL), so Lee let Tuberville talk to the President on his phone for 5 or 10 minutes until they were ordered to evacuate. Bryan Schott, "What Sen. Mike Lee Told Me about Trump's Call the Day of the Capitol Riot," *Salt Lake Tribune*, (Feb. 10, 2021, updated Feb. 11, 2021), available at https://www.sltrib.com/news/politics/2021/02/11/what-sen-mike-lee-told-me/; *see also* Kyle Cheney, "Tuberville Says He Informed Trump of Pence's Evacuation before Rioters Reached Senate," *Politico*, (Feb. 11, 2021), available at https://www.politico.com/news/2021/02/11/tuberville-pences-evacuation-trump-impeachment-468572.

471 167 Cong. Rec. S634 (daily ed. Feb. 10, 2021), available at https://www.congress.gov/117/crec/2021/02/10/CREC-2021-02-10-pt1-PgS615-4.pdf; Donald J. Trump (@realDonaldTrump), Twitter, Jan. 6, 2021 1:49 p.m. ET, available at http://web.archive.org/web/20210107235835/https://twitter.com/realDonaldTrump/status/1346891760174329859 (archived).

472 Select Committee to Investigate the January 6th Attack on the United States Capitol, Transcribed Interview of Pasquale Anthony "Pat" Cipollone, (July 8, 2022), pp. 149 50.

473 Select Committee to Investigate the January 6th Attack on the United States Capitol, Transcribed Interview of Pasquale Anthony "Pat" Cipollone, (July 8, 2022), pp. 150-51.

[474] Select Committee to Investigate the January 6th Attack on the United States Capitol, *Hearing on the January 6th Investigation*, 117th Cong., 2d sess., (June 28, 2022), at 1:39:03-1:40:42, available at https://youtu.be/HeQNV-aQ_jU?t=5943. Two witnesses recall writing this note: Cassidy Hutchinson and Eric Herschmann, although Hutchinson recalls that Herschmann was responsible for the revision made to the note. The Committee's review of Hutchinson's handwriting was consistent with the script of the note. Select Committee to Investigate the January 6th Attack on the United States Capitol, Transcribed Interview of Cassidy Hutchinson, (Feb. 23, 2022), p. 167; Select Committee to Investigate the January 6th Attack on the United States Capitol, Transcribed Interview of Eric Herschmann (Apr. 6, 2022), pp. 67-68. Who wrote the note is not material to the Select Committee—the important point is that it was prepared for the President.

[475] Select Committee to Investigate the January 6th Attack on the United States Capitol, Transcribed Interview of Pasquale Anthony "Pat" Cipollone, (July 8, 2022), p. 162.

[476] Select Committee to Investigate the January 6th Attack on the United States Capitol, *Hearing on the January 6th Investigation*, 117th Cong., 2d sess., (June 28, 2022), at 1:27:52-1:28:53, available at https://youtu.be/HeQNV-aQ_jU?t=5272; Select Committee to Investigate the January 6th Attack on the United States Capitol, Continued Interview of Cassidy Hutchinson, (June 20, 2022), pp. 25-26.

[477] Select Committee to Investigate the January 6th Attack on the United States Capitol, Transcribed Interview of Pasquale Anthony "Pat" Cipollone, (July 8, 2022), p. 161; Select Committee to Investigate the January 6th Attack on the United States Capitol, *Hearing on the January 6th Investigation*, 117th Cong., 2d sess., (July 21, 2022), at 1:29:30 - 1:31:51, available at https://www.youtube.com/watch?v=pbRVqWbHGuo.

[478] Select Committee to Investigate the January 6th Attack on the United States Capitol, Transcribed Interview of White House employee with national security responsibilities, (July 19, 2022), pp. 12-15, 98-99; Select Committee to Investigate the January 6th Attack on the United States Capitol, *Hearing on the January 6th Investigation*, 117th Cong., 2d sess., (July 21, 2022), at 38:02-38:44, available at https://youtu.be/pbRVqWbHGuo?t=2283.

[479] Select Committee to Investigate the January 6th Attack on the United States Capitol, Deposition of Judson P. Deere, (Mar. 3, 2022), pp. 108-09.

[480] Select Committee to Investigate the January 6th Attack on the United States Capitol, *Hearing on the January 6th Investigation*, 117th Cong., 2d sess., (July 21, 2022), available at https://www.govinfo.gov/committee/house-january6th.

[481] Select Committee to Investigate the January 6th Attack on the United States Capitol, Transcribed Interview of Pasquale Anthony "Pat" Cipollone, (July 8, 2022), p. 163.

[482] Third Superseding Indictment at 21, *United States v. Nordean et al.*, No. 1:21-cr-175 (D.D.C. June 6, 2022), ECF No. 380 (noting that Dominic Pezzola "used [a] riot shield … to break a window of the Capitol" at "2:13 p.m." and that "[t]he first members of the mob entered the Capitol through this broken window."); 167 Cong. Rec. S634 (daily ed. Feb. 10, 2021), available at https://www.congress.gov/117/crec/2021/02/10/CREC-2021-02-10-pt1-PgS615-4.pdf.

[483] Documents on file with the Select Committee to Investigate the January 6th Attack on the United States Capitol (Mark Meadows Production), MM014907.

[484] Documents on file with the Select Committee to Investigate the January 6th Attack on the United States Capitol (Mark Meadows Production), MM014912.

[485] Documents on file with the Select Committee to Investigate the January 6th Attack on the United States Capitol (Mark Meadows Production), MM014919.

[486] Documents on file with the Select Committee to Investigate the January 6th Attack on the United States Capitol (Mark Meadows Production), MM014925.

[487] Documents on file with the Select Committee to Investigate the January 6th Attack on the United States Capitol (Mark Meadows Production), MM014933.

[488] Documents on file with the Select Committee to Investigate the January 6th Attack on the United States Capitol (Mark Meadows Production), MM014935.

[489] Documents on file with the Select Committee to Investigate the January 6th Attack on the United States Capitol (Mark Meadows Production), MM014937.

[490] Documents on file with the Select Committee to Investigate the January 6th Attack on the United States Capitol (Mark Meadows Production), MM014939.

[491] Documents on file with the Select Committee to Investigate the January 6th Attack on the United States Capitol (Mark Meadows Production), MM014944.

[492] Documents on file with the Select Committee to Investigate the January 6th Attack on the United States Capitol (Mark Meadows Production), MM014961.

[493] Select Committee to Investigate the January 6th Attack on the United States Capitol, *Hearing on the January 6th Investigation*, 117th Cong., 2d sess., (July 21, 2022), available at https://www.govinfo.gov/committee/house-january6th.

[494] U.S. Senator Bill Cassidy, M.D. (@SenBillCassidy), Twitter, Jan. 6, 2021 4:03 p.m. ET, available at https://twitter.com/SenBillCassidy/status/1346925444189327361.

[495] Documents on file with the Select Committee to Investigate the January 6th Attack on the United States Capitol (Mark Meadows Production), MM014971.

[496] Select Committee to Investigate the January 6th Attack on the United States Capitol, Transcribed Interview of Jared Kushner, (Mar. 31, 2022), pp. 149-50; Select Committee to Investigate the January 6th Attack on the United States Capitol, Transcribed Interview of Julie Radford, (May 25, 2022), p. 37.

[497] Select Committee to Investigate the January 6th Attack on the United States Capitol, Transcribed Interview of Jared Kushner, (Mar. 31, 2022), pp. 145, 150.

[498] Leader McCarthy spoke on the air to Fox News starting at 3:05 p.m. ET and told the network that "I've already talked to the President. I called him. I think we need to make a statement, make sure that we can calm individuals down." Fox News (FoxNews), "LISTEN: Rep. Kevin McCarthy on protesters storming Capitol," Facebook, at 3:27-3:40, Jan. 6, 2021 (uploaded to Facebook at 3:35 p.m. ET), available at https://www.facebook.com/FoxNews/videos/listen-rep-kevin-mccarthy-on-protesters-storming-capitol/232725075039919/.

[499] CBS News, "Live coverage: Protesters Swarm Capitol, Abruptly Halting Electoral Vote Count," YouTube, at 3:29:02-3:29:15, 3:29:43-3:30:03, 3:31:28-3:32:07, 3:33:52-3:34:12, Jan. 6, 2021, available at https://youtu.be/3Fsf4aWudJk?t=12542.

[500] Rep. Herrera Beutler Describes Efforts to Get Trump to Intervene in Stopping Jan. 6 riot," WTHR (Feb. 13, 2021), at 1:20 - 1:50, available at https://www.wthr.com/video/news/nation-world/capitol-riot-herrera-beutler-trump-mccarthy-call/507-477fa84f-1277-444a-aad6-716c5ec9f66f.

[501] Select Committee to Investigate the January 6th Attack on the United States Capitol, Transcribed Interview of John Michael "Mick" Mulvaney, (July 28, 2022), p. 43. CNN's Jamie Gangel related that she also confirmed the account with multiple other sources, reporting that "I've spoken to multiple Republican Members of the House who have knowledge of that call, who tell us that after Trump tried to say to Kevin, 'these are not my people, it's Antifa,' Kevin McCarthy said to Trump, 'no, it's not Antifa. These are your people'…. We're also told by several other Republican Members that Kevin McCarthy wasn't shy about this heated exchange with Trump, that he wanted his Members to know about it." CNN, "New Details Emerge in McCarthy's Call with Trump on January 6," YouTube, at 0:25 - 1:50, Feb. 12, 2021, available at https://www.youtube.com/watch?v=Gy1FPNluoOE.

[502] Select Committee to Investigate the January 6th Attack on the United States Capitol, Transcribed Interview of John Michael "Mick" Mulvaney, (July 28, 2022), pp. 10-12 (describing calls and text messages to Dan Scavino and Mark Meadows).

[503] *See, e.g.*, Documents on file with the Select Committee to Investigate the January 6th Attack on the United States Capitol (HBO Production), Video file Reel_204I - All Clips Compilation.mp4 at 5:32–5:55 (January 6, 2021, footage of Nancy Pelosi and Chuck Schumer on phone call with Jeffrey Rosen); Documents on file with the Select Committee to Investigate the January 6th Attack on the United States Capitol (Mark Meadows Production), MM014906 (January 6, 2021 text message from Marjorie Taylor Greene to Mark Meadows), MM014919 (January 6, 2021 text message from William Timmons to Mark Meadows), MM014939 (January 6, 2021 text message from Chip Roy to Mark Meadows).

[504] Select Committee to Investigate the January 6th Attack on the United States Capitol, Transcribed Interview of Pasquale Anthony "Pat" Cipollone, (July 8, 2022), p. 151.

[505] Select Committee to Investigate the January 6th Attack on the United States Capitol, Transcribed Interview of Pasquale Anthony "Pat" Cipollone, (July 8, 2022), p. 162.

[506] Select Committee to Investigate the January 6th Attack on the United States Capitol, Transcribed Interview of Pasquale Anthony "Pat" Cipollone, (July 8, 2022), p. 152.

[507] Select Committee to Investigate the January 6th Attack on the United States Capitol, *Hearing on the January 6th Investigation*, 117th Cong., 2d sess., (July 21, 2022), at 0:57:48 - 0:58:19, available at https://youtu.be/pbRVqWbIIGuo?t=3468.

[508] Select Committee to Investigate the January 6th Attack on the United States Capitol, Transcribed Interview of White House Security Official, (July 11, 2022), pp. 81-83; Select Committee to Investigate the January 6th Attack on the United States Capitol, *Hearing on the January 6th Investigation*, 117th Cong., 2d sess., (July 21, 2022), available at https://www.govinfo.gov/committee/house-january6th. The Select Committee is not revealing the identity of this witness because of national security concerns as well as to guard against the risk of retaliation.

[509] Donald J. Trump (@realDonaldTrump), Twitter, Jan. 6, 2021 2:24 p.m. ET, available at https://media-cdn.factba.se/realdonaldtrump-twitter/1346900434540240897.jpg (archived).

[510] Select Committee to Investigate the January 6th Attack on the United States Capitol, *Hearing on the January 6th Investigation*, 117th Cong., 2d sess., (June 16, 2022), at 2:11:22-2:13:55, available at https://youtu.be/vBjUWVKuDj0?t=7882.

[511] Select Committee to Investigate the January 6th Attack on the United States Capitol, *Hearing on the January 6th Investigation*, 117th Cong., 2d sess., (June 16, 2022), at 2:26:06-2:26:26, available at https://youtu.be/IQvuBoLBuC0?t=8766; Sentencing Transcript at 19, *United States v. Young*, No. 1:21-cr-291 (D.D.C. Sept. 27, 2022), ECF No. 170 (testifying for a victim impact statement, Officer Michael Fanone said: "At approximately 1435 hours, with rapidly mounting injuries and most of the MPD less than lethal munitions expended, the defending officers were forced to conduct a fighting withdrawal back towards the United States Capitol Building entrance. This is the first fighting withdrawal in the history of the Metropolitan Police Department.").

[512] Select Committee to Investigate the January 6th Attack on the United States Capitol, *Hearing on the January 6th Investigation*, 117th Cong., 2d sess., (July 21, 2022), available at https://www.govinfo.gov/committee/house-january6th.

[513] Select Committee to Investigate the January 6th Attack on the United States Capitol, *Hearing on the January 6th Investigation*, 117th Cong., 2d sess., (July 21, 2022), available at https://www.govinfo.gov/committee/house-january6th.

[514] Select Committee to Investigate the January 6th Attack on the United States Capitol, Deposition of Judson P. Deere, (Mar. 3, 2022), p. 113.

[515] Select Committee to Investigate the January 6th Attack on the United States Capitol, Transcribed Interview of Pasquale Anthony "Pat" Cipollone, (July 8, 2022), p. 160.

[516] Documents on file with the Select Committee to Investigate the January 6th Attack on the United States Capitol (Hope Hicks Production), SC_HH_043-044 (January 6, 2021, text message from Hope Hicks to Julie Radford at 7:18 p.m.).

[517] 167 Cong. Rec. S635 (daily ed. Feb. 10, 2021), available at https://www.congress.gov/117/crec/2021/02/10/CREC-2021-02-10-pt1-PgS615-4.pdf; Spencer S. Hsu, "Pence Spent Jan. 6 at Underground Senate Loading Dock, Secret Service Confirms," *Washington Post*, (Mar. 21, 2022), available at https://www.washingtonpost.com/dc-md-va/2022/03/21/couy-griffin-cowboys-trump-jan6/.

[518] Select Committee to Investigate the January 6th Attack on the United States Capitol, Deposition of Molly Michael, (Mar. 24, 2022), p. 137.

[519] Select Committee to Investigate the January 6th Attack on the United States Capitol, *Hearing on the January 6th Investigation*, 117th Cong., 2d sess., (July 21, 2022), available at https://www.govinfo.gov/committee/house-january6th.

[520] Select Committee to Investigate the January 6th Attack on the United States Capitol, Continued Interview of Cassidy Hutchinson, (June 20, 2022), p. 27.

[521] Select Committee to Investigate the January 6th Attack on the United States Capitol, *Hearing on the January 6th Investigation*, 117th Cong., 2d sess., (June 28, 2022), at 1:31:25 – 1:32:22, available at https://youtu.be/HeQNV-aQ_jU?t=5359; Select Committee to Investigate the January 6th Attack on the United States Capitol, Continued Interview of Cassidy Hutchinson, (June 20, 2022), pp. 27-28.

[522] Select Committee to Investigate the January 6th Attack on the United States Capitol, Transcribed Interview of Pasquale Anthony "Pat" Cipollone, (July 8, 2022), p. 182.

[523] Select Committee to Investigate the January 6th Attack on the United States Capitol, Transcribed Interview of Eric Herschmann, (Apr. 6, 2022), pp. 68-69, 71.

[524] Donald J. Trump (@realDonaldTrump), Twitter, Jan. 6, 2021 2:38 p.m. ET, available at https://media-cdn.factba.se/realdonaldtrump-twitter/1346904110969315332.jpg (archived).

525 Select Committee to Investigate the January 6th Attack on the United States Capitol, *Hearing on the January 6th Investigation*, 117th Cong., 2d sess., (July 21, 2022), available at https://www.govinfo.gov/committee/house-january6th.

526 Donald J. Trump (@realDonaldTrump), Twitter, Jan. 6, 2021 3:13 p.m. ET, available at https://media-cdn.factba.se/realdonaldtrump-twitter/1346912780700577792.jpg (archived).

527 Documents on file with the Select Committee to Investigate the January 6th Attack on the United States Capitol (Mark Meadows Production), MM014925.

528 Documents on file with the Select Committee to Investigate the January 6th Attack on the United States Capitol (Mark Meadows Production), MM014944.

529 Select Committee to Investigate the January 6th Attack on the United States Capitol, *Hearing on the January 6th Investigation*, 117th Cong., 2d sess., (July 21, 2022), available at https://www.govinfo.gov/committee/house-january6th.

530 Select Committee to Investigate the January 6th Attack on the United States Capitol, *Hearing on the January 6th Investigation*, 117th Cong., 2d sess., (July 21, 2022), available at https://www.govinfo.gov/committee/house-january6th].

531 Documents on file with the Select Committee to Investigate the January 6th Attack on the United States Capitol (National Archives Production), 076P-R000004112_0001 (January 6, 2021 email at 3:05 p.m. notifying Beau Harrison of Ashli Babbitt shooting); Select Committee to Investigate the January 6th Attack on the United States Capitol, Transcribed Interview of William Beau Harrison (Aug. 18, 2022), pp. 73–76 (describing writing note and passing it to Mark Meadows or Tony Ornato); Documents on file with the Select Committee to Investigate the January 6th Attack on the United States Capitol (National Archives Production), P-R000241 (January 6, 2021 pocket card written by Beau Harrison with the message, "1x CIVILIAN GUNSHOT WOUND TO CHEST @ DOOR OF HOUSE CHABER [sic]"); Select Committee to Investigate the January 6th Attack on the United States Capitol, Transcribed Interview of White House Employee, (June 10, 2022), pp. 46–47 ("I remember seeing that [note] in front of [President Trump], yeah."). The Select Committee is not revealing the identity of this witness to guard against the risk of retaliation. *See also* Select Committee to Investigate the January 6th Attack on the United States Capitol, Transcribed Interview of Anthony Ornato, (January 28, 2022), p. 115; Select Committee to Investigate the January 6th Attack on the United States Capitol, Transcribed Interview of Eric Herschmann, (Apr. 6, 2022), p. 87 (recalling announcing during the afternoon that a Trump supporter had been killed).

532 "Department of Justice Closes Investigation into the Death of Ashli Babbitt," Department of Justice, (Apr. 14, 2021), available at https://www.justice.gov/usao-dc/pr/department-justice-closes-investigation-death-ashli-babbitt.

533 Select Committee to Investigate the January 6th Attack on the United States Capitol, *Hearing on the January 6th Investigation*, 117th Cong., 2d sess., (July 21, 2022), available at https://www.govinfo.gov/committee/house-january6th; Select Committee to Investigate the January 6th Attack on the United States Capitol, *Business Meeting on the January 6th Investigation*, 117th Cong., 2d sess., (Oct. 13, 2022), available at https://www.govinfo.gov/committee/house-january6th; ABC News, "Mike Pence Opens Up with David Muir on Jan. 6: Exclusive," YouTube, at 9:27-10:00, Nov. 14, 2022, available at https://youtu.be/-AAyKAoPFQs?t=567; Select Committee to Investigate the January 6th Attack on the United States Capitol, Transcribed Interview of General Mark A. Milley (Nov. 17, 2021), pp. 80-81; Select Committee to Investigate the January 6th Attack on the United States Capitol, Transcribed Interview of Christopher Charles Miller (Jan. 14, 2022), pp. 124-25; Select Committee to Investigate the January 6th Attack on the United States Capitol, Transcribed Interview of Jeffrey Rosen, (Oct. 13, 2021), pp. 172-73, 182-84; Select Committee to Investigate the January 6th Attack on the United States Capitol, Transcribed Interview of Richard Peter Donoghue, (Oct. 1, 2021), p. 186.

534 NBC News, "Biden Condemns Chaos at the Capitol as 'Insurrection,'" YouTube, Jan. 6, 2021, available at https://www.youtube.com/watch?v=FBCWTqJT7M4; Select Committee to Investigate the January 6th Attack on the United States Capitol, *Hearing on the January 6th Investigation*, 117th Cong., 2d sess., (July 21, 2022), available at https://www.govinfo.gov/committee/house-january6th.

535 "Trump Video Telling Protesters at Capitol Building to Go Home: Transcript," Rev, (Jan. 6, 2021), available at https://www.rev.com/blog/transcripts/trump-video-telling-protesters-at-capitol-building-to-go-home-transcript.

536 Select Committee to Investigate the January 6th Attack on the United States Capitol, *Hearing on the January 6th Investigation*, 117th Cong., 2d sess., (July 21, 2022), available at https://www.govinfo.gov/committee/house-january6th.

[537] Select Committee to Investigate the January 6th Attack on the United States Capitol, *Hearing on the January 6th Investigation*, 117th Cong., 2d sess., (July 21, 2022), available at https://www.govinfo.gov/committee/house-january6th

[538] Select Committee to Investigate the January 6th Attack on the United States Capitol, *Hearing on the January 6th Investigation*, 117th Cong., 2d sess., (July 12, 2022), at 2:36:58-2:37:30, 2:44:00-2:45:05, available at https://www.youtube.com/watch?v=rrUa0hfG6Lo ("[W]hen President Trump put his tweet out, we literally left right after that come out . . . As soon as that come out, everybody started talking about it . . . it definitely dispersed a lot of the crowd. . . . We left.").

[539] Select Committee to Investigate the January 6th Attack on the United States Capitol, *Hearing on the January 6th Investigation*, 117th Cong., 2d sess., (July 12, 2022), at 1:58:00, available at https://www.youtube.com/watch?v=pbRVqWbHGuo.

[540] Select Committee to Investigate the January 6th Attack on the United States Capitol, *Hearing on the January 6th Investigation*, 117th Cong., 2d sess., (July 12, 2022), at 1:58:00, available at https://www.youtube.com/watch?v=pbRVqWbHGuo.

[541] Donald J. Trump (@realDonaldTrump), Twitter, Jan. 6, 2021 at 6:01 p.m. ET, available at http://web.archive.org/web/20210106232133/https://twitter.com/realdonaldtrump/status/1346954970910707712 (archived).

[542] Select Committee to Investigate the January 6th Attack on the United States Capitol, *Hearing on the January 6th Investigation*, 117th Cong., 2d sess., (July 21, 2022), available at https://www.govinfo.gov/committee/house-january6th.

[543] Select Committee to Investigate the January 6th Attack on the United States Capitol, Transcribed Interview of Timothy Murtaugh, (May 19, 2022), p. 175; Select Committee to Investigate the January 6th Attack on the United States Capitol, *Hearing on the January 6th Investigation*, 117th Cong., 2d sess., (July 21, 2022), available at https://www.govinfo.gov/committee/house-january6th.

[544] Select Committee to Investigate the January 6th Attack on the United States Capitol, Transcribed Interview of Pasquale Anthony "Pat" Cipollone, (July 8, 2022), p. 194; Select Committee to Investigate the January 6th Attack on the United States Capitol, *Hearing on the January 6th Investigation*, 117th Cong., 2d sess., (July 21, 2022), available at https://www.govinfo.gov/committee/house-january6th.

[545] Select Committee to Investigate the January 6th Attack on the United States Capitol, Deposition of Greg Jacob, (Feb. 1, 2022), p. 192.

[546] Select Committee to Investigate the January 6th Attack on the United States Capitol, Transcribed Interview of White House Employee, (June 10, 2022), p. 53. The Select Committee is not revealing the identity of this witness to guard against the risk of retaliation.

[547] Documents on file with the Select Committee to Investigate the January 6th Attack on the United States Capitol, (Rudolph Giuliani Production, Mar. 11, 2022); Documents on file with the Select Committee to Investigate the January 6th Attack on the United States Capitol, (AT&T Production, Feb. 9, 2022).

[548] Select Committee to Investigate the January 6th Attack on the United States Capitol, Deposition of Rudolph Giuliani, (May 20, 2022), pp. 205-07; Sunlen Serfaty, Devan Cole, and Alex Rogers, "As Riot Raged at Capitol, Trump Tried to Call Senators to Overturn Election," CNN, (Jan. 8, 2021), available at https://www.cnn.com/2021/01/08/politics/mike-lee-tommy-tuberville-trump-misdialed-capitol-riot; Documents on file with the Select Committee to Investigate the January 6th Attack on the United States Capitol, (Rudolph Giuliani Production, Mar. 11, 2022); Documents on file with the Select Committee to Investigate the January 6th Attack on the United States Capitol, (AT&T Production, Feb. 9, 2022).

[549] Mike Pence, *So Help Me God* (New York: Simon & Schuster, 2022), p. 475.

[550] Mike Pence, *So Help Me God* (New York: Simon & Schuster, 2022), p. 474.

[551] Select Committee to Investigate the January 6th Attack on the United States Capitol, Transcribed Interview of Steven Andrew Sund, (Apr. 20, 2022), pp. 170-71; Select Committee to Investigate the January 6th Attack on the United States Capitol, Transcribed Interview of Pasquale Anthony "Pat" Cipollone, (Jul. 8, 2022), p. 174; Select Committee to Investigate the January 6th Attack on the United States Capitol, Deposition of Keith Kellogg Jr., (Dec. 14, 2021), pp. 126–27; Select Committee to Investigate the January 6th Attack on the United States Capitol, Deposition of Nicholas Luna, (Mar. 21, 2022), pp. 151-52; Select Committee to Investigate the January 6th Attack on the United States Capitol, Transcribed Interview of Christopher Charles Miller, (Jan. 14, 2022), pp. 124-26; Select Committee to Investigate the January 6th Attack on the United States Capitol, Transcribed Interview of General Mark A. Milley,

(Nov. 17, 2021), pp. 80-82; Select Committee to Investigate the January 6th Attack on the United States Capitol, Transcribed Interview of Richard Peter Donoghue, (Oct. 1, 2021), pp. 186-89; Select Committee to Investigate the January 6th Attack on the United States Capitol, Transcribed Interview of Muriel Bowser, (Jan. 12, 2022), pp. 21-22.

552 ABC News, "Pence Opens Up with David Muir on Jan. 6: Exclusive," YouTube, at 10:45-11:02, Nov. 14, 2022, available at https://www.youtube.com/watch?v=-AAyKAoPFQs.

553 Select Committee to Investigate the January 6th Attack on the United States Capitol, Transcribed Interview of Steven Andrew Sund, (Apr. 20, 2022), pp. 170-71; Select Committee to Investigate the January 6th Attack on the United States Capitol, Transcribed Interview of Pasquale Anthony "Pat" Cipollone, (Jul. 8, 2022), p. 174; Select Committee to Investigate the January 6th Attack on the United States Capitol, Deposition of Keith Kellogg Jr., (Dec. 14, 2021), pp. 126–27; Select Committee to Investigate the January 6th Attack on the United States Capitol, Deposition of Nicholas Luna, (Mar. 21, 2022), pp. 151-52; Select Committee to Investigate the January 6th Attack on the United States Capitol, Transcribed Interview of Christopher Charles Miller, (Jan. 14, 2022), pp. 124-26; Select Committee to Investigate the January 6th Attack on the United States Capitol, Transcribed Interview of General Mark A. Milley, (Nov. 17, 2021), pp. 80-82; Select Committee to Investigate the January 6th Attack on the United States Capitol, Transcribed Interview of Richard Peter Donoghue, (Oct. 1, 2021), pp. 186-89; Select Committee to Investigate the January 6th Attack on the United States Capitol, Transcribed Interview of Muriel Bowser, (Jan. 12, 2022), pp. 21-22.

554 Select Committee to Investigate the January 6th Attack on the United States Capitol, Transcribed Interview of General Mark A. Milley (Nov. 17, 2021), pp. 17, 268.

555 Select Committee to Investigate the January 6th Attack on the United States Capitol, Transcribed Interview of General Mark A. Milley (Nov. 17, 2021), p. 296; Select Committee to Investigate the January 6th Attack on the United States Capitol, *Hearing on the January 6th Investigation*, 117th Cong., 2d sess., (July 21, 2022), available at https://www.govinfo.gov/committee/house-january6th.

556 Glenn Kessler, "Trump Falsely Claims He 'Requested' 10,000 Troops Rejected by Pelosi," *Washington Post*, (Mar. 2, 2021), available at https://www.washingtonpost.com/politics/2021/03/02/trump-falsely-claims-he-requested-10000-troops-rejected-by-pelosi/; "Mark Meadows: Biden Administration Policies Put 'America Last'," Fox News, (Feb. 7, 2021), available at https://www.foxnews.com/transcript/mark-meadows-biden-administration-policies-put-america-last.

557 Select Committee to Investigate the January 6th Attack on the United States Capitol, Transcribed Interview of Christopher Charles Miller (Jan. 14, 2022), pp. 100-01. On January 4, 2021, Max Miller and Katrina Pierson exchanged text messages discussing their planning activities for the 6th. In those messages, Max Miller stated: "Just glad we killed the national guard and a procession" and that "… chief [Mark Meadows] already had said no for days!". Documents on file with the Select Committee to Investigate the January 6th Attack on the United States Capitol (Max Miller Production), Miller Production 0001 (January 4, 2021, text messages between Max Miller and Katrina Pierson).

558 Select Committee to Investigate the January 6th Attack on the United States Capitol, *Hearing on the January 6th Investigation*, 117th Cong., 2d sess., (July 12, 2022), at 2:22:45-2:23:22, available at https://youtu.be/rrUa0hfG6Lo?t=8565; Documents on file with the Select Committee to Investigate the January 6th Attack on the United States Capitol (Katrina Pierson Production), KPierson0717-719.

559 "House Republican Leader Kevin McCarthy on Asking President Trump for his Resignation," ed. Alex Burns and Jonathan Martin, ThisWillNotPass.com, (Jan. 8, 2021), available at https://www.thiswillnotpass.com/bookresources.

560 Documents on file with the Select Committee to Investigate the January 6th Attack on the United States Capitol (Mark Meadows Production), MM014456.

561 Documents on file with the Select Committee to Investigate the January 6th Attack on the United States Capitol (Mark Meadows Production), MM014858 - MM014861.

562 Documents on file with the Select Committee to Investigate the January 6th Attack on the United States Capitol (Mark Meadows Production), MM014467 (December 31, 2020, text message from telephone number assigned to Carrah Jo Roy, wife of Rep. Chip Roy. to Mark Meadows). The Select Committee believes that Rep. Chip Roy sent this message.

563 Documents on file with the Select Committee to Investigate the January 6th Attack on the United States Capitol (Mark Meadows Production), MM014503 (January 1, 2021, text message from telephone number assigned to Carrah Jo Roy, wife of Rep. Chip Roy. to Mark Meadows). The Select Committee believes that Rep. Chip Roy sent this message.

564 Documents on file with the Select Committee to Investigate the January 6th Attack on the United States Capitol (Kayleigh McEnany Production), CTRL0000925383, p. 3 (January 7, 2021, text message from Sean Hannity to Kayleigh McEnany)

565 Documents on file with the Select Committee to Investigate the January 6th Attack on the United States Capitol (Mark Meadows Production), MM015209 (January 10, 2021, text message Sean Hannity to Mark Meadows and Jim Jordan).

566 Documents on file with the Select Committee to Investigate the January 6th Attack on the United States Capitol (Mark Meadows Production), MM014906.

567 "U.S. House Impeaches President Trump for Second Time, 232-197," C-SPAN, at 4:14:56 - 4:15:31, Jan. 13, 2021, available at https://www.c-span.org/video/?507879-101/house-impeaches-president-trump-time-232-197&live=.

568 "Republican Leader Kevin McCarthy says Pres. Trump Admitted He Bears Some Responsibility for the January 6 Insurrection at the U.S. Capitol," ed. Alex Burns and Jonathan Martin, ThisWillNotPass.com, (Jan. 11, 2021), available at https://www.thiswillnotpass.com/bookresources.

569 "Statement by Mo Brooks," Mo Brooks for U.S. Senate, available at https://mobrooks.com/statement-by-mo-brooks/; Joe Walsh, "GOP Rep. Mo Brooks Claims Trump Asked Him to Reinstate Trump Presidency," *Forbes*, (Mar. 23, 2022), available at https://www.forbes.com/sites/joewalsh/2022/03/23/gop-rep-mo-brooks-claims-trump-asked-him-to-reinstate-trump-presidency/?sh=7264e1d91edd (noting that Rep. Mo Brooks issued this statement on Wednesday, March 23, 2022).

570 *See* Ryan Goodman and Josh Asabor, "In Their Own Words: The 43 Republicans' Explanations of Their Votes Not to Convict Trump in Impeachment Trial," Just Security, (Feb. 15, 2021), *available at* https://www.justsecurity.org/74725/in-their-own-words-the-43-republicans-explanations-of-their-votes-not-to-convict-trump-in-impeachment-trial/.

571 C-SPAN, "Senate Minority Leader Mitch McConnell Remarks Following Senate Impeachment Vote," YouTube, at 5:10 – 5:46, Feb. 13, 2021, available at https://www.youtube.com/watch?v=yxRMoqNnfvw.

572 "Republican Leader Kevin McCarthy Says Pres. Trump Admitted He Bears Some Responsibility for the January 6 Insurrection at the U.S. Capitol," ed. Alex Burns and Jonathan Martin, ThisWillNotPass.com, (Jan. 11, 2021), available at https://www.thiswillnotpass.com/bookresources; Melanie Zanona, "New Audio Reveals McCarthy said Trump Admitted Bearing Some Responsibility for Capitol Attack," CNN (April 22, 2022), available at https://www.cnn.com/2022/04/22/politics/trump-january-6-responsibility-book/index.html. McCarthy also relayed this conversation with President Trump to his Republican colleagues: "I asked him [Trump] personally today, does he hold responsibility for what happened. And he needs to acknowledge that." *Id.* The Committee believes that House Republican Leader Kevin McCarthy's testimony would be material to any criminal investigation of Donald Trump, not just to probe this apparent Trump acknowledgement of culpability, but also because Leader McCarthy spoke directly to Donald Trump and others who were in the White House on January 6th and unsuccessfully pleaded for the President's immediate assistance to halt the violence. Rep. McCarthy did not comply with the Select Committee's subpoena.

573 "U.S. House Impeaches President Trump for Second Time, 232-197," C-SPAN, at 4:14:56 - 4:15:31, Jan. 13, 2021, available at https://www.c-span.org/video/?507879-101/house-impeaches-president-trump-time-232-197&live=; 167 Cong. Rec. H172 (daily ed. Jan. 13, 2021), available at https://www.congress.gov/117/crec/2021/01/13/CREC-2021-01-13-pt1-PgH165.pdf.

574 *See supra* at _____.

575 *See supra* at _____.

576 Documents on file with the Select Committee (National Archives Production), VP-R0000156_0001 (January 6, 2021, email chain between John Eastman and Marc Jacob re: Pennsylvania letter).

577 Documents on file with Select Committee (Department of Justice Production), HCOR-Pre-Certification-Events-07282021-000738 - HCOR-Pre-Certification-Events-07282021-000739 (December 27, 2020, handwritten notes from Richard Donoghue).

578 *See supra* at _____. The State legislatures lacked authority to change the lawful outcome of the State elections at that point. Nevertheless Eastman, Trump, and others nevertheless pushed for such action.

579 *See supra* at _____.

580 *See* Executive Summary; Donald J. Trump (@realDonaldTrump), Twitter, Dec. 19, 2020 1:42 a.m. ET, available at http://web.archive.org/web/20201219064257/https://twitter.com/realDonaldTrump/status/1340185773220515840 (archived); *see also, e.g.*, Donald J. Trump (@realDonaldTrump), Twitter, Dec. 26, 2020 8:14 a.m. ET, available at

https://twitter.com/realDonaldTrump/status/1342821189077622792; Donald J. Trump (@realDonaldTrump), Twitter, Dec. 27, 2020 5:51 p.m. ET, available at https://twitter.com/realDonaldTrump/status/1343328708963299338; Donald J. Trump (@realDonaldTrump), Twitter, Dec. 30, 2020 2:06 p.m. ET, available at https://twitter.com/realDonaldTrump/status/1344359312878149634; Donald J. Trump (@realDonaldTrump), Twitter, Jan. 1, 2021 12:52 p.m. ET, available at https://www.thetrumparchive.com/?searchbox=%22RT+%40KylieJaneKremer%22 (retweeting @KylieJaneKremer, Dec. 19, 2020 3:50 p.m. ET, available at https://twitter.com/KylieJaneKremer/status/1340399063875895296); Donald J. Trump (@realDonaldTrump), Twitter, Jan. 1, 2021 2:53 p.m. ET, available at https://twitter.com/realDonaldTrump/status/1345095714687377418; Donald J. Trump (@realDonaldTrump), Twitter, Jan. 1, 2021 3:34 p.m. ET, available at https://twitter.com/realDonaldTrump/status/1345106078141394944; Donald J. Trump (@realDonaldTrump), Twitter, Jan. 1, 2021 6:38 p.m. ET, available at https://twitter.com/realDonaldTrump/status/1345152408591204352; Donald J. Trump (@realDonaldTrump), Twitter, Jan. 2, 2021 9:04 p.m. ET, available at https://twitter.com/realDonaldTrump/status/1345551634907209730; Donald J. Trump (@realDonaldTrump), Twitter, Jan. 3, 2021 1:29 a.m. ET, available at https://www.thetrumparchive.com/?searchbox=%22RT+%40realDonaldTrump%3A+https%3A%2F%2Ft.co%2FnslWcFwkCj%22 (retweeting Donald J. Trump (@realDonaldTrump), Jan. 2, 2021 9:04 p.m. ET, available at https://twitter.com/realDonaldTrump/status/1345551634907209730); Donald J. Trump (@realDonaldTrump), Twitter, Jan. 3, 2021 10:15 a.m. ET, available at https://www.thetrumparchive.com/?searchbox=%22RT+%40JenLawrence21%22 (retweeting Jennifer Lynn Lawrence (@JenLawrence21), Jan. 3, 2021 12:17 a.m. ET, available at https://twitter.com/JenLawrence21/status/1345600194826686464); Donald J. Trump (@realDonaldTrump), Twitter, Jan. 3, 2021 10:17 a.m. ET, available at https://www.thetrumparchive.com/?searchbox=%22RT+%40CodeMonkeyZ+if%22 (retweeting Ron Watkins (@CodeMonkeyZ) Jan. 2, 2021 9:14 p.m. ET, available at http://web.archive.org/web/20210103151826/https://twitter.com/CodeMonkeyZ/status/1345599512560078849 (archived)); Donald J. Trump, (@realDonaldTrump), Twitter, Jan. 3, 2021 10:24 a.m. ET, available at https://www.thetrumparchive.com/?searchbox=%22RT+%40realMikeLindell%22 (retweeting Mike Lindell (@realMikeLindell), Jan. 2, 2021 5:47 p.m. ET, available at http://web.archive.org/web/20210103152421/https://twitter.com/realMikeLindell/status/1345547185836978176 (archived)); Donald J. Trump (@realDonaldTrump), Twitter, Jan. 3, 2021 10:27 a.m. ET, available at https://twitter.com/realDonaldTrump/status/1345753534168506370; Donald J. Trump (@realDonaldTrump), Twitter, Jan. 3, 2021 10:28 a.m. ET, available at https://www.thetrumparchive.com/?searchbox=%22RT+%40AmyKremer+we%22 (retweeting Amy Kremer (@AmyKremer), Jan. 2, 2021 2:58 p.m. ET, available at https://twitter.com/AmyKremer/status/1345459488107749386); Donald J. Trump (@realDonaldTrump), Twitter, Jan. 4, 2021 9:46 a.m. ET, available at https://www.thetrumparchive.com/?searchbox=%22RT+%40realDonaldTrump+I+will+be+there.+Historic+day%21%22 (retweeting Donald J. Trump (@realDonaldTrump), Jan. 3, 2021 10:27 a.m. ET, available at https://twitter.com/realDonaldTrump/status/1345753534168506370); Donald J. Trump (@realDonaldTrump), Twitter, Jan. 5, 2021 10:27 a.m. ET, available at https://twitter.com/realDonaldTrump/status/1346478482105069568; Donald J. Trump (@realDonaldTrump), Twitter, Jan. 5, 2021 5:43 p.m. ET, available at https://twitter.com/realDonaldTrump/status/1346588064026685443.

[581] Donald J. Trump (@realDonldTrump), Twitter, Jan. 6, 2021 2:24 p.m. ET, available at https://www.thetrumparchive.com/?searchbox=%22mike+pence+%22&results=1 (archived) ("Mike Pence didn't have the courage to do what should have been done to protect our Country and our Constitution, giving States a chance to certify a corrected set of facts, not the fraudulent or inaccurate ones which they were asked to previously certify. USA demands the truth! "); USA Today Graphics (@usatgraphics), Twitter, Jan. 7, 2021 9:56 p.m. ET, available at https://twitter.com/usatgraphics/status/1347376642956603392 (screenshotting the since-deleted tweet).

[582] "Trump Video Telling Protesters at Capitol Building to Go Home: Transcript," Rev, (Jan. 6, 2021), available at https://www.rev.com/blog/transcripts/trump-video-telling-protesters-at-capitol-building-to-go-home-transcript;
Select Committee to Investigate the January 6th Attack on the United States Capitol, *Hearing on the January 6th Investigation*, 117th Cong., 2d sess., (July 12, 2022), at 2:36:58-2:37:30 and 2:44:00-2:45:05, available at https://www.youtube.com/watch?v=rrUa0hfG6Lo ("[W]hen President Trump put his tweet out, we literally left right

after that come out . . . As soon as that come out, everybody started talking about it . . . it definitely dispersed a lot of the crowd. . . . We left."). *See supra* at _____.

583 Order Re Privilege of Documents Dated January 4-7, 2021 at 3-16, *Eastman v. Thompson et al.*, 594 F. Supp. 3d 1156, (C.D. Cal. March 28, 2022) (No. 8:22-cv-99-DOC-DFM).

584 Order Re Privilege of Documents Dated January 4-7, 2021 at 53-53, 58, *Eastman v. Thompson et al.*, 594 F. Supp. 3d 1156, (C.D. Cal. March 28, 2022) (No. 8:22-cv-99-DOC-DFM) (referring to two Federal criminal statutes).

585 Order Re Privilege of 599 Documents Dated November 3, 2020 – January 20, 2021 at 24, *Eastman v. Thompson et al.*, No. 8:22-cv-99-DOC-DFM, (C.D. Cal. June 7, 2022), ECF No. 24.

586 Order Re Privilege of Documents Dated January 4-7, 2021 at 63-64, *Eastman v. Thompson et al.*, 594 F. Supp. 3d 1156, (C.D. Cal. March 28, 2022) (No. 8:22-cv-99-DOC-DFM).

587 Order Re Privilege of Documents Dated January 4-7, 2021 at 64, *Eastman v. Thompson et al.*, 594 F. Supp. 3d 1156, (C.D. Cal. March 28, 2022) (No. 8:22-cv-99-DOC-DFM).

588 *See* "23 Months Since the January 6th Attack on the Capitol," Department of Justice, (Dec. 8, 2022), available at https://www.justice.gov/usao-dc/23-months-january-6-attack-capitol.

589 Kyle Cheney, "Rep. Scott Perry Suing to Block DOJ Access to His Cell Phone," *Politico*, (Aug. 24, 2022), available at https://www.politico.com/news/2022/08/24/rep-scott-perry-suing-to-block-doj-access-to-his-cell-phone-00053486; Betsy Woodruff Swan, Josh Gerstein, and Kyle Cheney, "DOJ Searches Home of Former Official Who Aided Alleged Pro-Trump 'Coup'," *Politico*, (June 23, 2022), available at https://www.politico.com/news/2022/06/23/law-enforcement-trump-official-coup-00041767.

590 *See, e.g.*, Sarah Murray, Evan Perez, and Katelyn Polantz, "Federal Judge Orders Former Top Lawyers in Trump's White House to Testify in Criminal Grand Jury Probe," CNN, (Dec. 1, 2022), available at https://www.cnn.com/2022/12/01/politics/cipollone-philbin-trump-lawyers-testify.

591 Sara Murray and Jason Morris, "Fulton County Prosecutor Investigating Trump Aims for Indictments as Soon as December," CNN, (Oct. 6, 2022), available at https://www.cnn.com/2022/10/06/politics/fani-willis-georgia-prosecutor-trump-indictments-december/index.html.

592 The Special Counsel is to oversee the Department's ongoing investigation "into whether any person or entity unlawfully interfered with the transfer of power following the 2020 Presidential election or the certification of the Electoral College vote held on or about January 6, 2021." "Appointment of a Special Counsel," Department of Justice, (Nov. 18, 2022), available at https://www.justice.gov/opa/pr/appointment-special-counsel-0. In addition, the Special Counsel is to oversee the Department's "ongoing investigation involving classified documents and other Presidential records, as well as the possible obstruction of that investigation. . . ." *Id.*

593 The House of Representatives held Meadows in contempt for refusing to testify before the Committee, 167 Cong. Rec. H7814-7815 (daily ed. Dec. 14, 2021), but DOJ declined to prosecute him. *See* Josh Gerstein, Kyle Cheny, and Nicholas Wu, "DOJ Declines to Charge Meadows, Scavino with Contempt of Congress for Defying Jan. 6 Committee," *Politico*, (June 3, 2022), available at https://www.politico.com/news/2022/06/03/doj-declines-to-charge-meadows-scavino-with-contempt-of-congress-for-defying-jan-6-committee-00037230.

594 18 U.S.C. § 1512(c)(2).

595 According to DOJ, "[a] conviction under Section 1512(c)(2) requires proof that": (1) "the natural and probable effect of the defendant's actions were to obstruct [influence or impede] the official proceeding;" (2) "that [defendant] knew that his actions were likely to obstruct [influence or impede] that proceeding;" and (3) "that he acted with the wrongful or improper purpose of delaying or stopping the official proceeding." *United States v. Andries*, No. 21-93 (RC), 2022 U.S. Dist. LEXIS 44794 at *37 n.8 (D.D.C. Mar. 14, 2022) (quoting Government's Response to Defendant's Second Supplemental Brief at 6); *see United States v. Aguilar*; 515 U.S. 593, 616 (1995) (Scalia, J., concurring in part, dissenting in part) (describing the "longstanding and well-accepted meaning" of "corruptly" as denoting "an act done with an intent to give some advantage inconsistent with official duty and the rights of others" (quoting *United States v. Ogle*, 613 F.2d 233, 238 (10th Cir. 1979))).

596 *See, e.g., United States v. Gillespie*, No. 22-CR-60 (BAH), 2022 U.S. Dist. LEXIS 214833, at *7-8 (D.D.C. Nov. 29, 2022); *United States v. Seefried*, No. 1:21-cr-287 (TNM), 2022 U.S. Dist. LEXIS 196980, at *2-3 (D.D.C. Oct. 29, 2022); *United States v. Miller*, 589 F. Supp. 3d 60, 67 (D.D.C. 2022), *reconsideration denied*, No. 1:21-CR-119 (CJN), 589 F. Supp. 3d 60 (D.D.C. May 27, 2022); *United States v. Puma*, No. 1:21-CR-454 (PLF), 2022 U.S. Dist. LEXIS 48875, at *10 (D.D.C. Mar. 19, 2022); *United States v. McHugh*, 583 F. Supp. 3d 1, 14-15 (D.D.C. 2022). *See also* T. Kanefield, "January 6 Defendants Are Raising a Creative Defense. It Isn't Working," *Washington Post*, (Feb. 15, 2022), available at https://www.washingtonpost.com/outlook/2022/02/15/jan-6-official-proceeding/.

[597] *See supra* at ___.
[598] *See supra* at ___.
[599] *See supra* at ___.
[600] Documents on file with the Select Committee (National Archives Production), VP-R0000156_0001 (January 6, 2021, email chain between John Eastman and Marc Jacob re: Pennsylvania letter). One judge on the U.S. District Court for the District of Columbia, in the course of concluding that Section 1512(c) is not void for vagueness, interpreted the "corruptly" element as meaning "contrary to law, statute, or established rule." *United States v. Sandlin*, 575 F. Supp. 3d. 15-16, (D.D.C. 2021). As explained above, President Trump attempted to cause the Vice President to violate the Electoral Count Act, and even Dr. Eastman advised President Trump that the proposed course of action would violate the Act. We believe this satisfies the "corruptly" element of the offense under the *Sandlin* opinion.
[601] Indeed, it would not have been legally possible for a State to have done so in the days before January 6th.
[602] Order Re Privilege of Documents Dated January 4-7, 2021 at 49-50, *Eastman v. Thompson et al.*, 594 F. Supp. 3d 1156, (C.D. Cal. March 28, 2022) (No. 8:22-cv-99-DOC-DFM).
[603] *See supra* at ___.
[604] Documents on file with Select Committee (Department of Justice Production), HCOR-Pre-Certification-Events-07282021-000738 - COR-Pre-Certification-Events-07282021-000739 (December 27, 2020, handwritten notes from Richard Donoghue).
[605] *See supra* at ___.
[606] *See supra* at ___.
[607] *See E supra* at ___. Jeffrey Clark invoked his Fifth Amendment privilege against self-incrimination in response to questions regarding this letter. As already noted, the political appointee who assisted in drafting the letter was hired at the Justice Department on December 15, 2020, but had worked on behalf of President Trump on election challenges in the weeks beforehand (including, apparently, while simultaneously serving as Special Counsel for the White House Office of Management and Budget).
[608] *See supra* at ___.
[609] *See supra* at ___.
[610] *See supra* at ___.
[611] Select Committee to Investigate the January 6th Attack on the United States Capitol, Transcribed Interview of Eric Herschmann, (Apr. 6, 2022), p. 26.
[612] Documents on file with the Select Committee (National Archives Production), VP-R0000156_0001 (January 6, 2021, email chain between John Eastman and Marc Jacob re: Pennsylvania letter).
[613] Select Committee to Investigate the January 6th Attack on the United States Capitol, Transcribed Interview of Eric Herschmann, (Apr. 6, 2022), p. 44. Although Eastman invoked his Fifth Amendment rights as a reason not to answer any of this Committee's substantive questions during his deposition, he has recently suggested in public that he only wished to delay the count of votes by multiple days. As the evidence developed by this Committee demonstrates, Eastman knew that such an effort to delay the count would also be illegal. *See* Select Committee to Investigate the January 6th Attack on the United States Capitol, *Hearing on the January 6th Investigation*, 117th Cong., 2d sess., (June 16, 2022), at 1:32:00-1:35:13, available at https://www.youtube.com/watch?v=vBjUWVKuDj0 ("[D]id Dr. Eastman seem to admit that both of these theories suffered from similar legal flaws? [T]his new theory, as I was pointing out to him, or the procedural theory, still violates several provisions of the Electoral Count Act, as he acknowledged.... So, he acknowledged in those conversations that the underlying legal theory was the same...."). In addition, neither Eastman nor any other co-conspirator had information establishing that any delay in counting votes would or could have changed the outcome of the election in any State.
[614] *See supra* at ___. We also note that these Republican members of Congress, who had more knowledge of Trump's planning for January 6th than any other members of Congress, were also likely in a far superior position than any other members to warn the Capitol Police of the risks of violence at the Capitol on January 6th.
[615] *See* Select Committee to Investigate the January 6th Attack on the U.S. Capitol, *Hearing on the January 6th Investigation*, 117th Cong., 2d sess., (June 16, 2022), at 2:29:50, available at https://www.youtube.com/watch?v=vBjUWVKuDj0 ("I've decided that I should be on the pardon list, if that is still in the works.").
[616] The elements of a Section 371 conspiracy to defraud the United States are: (1) at least two people entered into an agreement to obstruct a lawful function of the government, (2) by deceitful or dishonest means, and (3) a member of the conspiracy engaged in at least one overt act in furtherance of the agreement. Order Re Privilege of Documents

Dated January 4-7, 2021 at 53, *Eastman v. Thompson et al.*, 594 F. Supp. 3d 1156, (C.D. Cal. Mar. 28, 2022) (No. 8:22-cv-99-DOC-DFM). Put similarly, to prove a violation Section 371's "defraud" provision, the government must prove that the defendant: (1) agreed with at least one other person to defraud the United States, (2) knowingly participated in the conspiracy with the intent to defraud the United States, and (3) that at least one overt act was taken in furtherance of the conspiracy. *See United States v. Dean*, 55 F.3d 640, 647 (D.C. Cir. 1995) (citing *United States v. Treadwell*, 760 F.2d 327, 333 (D.C. Cir. 1985)); *see also United States v. Mellen*, 158, 393 F.3d 175, 181 (D.C. Cir. 2004). An individual "defrauds" the government for purposes of Section 371 if he "interfere[s] with or obstruct[s] one of its lawful governmental functions by deceit, craft or trickery, or at least by means that are dishonest." *Hammerschmidt v. United States,* 265 U.S. 182, 188 (1924); *see also United States v. Haldeman*, 559 F.2d 31, 122 n.255 (D.C. Cir. 1976) (upholding jury verdict on instruction defining "defrauding the United States" as: "depriv[ing] the Government of its right to have the officials of its departments and agencies transact their official business honestly and impartially, free from corruption, fraud, improper and undue influence, dishonesty and obstruction").

[617] Order Re Privilege of Documents Dated January 4-7, 2021 at 54-55, *Eastman v. Thompson et al.*, 594 F. Supp. 3d 1156, (C.D. Cal. Mar. 28, 2022) (No. 8:22-cv-99-DOC-DFM).

[618] *See* Order Re Privilege of Documents Dated January 4-7, 2021 at 53, *Eastman v. Thompson et al.*, 594 F. Supp. 3d 1156, (C.D. Cal. Mar. 28, 2022) (No. 8:22-cv-99-DOC-DFM). ("An 'agreement' between co-conspirators need not be express and can be inferred from the conspirators' conduct.").

[619] *See infra*, Chapter 1.

[620] Order Re Privilege of Documents Dated January 4-7, 2021 at 55, *Eastman v. Thompson et al.*, 594 F. Supp. 3d 1156, (C.D. Cal. Mar. 28, 2022) (No. 8:22-cv-99-DOC-DFM).

[621] Order Re Privilege of Documents Dated January 4-7, 2021 at 57, *Eastman v. Thompson et al.*, 594 F. Supp. 3d 1156, (C.D. Cal. Mar. 28, 2022) (No. 8:22-cv-99-DOC-DFM).

[622] *See infra* Chapter 2. President Trump's call with Secretary Raffensperger may have violated several provisions of both Federal and Georgia law. We do not attempt to catalogue all the possible violations here.

[623] Order Re Privilege of Documents Dated January 4-7, 2021 at 57, *Eastman v. Thompson et al.*, 594 F. Supp. 3d 1156, (C.D. Cal. Mar. 28, 2022) (No. 8:22-cv-99-DOC-DFM).

[624] Order Re Privilege of Documents Dated January 4-7, 2021 at 59, *Eastman v. Thompson et al.*, 594 F. Supp. 3d 1156, (C.D. Cal. Mar. 28, 2022) (No. 8:22-cv-99-DOC-DFM).

[625] "908. ELEMENTS OF 18 U.S.C. § 1001," Department of Justice, (last accessed on Dec. 13, 2022), available at https://www.justice.gov/archives/jm/criminal-resource-manual-908-elements-18-usc-1001.

[626] The elements of a Section 371 conspiracy are discussed above.

[627] As explained in Chapter 5, staffers for Rep. Mike Kelly (R-PA) and Sen. Ron Johnson (R-WI) reached out to Vice President Pence's director of legislative affairs, apparently seeking to deliver fake certificates on January 6. Documents on file with the Select Committee to Investigate the January 6th Attack on the United States Capitol (Chris Hodgson Production), 00012 (January 6, 2021, text message from Rep. Kelly's Chief of Staff, Matt Stroia, to Chris Hodgson on January 6 at 8:41 a.m.), 00058 (January 6, 2021, text messages from Senator Johnson's Chief of Staff, Sean Riley, to Chris Hodgson around 12:37 p.m.).

[628] *See infra,* Chapter 3.

[629] 18 U.S.C. 1001 (emphasis added).

[630] *See, e.g., United States v. Bowser*, 964 F.3d 26, 31 (D.C. Cir. 2020), *cert. denied*, 141 S. Ct. 1390 (2021) ("[T]he False Statements Act applies to 'any investigation or review, conducted pursuant to the authority of any committee, subcommittee, commission *or office of the Congress.*' 18 U.S.C. § 1001(c)(2) (emphasis added)."); *United States v. Stone*, 394 F. Supp. 3d 1, 10 (D.D.C. 2019).

[631] *See* Select Committee to Investigate the January 6th Attack on the United States Capitol, *Business Meeting on the January 6th Investigation,* 117th Cong., 2d sess., (Oct. 13, 2022), at 1:14:59-1:15:22 available at https://www.youtube.com/watch?v=IQvuBoLBuC0 ("[President Trump] turned the call over to Mr. Eastman, who then proceeded to talk about the importance of the RNC helping the campaign gather these contingent electors, in case any of the legal challenges that were ongoing changed the result of any of the states.").

[632] 18 U.S. Code § 2383.

[633] *Thompson v. Trump*, 590 F. Supp. 3d 46, 115 (D.D.C. 2022).

[634] *See* Ryan Goodman and Josh Asabor, "In Their Own Words: The 43 Republicans' Explanations of Their Votes Not to Convict Trump in Impeachment Trial," Just Security (Feb. 15, 2021), available at

https://www.justsecurity.org/74725/in-their-own-words-the-43-republicans-explanations-of-their-votes-not-to-convict-trump-in-impeachment-trial/.

[635] *See supra* at ____.

[636] *See supra* at ____. The evidence suggests that the Vice President and certain members of President Trump's staff urged DOD to deploy the National Guard notwithstanding the President's wishes.

[637] A prominent U.S. professor of criminal law has opined that President Trump can be held criminally responsible under Section 2383 for his failure to act, when he had a duty to act given his constitutional obligation under Article II Section 3 of the Constitution to "take Care that the Laws be faithfully executed." *See* Albert W. Alschuler, "Trump and the Insurrection Act: The Legal Framework," Just Security, (Aug. 16, 2022), available at https://www.justsecurity.org/82696/trump-and-the-insurrection-act-the-true-legal-framework/. Professor Albert Alschuler, the Julius Kreeger Professor Emeritus at the University of Chicago Law School, taught criminal law for over 50 years at many of our nation's leading law schools. He has published a number of analytical pieces applying the "assists" and "aid and comfort" clauses of that provisions (which he analogizes to "aiding and abetting" accomplice liability) to the evidence presented at the Committee's hearings. In any event, as described above, President Trump *did* act, including through his 2:24 p.m. tweet about the Vice President that inflamed the crowd attacking the Capitol.

[638] Select Committee to Investigate the January 6th Attack on the United States Capitol, Continued Interview of Cassidy Hutchinson, (June 20, 2022,) p. 26.

[639] Select Committee to Investigate the January 6th Attack on the United States Capitol, *Hearing on the January 6th Investigation*, 117th Cong., 2d sess., (July 21, 2022), at 1:02:53, available at https://www.youtube.com/watch?v=pbRVqWbHGuo; Donald J. Trump (@realDonaldTrump), Twitter, Jan. 6, 2021 2:24 p.m. ET, *available at* https://www.thetrumparchive.com/?searchbox="didn't+have+the+courage+to+do+what+should+have+been+done" (archived).

[640] See *infra*, Chapter 8.

[641] *See supra* at ____.

[642] Select Committee to Investigate the January 6th Attack on the United States Capitol, Continued Interview of Cassidy Hutchinson, (June 20, 2022), p. 27.

[643] *See* Mariana Alfaro, "Trump Vows Pardons, Government Apology to Capitol Rioters if Elected," *Washington Post*, (Sept. 1, 2022), available at https://www.washingtonpost.com/national-security/2022/09/01/trump-jan-6-rioters-pardon/.

[644] Jordan Fischer, Eric Flack, and Stephanie Wilson, "Georgia Man Who Wanted to 'Remove Some Craniums' on January 6 Sentenced to More than 2 Years in Prison," WUSA9, (Dec. 14, 2021), available at https://perma.cc/RSY2-J3RU.

[645] Dan Mangan, "Capitol Rioter Garret Miller Says He Was Following Trump's Orders, Apologizes to AOC for Threat," CNBC, (Jan. 25, 2021), available at https://www.cnbc.com/2021/01/25/capitol-riots-garret-miller-says-he-was-following-trumps-orders-apologizes-to-aoc.html

[646] Donald J. Trump (@realDonaldTrump), Twitter, Jan. 6, 2021 6:01 p.m. ET, available at https://www.thetrumparchive.com/?searchbox=%22these+are+the+things+and+events%22 (archived).

[647] Select Committee to Investigate the January 6th Attack on the United States Capitol, Deposition of Nicholas Luna, (Mar. 21, 2022), pp. 166–67.

[648] Donald J. Trump (@realDonaldTrump), Twitter, Jan. 6, 2021 6:01 p.m. ET, available at https://www.thetrumparchive.com/?searchbox=%22these+are+the+things+and+events%22 (archived).

[649] 18 U.S.C. § 372.

[650] *See* "Leader of Oath Keepers and Oath Keepers Member Found Guilty of Seditious Conspiracy and Other Charges Related to U.S. Capitol Breach," Department of Justice, (Nov. 29, 2022), available at https://www.justice.gov/opa/pr/leader-oath-keepers-and-oath-keepers-member-found-guilty-seditious-conspiracy-and-other.

[651] 18 U.S.C. § 2384. To establish a violation of Section 2384, the government must establish (1) a conspiracy, (2) to overthrow, put down, or destroy by force the Government of the United States, or to levy war against them, or to oppose by force the authority thereof, or by force to prevent, hinder or delay the execution of any law of the United States, or by force to seize, take, or possess any property of the United States contrary to the authority thereof. *See United States v. Khan*, 461 F.3d 477, 487 (4th Cir. 2006).

[652] "Leader of Oath Keepers and Oath Keepers Member Found Guilty of Seditious Conspiracy and Other Charges Related to U.S. Capitol Breach," Department of Justice, (Nov. 29, 2022), available at https://www.justice.gov/opa/pr/leader-oath-keepers-and-oath-keepers-member-found-guilty-seditious-conspiracy-and-other.

[653] "Leader of Proud Boys and Four Other Members Indicted in Federal Court for Seditious Conspiracy and Other Offenses Related to U.S. Capitol Breach,"Department of Justice, (June 6, 2022), available at https://www.justice.gov/opa/pr/leader-proud-boys-and-four-other-members-indicted-federal-court-seditious-conspiracy-and.

[654] *See supra* at ___.

[655] Brian Naylor, "Read Trump's Jan. 6 Speech, A Key Part of Impeachment Trial," NPR, (Feb. 10, 2021), available at https://www.npr.org/2021/02/10/966396848/read-trumps-jan-6-speech-a-key-part-of-impeachment-trial.

[656] Kristen Holmes, "Trump Calls for the Termination of the Constitution in Truth Social Post," CNN, (Dec. 4, 2022), available at https://www.cnn.com/2022/12/03/politics/trump-constitution-truth-social/index.html.

[657] *See* Mariana Alfaro, "Trump Vows Pardons, Government Apology to Capitol Rioters if Elected," *Washington Post,* (Sept. 1, 2022), available at https://www.washingtonpost.com/national-security/2022/09/01/trump-jan-6-rioters-pardon/.

[658] *See infra,* Chapter 7.

[659] 167 Cong. Rec. H171-72 (daily ed. Jan. 13, 2021).

[660] *See supra* at ___.

[661] Select Committee to Investigate the January 6th Attack on the United States Capitol, Continued Interview of Cassidy Hutchinson, (June 20, 2022), pp. 84-87.

[662] Documents on file with the Select Committee to Investigate the January 6th Attack on the United States Capitol (National Archives Production), 076P-R000008962_0009 (January 2, 2021, White House Presidential Call Log).

[663] Documents on file with the Select Committee to Investigate the January 6th Attack on the United States Capitol (Mark Meadows Production), MM014864 (January 5, 2021, text message from Rep. Jim Jordan to Mark Meadows describing the Vice President's actions on January 6th).

[664] *See* Documents on file with the Select Committee to Investigate the January 6th Attack on the United States Capitol (National Archives Production), P-R000255-259 (January 6, 2021, Presidential Daily Diary); Felicia Somnez, "Rep. Jim Jordan Tells House Panel He Can't Recall How Many Times He Spoke with Trump on Jan. 6," *Washington Post* (Oct. 20, 2021), available at https://www.washingtonpost.com/politics/jordan-trump-calls-capitol-attack/2021/10/20/1a570d0e-31c7-11ec-9241-aad8e48f01ff_story.html.

[665] Documents on file with the Select Committee to Investigate the January 6th Attack on the United States Capitol, (AT&T Production, Feb. 9, 2022).

[666] Select Committee to Investigate the January 6th Attack on the United States Capitol, Deposition of Rudolph Giuliani, (May 20, 2022), 205-07.

[667] Select Committee to Investigate the January 6th Attack on the United States Capitol, Continued Interview of Cassidy Hutchinson, (May 17, 2022), p. 106.

[668] Select Committee to Investigate the January 6th Attack on the United States Capitol, Transcribed Interview of Cassidy Hutchinson, (Feb. 23, 2022), pp. 72-73.

[669] Select Committee to Investigate the January 6th Attack on the United States Capitol, Continued Interview of Cassidy Hutchinson, (Mar. 7, 2022), pp. 66-67.

[670] Select Committee to Investigate the January 6th Attack on the United States Capitol, Continued Interview of Cassidy Hutchinson, (June 20, 2022), pp. 62–64.

[671] *See* Sarah Lynch and David Shepardson, "Watchdog to Probe if Justice Dept. Officials Improperly Tried to Alter 2020 Election," *Reuters,* (Jan. 25, 2021), available at https://www.reuters.com/article/us-usa-trump-justice/watchdog-to-probe-if-justice-dept-officials-improperly-tried-to-alter-2020-election-idUSKBN29U21E ("'Throughout the past four years, I worked with Assistant Attorney General Clark on various legislative matters. When President Trump asked if I would make an introduction, I obliged,' Perry said in a statement.").

[672] Select Committee to Investigate the January 6th Attack on the United States Capitol, Continued Interview of Cassidy Hutchinson, (June 20, 2022), p. 48.

[673] Select Committee to Investigate the January 6th Attack on the United States Capitol, Transcribed Interview of Cassidy Hutchinson, (Feb. 23, 2022), p. 45.

[674] Select Committee to Investigate the January 6th Attack on the United States Capitol, Continued Interview of Cassidy Hutchinson, (May 17, 2022), pp. 106–07.
[675] Documents on file with the Select Committee to Investigate the January 6th Attack on the United States Capitol (Mark Meadows Production), MM011449.
[676] Documents on file with the Select Committee to Investigate the January 6th Attack on the United States Capitol (Mark Meadows Production), MM011506, (November 2020 text messages from Rep. Andy Biggs to Mark Meadows).
[677] Josh Kelety, "Congressman Andy Biggs Coordinated Efforts with Mark Finchem before Capitol Riot," *Phoenix New Times*, (Feb. 18, 2021), available at https://www.phoenixnewtimes.com/news/congressman-andy-biggs-coordinated-with-mark-finchem-before-capitol-riot-11532527.
[678] Documents on file with the Select Committee to Investigate the January 6th Attack on the United States Capitol (Jim DeGraffenreid Production), DEGRAFFENREID 000554 (December 18, 2020, text messages between James DeGraffenreid, a Nevada fake elector for Trump, and another remarking that "Andy Biggs ... has reached out to NV to ask about our evidence").
[679] Audrey Fahlberg, "January 6 Hearings Become Fundraising Fodder," *The Dispatch*, (July 7, 2022), available at https://thedispatch.com/p/january-6-hearings-become-fundraising; Archive of Political Emails, Jim Jordan, "The January 6th Committee Is After Me," June 9, 2022 12:41 p.m., available at https://politicalemails.org/messages/686023.
[680] John Rowley III to the Honorable Bennie G. Thompson re: "Subpoena to Representative Scott Perry," (May 24, 2022), available at https://www.documentcloud.org/documents/22061774-scott-perry-j6-response.
[681] Committee on Standards of Official Conduct, *House Ethics Manual*, p. 13 (2008).
[682] Documents on file with the Select Committee to Investigate the January 6th Attack on the United States Capitol (National Archives Production), 076P-R001080 (December 21, 2020, WAVES records showing Representatives Babin, Biggs, Brooks, Gaetz, Gohmert, Gosar, Taylor Greene, Harris, Hice, Jordan, and Perry entering the White House).
[683] *See* Select Committee to Investigate the January 6th Attack on the United States Capitol, Deposition of John Eastman, (Dec. 9, 2021); Select Committee to Investigate the January 6th Attack on the United States Capitol, Deposition of Roger Stone, (Dec. 17, 2021); Select Committee to Investigate the January 6th Attack on the United States Capitol, Deposition of Jeffrey Clark, (Feb. 2, 2022); Select Committee to Investigate the January 6th Attack on the United States Capitol, Deposition of Michael Flynn, (Mar. 10, 2022).
[684] *Latif v. Obama*, 677 F.3d 1175, 1193 (D.C. Cir. 2012) (quoting *Mitchell v. United States*, 526 U.S. 314, 328 (1999)). Justice Scalia not only agreed with this principle, but he also reasoned that the Fifth Amendment does not prevent an adverse inference in even criminal cases. This is because the text of that Amendment does not require such a rule and applying an adverse inference to a refusal to testify is exactly in keeping with "normal evidentiary inferences." *See Mitchell*, 526 U.S. at 332 (Scalia, J., dissenting). Justice Thomas agreed with Justice Scalia. *See id.* at 341-42 (Thomas, J., dissenting).
[685] Select Committee to Investigate the January 6th Attack on the United States Capitol, Deposition of Michael Flynn, (Mar. 10, 2022), p. 82.
[686] *Trump v. Thompson*, 20 F.4th 10, 15-16 (D.C. Cir. 2021), *cert. denied*, 142 S.Ct. 1350 (2022).
[687] *Trump v. Thompson*, 20 F.4th 10, 89 (D.C. Cir. 2021) (citation omitted), *cert. denied*, 142 S.Ct. 1350 (2022). Former President Trump also asked the United State Supreme Court to block the Select Committee from accessing his documents. The Supreme Court denied that request stating, "Because the Court of Appeals concluded that President Trump's claims would have failed even if he were the incumbent, his status as a former President necessarily made no difference to the court's decision." *Trump v. Thompson*, 142 S.Ct. 680, 680 (2022) (citation omitted).
[688] H. Res. 851, 117th Cong., (2021); H. Rept. 117-216, Resolution Recommending that the House of Representatives Find Mark Randall Meadows in Contempt of Congress for Refusal to Comply with a Subpoena Duly Issued by the Select Committee to Investigate the January 6th Attack on the United States Capitol, 117th Cong., 1st Sess. (2021), available at https://www.congress.gov/117/crpt/hrpt216/CRPT-117hrpt216.pdf.
[689] Statement of Interest of the United States at 9-10, *Meadows v. Pelosi et al.*, No. 1:21-cv-03217 (CJN) (D.D.C. July 15, 2022), ECF No. 42.
[690] "Thompson & Cheney Statement on Justice Department Decisions on Contempt Referrals," Select Committee to Investigate the January 6th Attack on the United States Capitol, (June 3, 2022), available at https://january6th.house.gov/news/press-releases/thompson-cheney-statement-justice-department-decisions-contempt-referrals.

[691] Dennis Aftergut, "Why the DOJ Did Not Indict Mark Meadows (and What It Should Do Next)," NBC News, (June 7, 2022), available at https://www.nbcnews.com/think/opinion/trump-lackey-mark-meadows-escaped-january-6-prosecution-peter-navarro-rcna32319.

[692] H. Res. 1037, 117th Cong., (2022); H. Rept. 117-284, Resolution Recommending that the House of Representatives Find Peter K. Navarro and Daniel Scavino, Jr., in Contempt of Congress for Refusal to Comply with a Subpoena Duly Issued by the Select Committee to Investigate the January 6th Attack on the United States Capitol, 117th Cong., 2d Sess. (2022), available at https://www.congress.gov/117/crpt/hrpt284/CRPT-117hrpt284.pdf. In particular, Scavino may have further information on President Trump's advance knowledge from social media posts of the rioters' plans to invade the Capitol. See *supra* __.

[693] H. Res. 730, 117th Cong., (2021); H. Rept. 117-152, Resolution Recommending that the House of Representatives Find Stephen K. Bannon in Contempt of Congress for Refusal to Comply with a Subpoena Duly Issued by the Select Committee to Investigate the January 6th Attack on the United States Capitol, 117th Cong., 1st Sess. (2021), available at https://www.congress.gov/117/crpt/hrpt152/CRPT-117hrpt152.pdf.

[694] H. Res. 1037, 117th Cong., (2022); "Peter Navarro Indicted for Contempt of Congress," Department of Justice, (June 3, 2022), available at https://www.justice.gov/usao-dc/pr/peter-navarro-indicted-contempt-congress; H. Rept. 117-284, Resolution Recommending that the House of Representatives Find Peter K. Navarro and Daniel Scavino, Jr., in Contempt of Congress for Refusal to Comply with a Subpoena Duly Issued by the Select Committee to Investigate the January 6th Attack on the United States Capitol, 117th Cong., 2d Sess. (2022), available at https://www.congress.gov/117/crpt/hrpt284/CRPT-117hrpt284.pdf.

[695] See *infra* __.

[696] Select Committee to Investigate the January 6th Attack on the United States Capitol, *Hearing on the January 6th Investigation*, 117th Cong., 2d sess., (July 12, 2022), at 2;14:00-2:14:50, available at https://youtu.be/rrUa0hfG6Lo.

[697] Select Committee to Investigate the January 6th Attack on the United States Capitol, Deposition of John McEntee, (Mar. 28, 2022), pp. 153-55; Select Committee to Investigate the January 6th Attack on the United States Capitol, Transcribed Interview of Eric Herschmann, (Apr. 6, 2022), pp. 129-35; Select Committee to Investigate the January 6th Attack on the United States Capitol, Transcribed Interview of Pasquale Anthony "Pat" Cipollone, (July 8, 2022), pp. 176-77; Select Committee to Investigate the January 6th Attack on the United States Capitol, Continued Interview of Cassidy Hutchinson, (May 17, 2022), pp. 104-06.

[698] Select Committee to Investigate the January 6th Attack on the United States Capitol, *Hearing on the January 6th Investigation*, 117th Cong., 2d sess., (June 23, 2022), at 2:22:05-2:23:41, available at https://www.youtube.com/live/Z4535-VW-bY?feature=share&t=8525.

[699] Select Committee to Investigate the January 6th Attack on the United States Capitol, Deposition of John McEntee, (Mar. 28, 2022), pp. 153-55; Select Committee to Investigate the January 6th Attack on the United States Capitol, *Hearing on the January 6th Investigation*, 117th Cong., 2d sess., (June 23, 2022), at 2:23:41-2:24:42, available at https://www.youtube.com/watch?v=Z4535-VW-bY&t=8620s.

[700] Select Committee to Investigate the January 6th Attack on the United States Capitol, Transcribed Interview of Eric Herschmann, (Apr. 6, 2022), pp. 129-35, esp. pp. 130-131; Select Committee to Investigate the January 6th Attack on the United States Capitol, *Hearing on the January 6th Investigation*, 117th Cong., 2d sess., (June 23, 2022), at 2:21:26-2:22:04, available at https://www.youtube.com/live/Z4535-VW-bY?feature=share&t=8486.

[701] Select Committee to Investigate the January 6th Attack on the United States Capitol, Transcribed Interview of Eric Herschmann, (Apr. 6, 2022), p. 133.

[702] Documents on file with the Select Committee to Investigate the January 6th Attack on the United States Capitol (National Archives Production), 076P-R000005854_0001 (January 11, 2021, email from Molly Michael to Rep. Mo Brooks, confirming receipt of email from Brooks recommending pardons, including for "Every Congressman and Senator who voted to reject the electoral college vote submissions of Arizona and Pennsylvania"); Select Committee to Investigate the January 6th Attack on the United States Capitol, *Hearing on the January 6th Investigation*, 117th Cong., 2d sess., (June 23, 2022), at 2:20:52-2:21:12, available at https://www.youtube.com/live/Z4535-VW-bY?feature=share&t=8452.

[703] Select Committee to Investigate the January 6th Attack on the United States Capitol, *Hearing on the January 6th Investigation*, 117th Cong., 2d sess., (June 28, 2022), available at https://www.govinfo.gov/committee/house-january6th.

[704] The Committee has enormous respect for the U.S. Secret Service and recognized that the testimony regarding their work is sensitive for law enforcement, protectee security, and national security reasons. *See, e.g.*, Select Committee

to Investigate the January 6th Attack on the United States Capitol, Transcribed Interview of USSS Employee "Driver", (Nov. 7, 2022), p. 4 (the Select Committee is not releasing the name of this individual); Select Committee to Investigate the January 6th Attack on the United States Capitol, Continued Interview of Anthony Ornato, (Nov. 28, 2022), p. 4; Select Committee to Investigate the January 6th Attack on the United States Capitol, Transcribed Interview of USSS Employee, (Nov. 21, 2022), p. 4; Select Committee to Investigate the January 6th Attack on the United States Capitol, Transcribed Interview of USSS Employee, (Nov. 18, 2022), p. 4 Select Committee to Investigate the January 6th Attack on the United States Capitol, Transcribed Interview of Robert Engel, (Nov. 17, 2022), p. 4; Select Committee to Investigate the January 6th Attack on the United States Capitol, Transcribed Interview of Brandon Cecil, (Nov. 4, 2022), p. 4.

[705] Select Committee to Investigate the January 6th Attack on the United States Capitol, Transcribed Interview of USSS Employee "Driver", (Nov. 7, 2022), pp. 4, 86-87.

[706] *See, e.g.*, Devlin Barrett, Jacqueline Alemany, Josh Dawsey, and Rosalind S. Heldeman, "The Justice Dept.'s Jan. 6 Investigation Is Looking at … Everything," *Washington Post*, (Sept. 16, 2022), available at https://www.washingtonpost.com/national-security/2022/09/15/trump-january-6-subpoenas-meadows/; Josh Dawsey and Isaac Arnsdorf, "Prosecutors Seek Details from Trump's PAC in Expanding Jan. 6 Probe," *Washington Post*, (Sept. 8, 2022), available at https://www.washingtonpost.com/national-security/2022/09/08/trump-subpoenas-pac-jan-6/.

[707] *See* Devlin Barrett, Josh Dawsey, and Isaac Stanley-Becker, "Trump's Committee Paying for Lawyers of Key Mar-a-Lago Witnesses," *Washington Post*, (Dec. 5, 2022), available at https://www.washingtonpost.com/national-security/2022/12/05/trump-witnesses-legal-bills-pac/.

[708] The Committee sat for dozens of hours with Hutchinson and concluded that she is brave and earnest, and understood the intense backlash that would inevitably result from those who were enlisted to defend President Trump's behavior. [See Chapter 7 at XX.]. The thuggish behavior from President Trump's team, including efforts to intimidate described elsewhere in this report (*see e.g.* Chapter 3), gave rise to many concerns about Hutchinson's security, both in advance of and since her public testimony. (We note that multiple members of the Committee were regularly receiving threats of violence during this period.) Accordingly, the Committee attempted to take appropriate measures to help ensure her safety in advance of her testimony, including measures designed to minimize the risk of leaks that might put her safety at risk.

[709] *See, e.g.*, Select Committee to Investigate the January 6th Attack on the United States Capitol, Transcribed Interview of Pasquale Anthony "Pat" Cipollone, (July 8, 2022), pp. 71-72 (noting that another witness reference may have been to Pat Philbin).

[710] Select Committee to Investigate the January 6th Attack on the United States Capitol, Deposition of Kayleigh McEnany, (Jan. 12, 2022), pp. 264-65.

[711] Select Committee to Investigate the January 6th Attack on the United States Capitol, Deposition of Kayleigh McEnany, (Jan. 12, 2022), pp. 52-57, 70-74, 282-88.

[712] Select Committee to Investigate the January 6th Attack on the United States Capitol, Deposition of Kayleigh McEnany, (Jan. 12, 2022), pp. 142-45, 288-92. *See also* Select Committee to Investigate the January 6th Attack on the United States Capitol, Transcribed Interview of Sarah Matthews, (Feb. 8, 2022), pp. 12-15.

[713] Select Committee to Investigate the January 6th Attack on the United States Capitol, Deposition of Kayleigh McEnany, (Jan. 12, 2022), pp. 183-86.

[714] Select Committee to Investigate the January 6th Attack on the United States Capitol, Transcribed Interview of Sarah Matthews, (Feb. 8, 2022), pp. 39-41.

[715] Select Committee to Investigate the January 6th Attack on the United States Capitol, Transcribed Interview of Sarah Matthews, (Feb. 8, 2022), p. 41.

[716] Select Committee to Investigate the January 6th Attack on the United States Capitol, Transcribed Interview of Ivanka Trump, (Apr. 5, 2022), pp. 38-39, 120, 205, 210, 213-14.

[717] Select Committee to Investigate the January 6th Attack on the United States Capitol, Transcribed Interview of Ivanka Trump, (Apr. 5, 2022), p. 27.

[718] Select Committee to Investigate the January 6th Attack on the United States Capitol, Transcribed Interview of Julie Radford, (May 24, 2022), p. 19.

[719] Select Committee to Investigate the January 6th Attack on the United States Capitol, Transcribed Interview of Ivanka Trump, (Apr. 5, 2022), p. 40.

[720] Mark Meadows, *The Chief's Chief* (Ft. Lauderdale, FL: All Seasons Press, 2021).

721 Mark Meadows, *The Chief's Chief* (Ft. Lauderdale, FL: All Seasons Press, 2021), p. 259.
722 Mark Meadows, *The Chief's Chief* (Ft. Lauderdale, FL: All Seasons Press, 2021), p. 259.
723 Select Committee to Investigate the January 6th Attack on the United States Capitol, Continued Interview of Cassidy Hutchinson, (June 20, 2022), pp. 47-49.
724 Select Committee to Investigate the January 6th Attack on the United States Capitol, Transcribed Interview of Anthony Ornato, (Jan.y 28, 2022), pp. 76-77.
725 Select Committee to Investigate the January 6th Attack on the United States Capitol, Continued Interview of Anthony Ornato, (Mar. 29, 2022), pp. 46-47. Ornato was interviewed at length by the Select Committee in November 2022, after the Secret Service produced nearly a million new internal documents in August and September of this year.
726 Select Committee to Investigate the January 6th Attack on the United States Capitol, Continued Interview of Anthony Ornato, (Nov. 29, 2022), p. 92; *see also* Select Committee to Investigate the January 6th Attack on the United States Capitol, Continued Interview of Anthony Ornato, (Mar.ch 29, 2022), pp. 45-46 (stating that he had not heard about President Trump's instruction to others to ask Ornato about going to the Capitol).
727 Select Committee to Investigate the January 6th Attack on the United States Capitol, Interview of White House employee with national security responsibilities, (July 19, 2022), pp. 69-70; Select Committee to Investigate the January 6th Attack on the United States Capitol, Continued Interview of Cassidy Hutchinson, (June 20, 2022), pp. 4-6.
728 Select Committee to Investigate the January 6th Attack on the United States Capitol, Interview of White House employee with national security responsibilities, (July 19, 2022), pp. 69-70; Select Committee to Investigate the January 6th Attack on the United States Capitol, Continued Interview of Cassidy Hutchinson, (June 20, 2022), pp. 4-6.
729 Select Committee to Investigate the January 6th Attack on the United States Capitol, Transcribed Interview of White House employee with national security responsibilities, (July 19, 2022), pp. 69-70; Select Committee to Investigate the January 6th Attack on the United States Capitol, Continued Interview of Cassidy Hutchinson, (June 20, 2022), pp. 4-7; Select Committee to Investigate the January 6th Attack on the United States Capitol, Transcribed Interview of USSS Employee "Driver", (Nov. 7, 2022), pp. 77-80, 92-93; Select Committee to Investigate the January 6th Attack on the United States Capitol, Transcribed Interview of Mark Robinson, (July 7, 2022), pp. 17-18.
730 Select Committee to Investigate the January 6th Attack on the United States Capitol, Continued Interview of Anthony Ornato, (Nov. 29, 2022), pp. 104-105, 131-32, 135-36. *See also* Chapter 7.
731 *See, e.g.*, Select Committee to Investigate the January 6th Attack on the United States Capitol, Transcribed Interview of General Mark A. Milley, (Nov. 17, 2021), p. 199 (describing another senior intelligence official worrying, ahead of January 6th, about violence at the Capitol); Select Committee to Investigate the January 6th Attack on the United States Capitol, Transcribed Interview of Donnell Harvin, (Jan. 24, 2022), pp. 22-23 (former Chief of Homeland Security and Intelligence for the District of Columbia describing the threat scene ahead of January 6th); Documents on file with the Select Committee to Investigate the January 6th Attack on the United States Capitol (Capitol Police Production), CTRL0000001532.0001, p.2 (January 5, 2021, FBI Situational Information Report).
732 Select Committee to Investigate the January 6th Attack on the United States Capitol, Continued Interview of Anthony Ornato, (Nov. 29, 2022), pp. 54-56.
733 Select Committee to Investigate the January 6th Attack on the United States Capitol, Continued Interview of Anthony Ornato, (Nov. 29, 2022), pp. 55-56.
734 See *supra* pp. 81-83. *See also* Select Committee to Investigate the January 6th Attack on the United States Capitol, Continued Interview of Anthony Ornato, (Nov. 29, 2022), p. 13 (Ornato confirming that one of his responsibilities was briefing the chief of staff and, through the chief of staff at times, the President on security-related issues).
735 "U.S. House of Representatives Debate on Impeachment of President Trump," C-SPAN, at 1:03:53 - 1:13:42, Jan. 13, 2021, available at https://www.c-span.org/video/?507879-4/debate-impeachment-president-trump; Tyler Moyer, "McCarthy: "President Bears Responsibility for Wednesday's Attack"," *Bakersfield Now*, (Jan. 13, 2021), available at https://bakersfieldnow.com/news/local/mccarthy-president-bears-responsibility-for-wednesdays-attack.
736 "House Minority Leader Weekly Briefing." C-SPAN, at 7:30 - 8:44, Jan. 21, 2021, available at https://www.c-span.org/video/?508185-1/minority-leader-mccarthy-backs-gop-conference-chair-liz-cheney; Rudy Talaka, "GOP Leader McCarthy Calls for Bipartisan Commission to Investigate Allegations of Members Helping Rioters," Mediaite, (Jan. 21, 2021), available at https://www.mediaite.com/news/gop-leader-mccarthy-calls-for-bipartisan-commission-to-investigate-allegations-of-members-helping-rioters/; "Rep. McCarthy Calls for Bipartisan Commission to Probe

Capitol Riot," Newsmax, (Jan. 22, 2021), available at https://www.newsmax.com/politics/kevin-mccarthy-capitol-riot-boebert-probe/2021/01/21/id/1006648/.

[737] Clare Foran, Ryan Nobles, and Annie Grayer, "Pelosi Announces Plans for '9/11-Type Commission' to Investigate Capitol Attack," CNN, (Feb. 15, 2021), available at https://www.cnn.com/2021/02/15/politics/pelosi-capitol-attack-commission/index.html.

[738] "Letter to The Honorable Speaker Nancy Pelosi," House Republican Leader Kevin McCarthy, (Feb. 22, 2021), available at https://www.speaker.gov/sites/speaker.house.gov/files/Sharp%20MX-4141_20210518_081238.pdf.

[739] "Letter to The Honorable Speaker Nancy Pelosi," House Republican Leader Kevin McCarthy, (Feb. 22, 2021), available at https://www.speaker.gov/sites/speaker.house.gov/files/Sharp%20MX-4141_20210518_081238.pdf.

[740] "Letter to The Honorable Speaker Nancy Pelosi," House Republican Leader Kevin McCarthy, (Feb. 22, 2021), available at https://www.speaker.gov/sites/speaker.house.gov/files/Sharp%20MX-4141_20210518_081238.pdf.

[741] Ryan Nobles, Annie Grayer, and Jeremy Herb, "Pelosi Concedes to Even Partisan Split on 1/6 Commission in Effort to Jumpstart Talks," CNN, (Apr. 20, 2021), available at https://www.cnn.com/2021/04/20/politics/nancy-pelosi-january-6-commission-talks/index.html; Ryan Nobles and Daniella Diaz, "Pelosi Makes Concession on Subpoenas for 9/11 Style Commission to Investigate Insurrection," CNN, (Apr. 22, 2021), available at https://www.cnn.com/2021/04/22/politics/nancy-pelosi-911-style-commission-insurrection-subpoenas/index.html.

[742] John Bresnahan, Anna Palmer, and Jake Sherman, "Pelosi Taps Top Dem to Negotiate on Jan. 6 Commission," *Punchbowl News*, (May 11, 2021), available at https://punchbowl.news/archive/punchbowl-news-am-5-11/.

[743] "Chairman Thompson Announces Bipartisan Agreement with Ranking Member Katko to Create Commission to Investigate the January 6 Attack on the Capitol," House Committee on Homeland Security, (May 14, 2021), available at https://homeland.house.gov/news/press-releases/chairman-thompson-announces-bipartisan-agreement-with-ranking-member-katko-to-create-commission-to-investigate-the-january-6-attack-on-the-capitol.

[744] "McCarthy Statement on January 6 Commission Legislation," House Republican Leader Kevin McCarthy, (May 18, 2021), available at https://www.republicanleader.gov/mccarthy-statement-on-january-6-commission-legislation/.

[745] "Pelosi Statement on McCarthy Opposition to January 6th Commission," Speaker of the House Nancy Pelosi, (May 18, 2021), available at https://www.speaker.gov/newsroom/51821.

[746] "Pelosi Statement on McCarthy Opposition to January 6th Commission," Speaker of the House Nancy Pelosi, (May 18, 2021), available at https://www.speaker.gov/newsroom/51821; "Letter to The Honorable Speaker Nancy Pelosi," House Republican Leader Kevin McCarthy, (Feb. 22, 2021), available at https://www.speaker.gov/sites/speaker.house.gov/files/Sharp%20MX-4141_20210518_081238.pdf.

[747] "Pelosi Statement on McCarthy Opposition to January 6th Commission," Speaker of the House Nancy Pelosi, (May 18, 2021), available at https://www.speaker.gov/newsroom/51821.

[748] "U.S. House of Representatives House Session," C-SPAN, at 4:12:23-4:12:55, May 19, 2021, available at https://www.c-span.org/video/?511820-2/houses-passes-bill-create-january-6-commission-252-175.

[749] "Roll Call 154 | Bill Number: H. R. 3233," Clerk of the U.S. House of Representatives, (May 19, 2021), available at https://clerk.house.gov/Votes/2021154?Page=1&Date=05%2F19%2F2021.

[750] "Roll Call Vote 117th Congress - 1st Session," Question: On the Cloture Motion (Motion to Invoke Cloture Re: Motion to Proceed to H.R. 3233), H.R. 3233 - 117th Congress (2021): National Commission to Investigate the January 6 Attack on the United States Capitol Complex Act, H.R.3233, 117th Cong. (2021), available at https://www.senate.gov/legislative/LIS/roll_call_votes/vote1171/vote_117_1_00218.htm.

[751] "House Speaker Nancy Pelosi Announces Select Committee on the January 6th Insurrection," C-SPAN, at 4:44-5:26, June 24, 2021, available at https://www.youtube.com/watch?v=guCcy9tUfn8.

[752] Manu Raju and Clare Foran, "Officer Injured in Capitol Riot asks McCarthy to Denounce GOP January 6 Conspiracies," CNN, (June 25, 2021), available at https://www.cnn.com/2021/06/25/politics/michael-fanone-kevin-mccarthy-meeting/index.html.

[753] Manu Raju and Clare Foran, "Officer Injured in Capitol Riot asks McCarthy to Denounce GOP January 6 Conspiracies," CNN, (June 25, 2021), available at https://www.cnn.com/2021/06/25/politics/michael-fanone-kevin-mccarthy-meeting/index.html.

[754] "Roll Call 197 | Bill Number: H. Res. 503," Clerk of the U.S. House of Representatives, (June 30, 2021), available at https://clerk.house.gov/Votes/2021197.

[755] "Pelosi Names Members to Select Committee to Investigate January 6th Attack on the U.S. Capitol," House Speaker Nancy Pelosi, (July 1, 2021), available at https://www.speaker.gov/newsroom/7121-0.

[756] "McCarthy Names House Republicans to Serve on Select Committees," House Republican Leader Kevin McCarthy, (July 19, 2021), available at https://www.republicanleader.gov/mccarthy-names-house-republicans-to-serve-on-select-committees/.

[757] "McCarthy Taps Banks to Lead Republicans on Jan 6 Committee," Congressman Jim Banks, (Jul. 19, 2021), available at https://banks.house.gov/news/documentsingle.aspx?DocumentID=1921.

[758] "Pelosi Statement on Republican Recommendations to Serve on the Select Committee to Investigate the January 6th Attack on the U.S. Capitol," Speaker of the House Nancy Pelosi, (Jul. 21, 2021), available at https://www.speaker.gov/newsroom/72121-2.

[759] "Pelosi Statement on Republican Recommendations to Serve on the Select Committee to Investigate the January 6th Attack on the U.S. Capitol," Speaker of the House Nancy Pelosi, (Jul. 21, 2021), available at https://www.speaker.gov/newsroom/72121-2.

[760] "McCarthy Statement about Pelosi's Abuse of Power on January 6th Select Committee," Republican Leader Kevin McCarthy, (July 21, 2021), available at https://republicanleader.house.gov/mccarthy-statement-about-pelosis-abuse-of-power-on-january-6th-select-committee/; "McCarthy Pulls Republicans from Jan. 6 Select Committee after Pelosi Rejects Picks," *Axios*, (July 21, 2021), available at https://www.axios.com/2021/07/21/pelosi-jim-jordan-banks-select-committee.

[761] "Pelosi Announces Appointment of Congressman Adam Kinzinger to Select Committee to Investigate the January 6th Attack on the U.S. Capitol," House Speaker Nancy Pelosi, (July 25, 2021), available at https://www.speaker.gov/newsroom/72521.

[762] *See, e.g., Eastman v. Thompson et al.*, No. 8:22-cv-99-DOC-DFM, 2022 U.S. Dist. LEXIS 25546, at *12-14 (C.D. Cal. Jan. 25, 2022); Memorandum Opinion, Republican National Committee v. Nancy Pelosi et al.. https://storage.courtlistener.com/recap/gov.uscourts.dcd.241102/gov.uscourts.dcd.241102.33.0.pdf.

Visit us at *www.quidprobooks.com*.